MULTICULTURAL EDUCATION: STRATEGIES FOR IMPLEMENTATION IN COLLEGES AND UNIVERSITIES

Volume 4

Edited by
J. Q. Adams
Janice R. Welsch

Prepared with Higher Education Cooperation Act Funds
Awarded by the Illinois Board of Higher Education

to

Board of Governors of State Colleges
and Universities Acting on Behalf of
Western Illinois University

for a project titled

Expanding Cultural Diversity
in the Curriculum and in the Classroom

HECA GRANT
COOPERATING INSTITUTIONS
1994-95

Eastern Illinois University ....Dr. David Jorns, President
Illinois State University ....Dr. David Strand, President
Illinois Valley Community College ....Dr. Alfred E. Wisgoski, President
McHenry County College ....Dr. Robert C. Bartlett, President
Southern Illinois University Carbondale ....Dr. Ted Sanders, Chancellor
Western Illinois University ....Dr. Donald S. Spencer, President

Previous *Expanding Cultural Diversity* Publications

Adams, J. Q., Niss, J. F., & Suarez, C. (Eds.). (1991). *Multicultural Education: Strategies for Implementation in Colleges and Universities. (Vol. 1).* Macomb, IL: Western Illinois University. (ERIC Document Reproduction Service No. 346 811)

Adams, J. Q., & Welsch, J. R. (Eds.). (1992). *Multicultural Education: Strategies for Implementation in Colleges and Universities (Vol. 2).* Macomb, IL: Illinois Staff and Curriculum Developers Association. (ERIC Document Reproduction Service No. ED 351 921)

Adams, J. Q., & Welsch, J. R. (Eds.). (1993). *Multicultural Education: Strategies for Implementation in Colleges and Universities (Vol. 3).* Macomb, IL: Illinois Staff and Curriculum Developers Association. (ERIC Document Reproduction Service No. 363 211)

Adams, J. Q., & Welsch, J. R. (Eds.). (1994). *Multicultural Prism: Voices from the Field* [Handbook]. Macomb, IL: Illinois Staff and Curriculum Developers Association.

Williams, E. C. (Producer), and Adams, J. Q., & Welsch, J. R. (Project Directors). (1994). *Multicultural Prism: Voices from the Field* [Videotape]. Macomb, IL: Illinois Staff and Curriculum Developers Association.

For further information contact the Multicultural Resource Development and Advising Center, HH 80, Western Illinois University, 1 University Circle, Macomb, IL 61455.

IBHN 1-885890-05-2

DEDICATION

To the officials and administrators

on every level --

local, regional, state, national, international --

in government and education,

who see the future in our students

and are working for the success of each one of them,

recognizing and respecting

their varied histories and cultures,

genders, ages and abilities, needs and goals.

ACKNOWLEDGEMENTS

We want to recognize and thank the institutions and the individuals that have made this fourth volume of *Multicultural Education* possible: the Illinois Board of Higher Education for its continued backing through a Higher Education Cooperation Grant; James C. Forstall for his advice and encouragement; Yvonne Singley for her constant support; our contributors for generously sharing their knowledge, understanding, and experience; behind-the-scenes colleagues, particularly Jean Kipling, Joanne Jahraus, and Nita Burg for their invaluable assistance; and our friends and families who listened or lent a hand when we needed a boost.

J.Q.A.
J.R.W.
August 1995

PERMISSIONS

We gratefully acknowledge permission to reprint the following articles.

Alexander W. Astin, "Diversity and multiculturalism on the campus: How are students affected?" Originally published in *Change* (Vol. 25, No. 2, pp. 44-49, March/ April 1993).

James A. Banks, "Multicultural education: Development, dimensions, and challenges." Reprinted with permission of the author and of the *Phi Delta Kappan* (Vol. 75, No. 1, pp. 22-28, September 1993).

Carlos E. Cortés, "Media literacy: An educational basic for the information age." Published in a slightly different form in *Education and Urban Society* (Vol. 24, No. 4, pp. 489-497, August 1992). ©1992 by Carlos E. Cortés. All rights reserved. Reprinted by permission of Corwin Press, Inc. and with the permission of the author.

Geneva Gay, "Building cultural bridges: A bold proposal for teacher education." Originally published in *Education and Urban Society* (Vol. 25, No. 3, pp. 285-299, May 1993). ©1993 Sage Publications, Inc. Reprinted by permission of Corwin Press, Inc. and with the permission of the author.

Jack G. Shaheen, "Media depictions of Arabs." An earlier version appeared, under the title "The Persian Gulf crisis gives scholars a chance to encourage more accurate depictions of Arabs," in *The Chronicle of Higher Education* (Vol. 37, No. 9, pp. B1, B3, October 31, 1990).

Lawrence White, "Hate-speech codes that will pass Constitutional muster" *The Chronicle of Higher Education* (Vol. 40, No. 38, p. A48, May 25, 1994).

TABLE OF CONTENTS

STATEMENT ON MULTICULTURAL EDUCATION

by
Senator Carol Moseley-Braun

We are currently experiencing a new era in economic competition. All over the world, barriers to trade between nations are falling. We are witnessing the development of a truly global marketplace. I believe that the United States can lead the way in this marketplace. But if we are to succeed, if we are to retain our competitiveness into the 21st century, there must be a renewed commitment to education in this country.

If there is any objective that should command complete American consensus, it is to ensure that every American has a chance to succeed. That is the core concept of the American dream—the chance to go as far as your ability and talent will take you. Education has always been a part of that core concept. In this country, the chance to be educated has always gone hand in hand with the chance to succeed.

Yet, education is more than a private benefit; it is a public good. The quality of education affects the entire community. Education promotes the standard and quality of living for our people. It increases our productivity and competitive advantage in world markets. It also prepares our workforce to compete in the emerging global economy.

Multicultural education helps our nation compete in the emerging global economy, for example, by allowing us to make full use of the talents and skills of every one of our citizens and the enormous cultural diversity within our borders. By giving all Americans the opportunity to share what is best about their heritage with the community at large, multicultural education helps us take advantage of our most precious natural resource—our human capital.

A central task of our time is to learn how to live together in our increasingly multiethnic, multicultural society. By giving our young people an opportunity to learn about each other in our nation's classrooms, they will come to understand for themselves that we are stronger as a nation and stronger as a people if we work together, if we utilize the talents of every one of our people, if we put aside racism, sexism, and all of the "isms" that separate us from one another. I am convinced that, more than any other group in our society, our young people can break the cycle of cultural isolation and persistent bias that creates barriers to full participation of all Americans.

If we do not make full use of the talents and skills of every one of our citizens, they are hurt as individuals, but we are hurt as a nation as well. I truly believe that if we come together, to work for our common good, we cannot fail. In the words of my mother, we may be as different as each of the five fingers, but we are all parts of one hand.

CONTRIBUTORS

J. Q. Adams

J. Q. Adams is an Associate Professor in the Department of Educational Foundations at Western Illinois University, Macomb, Illinois. He has worked extensively in the area of multicultural education as a consultant, lecturer, and curriculum development specialist. His recent publications include three volumes of *Multicultural Education: Strategies for Implementation in Colleges and Universities,* for which he is co-editor as well as a contributor. He has also developed and taught *"Dealing with Diversity,"* a Board of Governors Universities teleclass distributed nationally by PBS.

Bem P. Allen

Bem P. Allen (Ph.D. Experimental Psychology, University of Huston) is a Professor of Psychology at Western Illinois University and has studied and researched prejudice, racism, and sexism throughout his 27-year career. He has a number of journal publications on these topics and has written about them in his published texts. He also has a strong interest in multicultural issues. His teaching, publication, and conference attendance record includes many entries relevant to multicultural matters.

Alexander W. Astin

Alexander W. Astin is Professor of Higher Education and Director of the Higher Education Research Institute at the University of California, Los Angeles. A highly respected researcher and scholar in several areas of higher education, among his publications are *Assessment for Excellence: The Philosophy and Practice of Assessment and Evaluation in Higher Education; What Matters in College? Four Critical Years Revisited;* and "What Matters in General Education: Provocative Findings from a National Study of Student Outcomes" *(Perspectives,* Fall 1992).

James A. Banks

James A. Banks is Professor of Education and Director of the Center for Multicultural Education at the University of Washington. His numerous articles and books as well as presentations and workshops on multicultural education attest to his knowledge and leadership in this area. His books, many in multiple editions and used widely as textbooks, include *Multicultural Education: Theory and Practice; Teaching Strategies for Ethnic Studies; Multicultural Education: Issues and Perspectives;* and the *Handbook of Research on Multicultural Education.*

Nancy "Rusty" Barceló

Nancy "Rusty" Barceló is Assistant Provost in the Office of the Provost and Director of Opportunity at Iowa" at the University of Iowa. Well known for her work in organizing and coordinating outreach and retention programs for underrepresented students, she has created programs and developed university policy related to these students. She teaches courses in human relations, human rights and equity, and in Chicano and Puerto Rican cultures. She frequently lectures on multicultural issues and recently co-edited *Parallels and Intersections:*

The Experience of the Women Against Racism Committee in Iowa City.

Samuel Betances

Samuel Betances is Professor Emeritus of Sociology at Northeastern Illinois University where he taught undergraduate and graduate students for twenty years. He is a well-known and frequent lecturer on topics of diversity, social change, gender and race relations, demographic changes, and the impact of the global economy on group relations in the USA. He is committed to building positive synergy through ethnic diversity and is noted for the ease and effectiveness with which he weaves humor into his discussions of critical diversity issues.

James B. Boyer

James B. Boyer, Professor of Curriculum and American Ethnic Studies at Kansas State University, teaches courses in Manhattan, Kansas, while also coordinating and teaching in KSU's urban masters degree program in Kansas City. He is a founding member of the National Association of Multicultural Education and has been active in multicultural education for many years. He continues to direct training institutes in educational equity and cultural understanding and to develop teacher education projects that focus on equity for all populations.

Gayle Tronvig Carper

Gayle Tronvig Carper (J.D., DePaul University College of Law) is a Professor in the Law Enforcement and Justice Administration Department at Western Illinois University and a lawyer concentrating in criminal defense and juvenile justice. Her research interests include First Amendment and reproductive rights issues. She has chaired WIU's Women's Center Advisory Board and is currently developing a course on Women and the Law.

Carlos E. Cortés

Carlos E. Cortés is Professor Emeritus of History at the University of California, Riverside. His research encompasses multicultural education, ethnicity issues, and media as a force in conveying information (and misinformation) as well as in shaping attitudes. He has published in all of these areas as well as in history. Among his books are *Three Perspectives on Ethnicity: Blacks, Chicanos, and Native Americans, Understanding You and Them,* and *A Filmic Approach to the Study of Historical Dilemmas.* He is currently writing *Backing into the Future: A Brief History of Multicultural 21st-Century America.*

Nada Elia

Nada Elia (Ph.D., Comparative Literature, Purdue University) is an Assistant Professor at Western Illinois University, where she teaches non-Western Literature. Her areas of interest and research are counter-hegemonic, especially postcolonial and feminist, narratives. She is editing an anthology of narratives that describe a range of first generation immigrant experiences and recently contributed to *Food for Our Grandmothers: Writings for Arab-American and Arab-Canadian Feminists.*

Geneva Gay

Geneva Gay is Professor of Education and Associate with the Center of Multicultural Education at the University of Washington-Seattle. Known internationally for her scholarship in multicultural education, she received the 1990 Distinguished Scholar Award of the American Educational Research Association and the 1994 Multicultural Educator Award, the first presented by the National Association of Multicultural Education. Her writings include over 90 articles and chapters as well as the recently published *At the Essence of Learning: Multicultural Education.*

Howard L. Hansen

Howard L. Hansen (Ph.D. candidate, University of Nebraska-Lincoln) is an Assistant Professor of Mathematics at Western Illinois University. He has been actively involved with in-service and pre-service preparation of both elementary and secondary teachers of mathematics. He is especially interested in assuring equal access to the use of technology in the mathematics curriculum.

Duane M. Jackson

Duane M. Jackson is Chair of the Department of Psychology at Morehouse College. A graduate of the University of Illinois' Comparative Psychology and Behavior-Genetics program, his research and publications focus on various aspects of animal behavior, including relationships between learning and memory. He is a member of the Board of Governors for the National Conference on Undergraduate Research. As a teacher and scientist he is interested in incorporating multicultural perspectives into the teaching of science and into scientific research.

Hallie S. Lemon

Hallie S. Lemon (M.A., English, University of Illinois, Urbana) teaches writing at Western Illinois University. She coordinates the Collaborative Learning Across the Curriculum support group at Western for faculty interested in implementing successful collaborative learning strategies. She is currently writing articles and presenting workshops on the use of portfolios to teach writing and to assess teaching and learning.

Reinhard W. Lindner

Reinhard W. Lindner (Ph.D., Cognition/Instruction, University of Connecticut, Storrs) is Associate Professor in the Department of Educational Foundations at Western Illinois University. Dr. Lindner is a member of a number of professional research organizations, including the American Educational Research Association. His primary area of research involves the study of self-regulated learning. He publishes and presents at professional conferences regularly on this and related topics.

Savario Mungo

Savario Mungo (Ph.D., Curriculum and Instruction, New York University, New York) is a Professor of Education in the Department of Curriculum and Instruction at Illinois State

University, Normal. He has worked extensively in the field of cross-cultural communication and education as a presenter, consultant, and curriculum development specialist. His current research efforts include the development of multicultural strategies for use in classroom settings.

Judith K. Olson

Judith K. Olson (Ed.D., Curriculum and Instruction, Oklahoma State University, Stillwater) is a Professor of Mathematics at Western Illinois University. She teaches mathematics and mathematics education courses for pre-service and in-service teachers while actively promoting the importance of mathematics for all, especially women and members of traditionally underrepresented groups. She is director of "Connecting the Past with the Future: Women in Mathematics and Science," a National Science Foundation project that encourages the participation of women in mathematics and science.

Melfried Olson

Melfried Olson (Ed.D., Curriculum and Instruction - Secondary Mathematics, Oklahoma State University) is a Professor of Mathematics and Mathematics Education at Western Illinois University. He works with pre-service and in-service elementary, middle, and high school teachers of mathematics. He has been successful in securing funding for several school-based in-service projects and has written mathematics materials for "Connecting the Past with the Future: Women in Mathematics and Science."

Jacqueline C. Rickman

Jacqueline C. Rickman (Ed.D., Educational Psychology, Northern Illinois University) is an Assistant Professor in the Department of Educational Foundations at Western Illinois University. She teaches courses in human development, emphasizing the integration of technology, multicultural perspectives, and the concepts of collaboration and multiple intelligences into teacher preparation. Her current research involves the relationships in higher education among curriculum and program development, counseling and advisement, and retention, ableism, prodigiousness, and equity.

Brenda M. Rodriguez

Brenda M. Rodriguez is an educational consultant with the InterAmerica Midwest Multifunctional Resource Center and Director of Training and Special Programs for the InterAmerica Intercultural Training Institute. She has developed and conducted leadership training on a broad range of diversity and equity issues, including intercultural conflict resolution, the recognition and reduction of personal and institutional prejudice, cross-cultural counseling, the creation of inclusive communities, and multicultural curriculum transformation.

BarBara M. Scott

BarBara M. Scott is an Associate Professor of Sociology and Women's Studies and Chair of the Criminal Justice, Social Work, and Sociology Department at Northeastern Illinois University. She is the co-author of *Marriages and Families: Diversity and Change* and is a founding member of Sisters of Color International, an activist organization bringing Women of Color together in sisterhood to explore and affirm multicultural perspectives and to provide leadership within academic and ethnic communities.

Jack G. Shaheen

Jack G. Shaheen, Professor Emeritus of Mass Communications at Southern Illinois University, Edwardsville, has written and spoken often on portraits of Arabs and Muslims in U. S. popular culture. He is the author of two books, *Nuclear War Films* and *The TV Arab,* as well as numerous essays. A consultant on Arab issues with CBS News and a Department of State Scholar Diplomat, his work reflects his conviction that stereotypes of any group narrow vision and blur reality.

Pearlie Strother-Adams

Pearlie Strother-Adams is an Assistant Professor in the Department of English and Journalism at Western Illinois University. She has taught courses in both English composition and in African American literature. Her current assignment involves teaching courses in journalism, mass communications, and news reporting and writing. She enjoys writing and plans to channel much of her energy in that direction.

Martha E. Thompson

Martha E. Thompson is a Professor of Sociology and Women's Studies at Northeastern Illinois University in Chicago. Her commitment to curriculum development and pedagogical strategies for women's studies courses is longstanding. In her publications she has focused on ways to structure a classroom to build a community among students who vary in age, ethnicity, gender, literacy skills, physical ability, sexual orientation, and social class. *Women and Social Action,* the Board of Governors teleclass that she developed, provides an example of her approach.

Janice R. Welsch

Janice R. Welsch is a Professor in the Department of English and Journalism and Director of Faculty Development at Western Illinois University. She teaches courses in film history and criticism, women's studies, and cultural diversity and has coordinated many multicultural initiatives for the Society for Cinema Studies as well as for Western. She recently co-edited and contributed essays to *Multiple Voices in Feminist Film Criticism* and two volumes of *Multicultural Education: Strategies for Implementation in Colleges and Universities.*

Lawrence White

Lawrence White is University Counsel at Georgetown University, Washington, D.C. His article on hate-speech codes was adopted from a presentation at the Stetson University College of Law's National Conference on Law and Higher Education for publication in *The Chronicle of Higher Education.*

Section I: Establishing the Context for Multicultural Education

MULTICULTURAL EDUCATION:
DEVELOPMENT, DIMENSIONS, AND CHALLENGES

by
James A. Banks

The bitter debate over the literary and historical canon that has been carried on in the popular press and in several widely reviewed books has overshadowed the progress that has been made in multicultural education during the last two decades. The debate has also perpetuated harmful misconceptions about theory and practice in multicultural education. Consequently, it has heightened racial and ethnic tension and trivialized the field's remarkable accomplishments in theory, research, and curriculum development. The truth about the development and attainments of multicultural education needs to be told for the sake of balance, scholarly integrity, and accuracy. But if I am to reveal the truth about multicultural education, I must first identify and debunk some of the widespread myths and misconceptions about it.

Myths About Multicultural Education

<u>Multicultural Education Is for the Others</u>

One misconception about multicultural education is that it is an entitlement program and curriculum movement for African Americans, Hispanics, the poor, women, and other victimized groups.[1] The major theorists and researchers in multicultural education agree that the movement is designed to restructure educational institutions so all students, including middle-class white males, will acquire the knowledge, skills, and attitudes needed to function effectively in a culturally and ethnically diverse nation and world.[2] Multicultural education, as its major architects have conceived it during the last decade, is not an ethnic- or genderspecific movement. It is a movement designed to empower all students to become knowledgeable, caring, and active citizens in a deeply troubled and ethnically polarized nation and world.

The claim that multicultural education is only for people of color and for the disenfranchised is one of the pernicious and damaging misconceptions with which the movement has had to cope. It has caused intractable problems and has haunted multicultural education since its inception. Despite all that has been written and spoken about multicultural education being for all students, the image of multicultural education as an entitlement program for the "others" remains strong and vivid in the public imagination, as well as in the hearts and minds of many teachers and administrators. Teachers who teach in predominantly white schools and districts often state that they don't have a program or plan for multicultural education because they have few African American, Hispanic, or Asian American students.

When educators view multicultural education as the study of the "others," it is marginalized and held apart from mainstream education reform. Several critics of multicultural education, such as Arthur Schlesinger, John Leo, and Paul Gray, have perpetuated the idea that multicultural education is the study of the "other" by defining it as synonymous with Afrocentric education.[3] The history of intergroup education teaches us that only when education reform related to diversity is viewed as essential for all students—and as promoting the broad public interest—will it have a reasonable chance of becoming institutionalized in the nation's schools, colleges, and universities.[4] The intergroup education movement of the 1940s and 1950s failed in large part because intergroup educators were never able to persuade mainstream educators to believe that the approach was needed by and designed for all students. To its bitter but quiet end, mainstream educators viewed intergroup education as something for schools with racial problems and as something for "them" and not for "us."

Multicultural Education Is Opposed to the Western Tradition

Another harmful misconception about multicultural education has been repeated so often by its critics that many people take it as self-evident. This is the claim that multicultural education is a movement that is opposed to the West and to Western civilization. Multicultural education is not anti-West, because most writers of color—such as Rudolfo Anaya, Paula Gunn Allen, Maxine Hong Kingston, Maya Angelou, and Toni Morrison—are Western writers. Multicultural education itself is a thoroughly Western movement. It grew out of a civil rights movement grounded in such democratic ideals of the West as freedom, justice, and equality. Multicultural education seeks to extend to all people the ideals that were meant only for an elite few at the nation's birth.

Although multicultural education is not opposed to the West, its advocates do demand that the truth about the West be told, that its debt to people of color and women be recognized and included in the curriculum, and that the discrepancies between the ideals of freedom and equality and the realities of racism and sexism be taught to students. Reflective action by citizens is also an integral part of multicultural theory. Multicultural education views citizen action to improve society as an integral part of education in a democracy; it links knowledge, values, empowerment, and action. Multicultural education is also postmodern in its assumptions about knowledge and knowledge construction; it challenges positivist assumptions about the relationships between human values, knowledge, and action.

Positivists, who are the intellectual heirs of the Enlightenment, believe that it is possible to structure knowledge that is objective and beyond the influence of human values and interests. Multicultural theorists maintain that knowledge is positional, that it relates to the knower's values and experiences, and that knowledge implies action. Consequently, different concepts, theories, and paradigms imply different kinds of actions. Multiculturalists believe that, in order to have valid knowledge, information about the social condition and experiences of the knower are essential.

A few critics of multicultural education, such as John Leo and Dinesh D'Souza, claim that multicultural education has reduced or displaced the study of Western civilization in the nation's schools and colleges. However, as Gerald Graff points out in his welcome book *Beyond the Culture Wars*, this claim is simply not true. Graff cites his own research at the college level and that of Arthur Applebee at the high school level to substantiate his conclusion that European and American male authors—such as Shakespeare, Dante, Chaucer, Twain, and Hemingway—still dominate the required reading lists in the nation's high schools and colleges.[5] Graff found that, in the cases he examined, most of the books by authors of color were optional rather than required reading. Applebee found that, of the ten book-length works most frequently required in the high school grades, only one title was by a female author (Harper Lee's *To Kill a Mockingbird),* and not a single work was by a writer of color. Works by Shakespeare, Steinbeck, and Dickens headed the list.

Multicultural Education Will Divide the Nation

Many of its critics claim that multicultural education will divide the nation and undercut its unity. Schlesinger underscores this view in the title of his book, *The Disuniting of America: Reflections on a Multicultural Society.* This misconception is based partly on questionable assumptions about the nature of U. S. society and partly on a mistaken understanding

4

of multicultural education. The claim that multicultural education will divide the nation assumes that the nation is already united. While we are one nation politically, sociologically our nation is deeply divided along lines of race, gender, and class. The current debate about admitting gays into the military underscores another deep division in our society.

Multicultural education is designed to help unify a deeply divided nation rather than to divide a highly cohesive one. Multicultural education supports the notion of *e pluribus unum*—out of many, one. The multiculturalists and the Western traditionalists, however, often differ about how the *unum* can best be attained. Traditionally, the larger U. S. society and the schools tried to create unity by assimilating students from diverse racial and ethnic groups into a mythical Anglo American culture that required them to experience a process of self-alienation. However, even when students of color became culturally assimilated, they were often structurally excluded from mainstream institutions.

The multiculturalists view *e pluribus unum* as an appropriate national goal but they believe that the *unum* must be negotiated, discussed, and restructured to reflect the nation's ethnic and cultural diversity. The reformulation of what it means to be united must be a process that involves the participation of diverse groups within the nation, such as people of color, women, straights, gays, the powerful, the powerless, the young, and the old. The reformulation must also involve power sharing and participation by people from many different cultures who must reach beyond their cultural and ethnic borders in order to create a common civic culture that reflects and contributes to the well-being of all. This common civic culture will extend beyond the cultural borders of any single group and constitute a civic "borderland" culture.

In *Borderlands,* Gloria Anzaldúa contrasts cultural borders and borderlands and calls for a weakening of the former in order to create a shared borderland culture in which people from many different cultures can interact, relate, and engage in civic talk and action. Anzaldua states that "borders are set up to define the places that are safe and unsafe, to distinguish us from them. A border is a dividing line, a narrow strip along a steep edge. A borderland is a vague and undetermined place created by the residue of an unnatural boundary. It is in a constant state of transition."[6]

Multicultural Education Has Made Progress

While it is still on the margins rather than in the center of the curriculum in most schools and colleges, multicultural content has made significant inroads into both the school and the college curricula within the last two decades. The truth lies somewhere between the claim that no progress has been made in infusing the school and college curricula with multiethnic content and the claim that such content has replaced the European and American classics

In the elementary and high schools, much more ethnic content appears in social studies and language arts textbooks today than was the case 20 years ago. In addition, some teachers assign works written by authors of color along with the more standard American classics. In his study of book-length works used in the high schools, Applebee concluded that his most striking finding was how similar present reading lists are to past ones and how little change has occurred. However, he did note that many teachers use anthologies as a mainstay of their literature programs and that 21% of the anthology selections were written by women and 14% by authors of color.[7]

More classroom teachers today have studied the concepts of multicultural education than at any previous point in our history. A significant percentage of today's classroom teachers took a required teacher education course in multicultural education when they were in college. The multicultural education standard adopted by the National Council for Accreditation of Teacher Education in 1977, which became effective in 1979, was a major factor that stimulated the growth of multicultural education in teacher education programs. The standard stated: "The institution gives evidence of planning for multicultural education in its teacher education curricula including both the general and professional studies components."[8]

The market for teacher education textbooks dealing with multicultural education is now a substantial one. Most major publishers now have at least one text in the field. Textbooks in other required courses, such as educational psychology and the foundations of education, frequently have separate chapters or a significant number of pages devoted to examining concepts and developments in multicultural education.

Some of the nation's leading colleges and universities, such as the University of California at Berkeley, the University of Minnesota, and Stanford University, have either revised their general core curriculum to include ethnic content or have established an ethnic studies course requirement. The list of universities with similar kinds of requirements grows longer each year. However, the transformation of the traditional canon on college and university campuses has often been bitter and divisive. All changes in curriculum come slowly and painfully to university campuses, but curriculum changes that are linked with issues related to race evoke primordial feelings and reflect the racial crisis in American society. For example, at the University of Washington a bitter struggle ended with the defeat of the ethnic studies requirement.

Changes are also coming to elementary and high school textbooks. I believe that the demographic imperative is the major factor driving the changes in school textbooks. The color of the nation's student body is changing rapidly. Nearly half (about 45.5%) of the nation's school-age youths will be young people of color by 2020.[9] Black parents and brown parents are demanding that their leaders, their images, their pain, and their dreams be mirrored in the textbooks that their children study in school.

Textbooks have always reflected the myths, hopes, and dreams of people with money and power. As African Americans, Hispanics, Asians, and women become more influential, textbooks will increasingly reflect their hopes, dreams, and disappointments. Textbooks will have to survive in the marketplace of a browner America. Because textbooks still carry the curriculum in the nation's public schools, they will remain an important focus for multicultural curriculum reformers.

The Dimensions of Multicultural Education

One of the problems that continues to plague the multicultural education movement, both from within and without, is the tendency of teachers, administrators, policy makers, and the public to oversimplify the concept. Multicultural education is a complex and multidimensional concept, yet media commentators and educators alike often focus on only one of its many dimensions. Some teachers view it only as the inclusion of content about ethnic groups into the curriculum; others view it as an effort to reduce prejudice; still others view it as the celebration of ethnic holidays and events. After I made a presentation in which I described the major goals of multicultural education, a math teacher told me that what I said was fine and appropriate for language arts and social studies teachers, but it had nothing to do with him. After all, he said, math was math, regardless of the color of the kids.

This reaction on the part of a respected teacher caused me to think more deeply about the images of multicultural education that had been created by the key actors in the field. I wondered whether we were partly responsible for this teacher's narrow conception of multicultural education as merely content integration. It was in response to such statements by classroom teachers that I conceptualized the dimensions of multicultural education. I will use the following five dimensions to describe the field's major components and to highlight important developments within the last two decades: 1) content integration, 2) the knowledge construction process, 3) prejudice reduction, 4) an equity pedagogy, and 5) an empowering school culture and social structure.[10] I will devote most of the rest of this article to the second of these dimensions.

Content Integration

Content integration deals with the extent to which teachers use examples, data and information from a variety of cultures and groups to illustrate the key concepts, principles, generalizations, and theories in their subject area or discipline. In many school districts as well as in popular writing, multicultural education is viewed almost solely as content integration. This narrow conception of multicultural education is a major reason why many teachers in such subjects as biology, physics, and mathematics reject multicultural education as irrelevant to them and their students.

In fact, this dimension of multicultural education probably has more relevance to social studies and language arts teachers than it does to physics and math teachers. Physics and math teachers can insert multicultural content into their subjects—e.g., by using biographies of physicists and mathematicians of color and examples from different cultural groups. However, these kinds of activities are probably not the most important multicultural tasks that can be undertaken by science and math teachers. Activities related to the other dimensions of multicultural education, such as the knowledge construction process, prejudice reduction, and an equity pedagogy, are probably the most fruitful areas for the multicultural involvement of science and math teachers.

Knowledge Construction

The *knowledge construction process* encompasses the procedures by which social, behavioral, and natural scientists create knowledge in their disciplines. A multicultural focus on knowledge construction includes discussion of the ways in which the implicit cultural assumptions, frames of reference, perspectives, and biases within a discipline influence the construction of knowledge. An examination of the knowledge construction process is an important part of multicultural teaching. Teachers help students to understand how knowledge is created and how it is influenced by factors of race, ethnicity, gender, and social class.

Within the last decade, landmark work related to the construction of knowledge has been done by feminist social scientists and epistemologists, as well as by scholars in ethnic studies. Working in philosophy and sociology, Sandra Harding, Lorraine Code, and Patricia Hill Collins have done some of the most important work related to knowledge construction.[11] This ground-breaking work, although influential among scholars and curriculum developers, has been overshadowed in the popular media by the heated debates about the canon. These writers and researchers have seriously challenged the claims made by the positivists that knowledge can be value-free and have described the ways in which knowledge claims are influenced by the gender and ethnic characteristics of the knower. These scholars argue that the human interests and value assumptions of those who create knowledge should be identified, discussed, and examined.

Code states that the sex of the knower is epistemologically significant because knowledge is both subjective and objective. She maintains that both aspects should be recognized and discussed. Collins, an African American sociologist, extends and enriches the works of writers such as Code and Harding by describing the ways in which race and gender interact to influence knowledge construction. Collins calls the perspective of African American women

7

the perspective of "the outsider within." She writes, "As outsiders within, Black women have a distinct view of the contradictions between the dominant group's actions and ideologies."[12]

Curriculum theorists and developers in multicultural education are applying to the classroom the work being done by the feminist and ethnic studies epistemologists. In *Transforming Knowledge,* Elizabeth Minnich, a professor of philosophy and women's studies, has analyzed the nature of knowledge and described how the dominant tradition, through such logical errors as faulty generalization and circular reasoning, has contributed to the marginalization of women.[13]

I have identified five types of knowledge and described their implications for multicultural teaching.[14] Teachers need to be aware of the various types of knowledge so they can structure a curriculum that helps students to understand each type. Teachers also need to use their own cultural knowledge and that of their students to enrich teaching and learning. The types of knowledge I have identified and described are: 1) personal/cultural, 2) popular, 3) mainstream academic, 4) transformative, and 5) school. (I will not discuss school knowledge in this article.)

Personal/cultural knowledge consists of the concepts, explanations, and interpretations that students derive from personal experiences in their homes, families, and community cultures. Cultural conflict occurs in the classroom because much of the personal/cultural knowledge that students from diverse cultural groups bring to the classroom is inconsistent with school knowledge and with the teacher's personal and cultural knowledge. For example, research indicates that many African American and Mexican American students are more likely to experience academic success in cooperative rather than in competitive learning environments.[15] Yet the typical school culture is highly competitive, and children of color may experience failure if they do not figure out the implicit rules of the school culture.[16]

The popular knowledge that is institutionalized by the mass media and other forces that shape the popular culture has a strong influence on the values, perceptions, and behavior of children and young people. The messages and images carried by the media, which Carlos Cortés calls the societal curriculum,[17] often reinforce the stereotypes and misconceptions about racial and ethnic groups that are institutionalized within the larger society.

Of course, some films and other popular media forms do make positive contributions to racial understanding. *Dances with Wolves, Glory,* and *Malcolm X* are examples. However, there are many ways to view such films, and both positive and negative examples of popular culture need to become a part of classroom discourse and analysis. Like all human creations, even these positive films are imperfect. The multiculturally informed and sensitive teacher needs to help students view these films, as well as other media productions, from diverse cultural, ethnic, and gender perspectives.

The concepts, theories, and explanations that constitute traditional Westerncentric knowledge in history and in the social and behavioral sciences constitute mainstream academic knowledge. Traditional interpretations of U.S. history—embodied in such headings as "The European Discovery of America" and "The Westward Movement"—are central concepts in mainstream academic knowledge. Mainstream academic knowledge is established within mainstream professional associations, such as the American Historical Association and the American Psychological Association. It provides the interpretations that are taught in U. S. colleges and universities.

The literary legacy of mainstream academic knowledge includes such writers as Shakespeare, Dante, Chaucer, and Aristotle. Critics of multicultural education, such as Schlesinger, D'Souza, and Leo, believe that mainstream academic knowledge in the curriculum is being displaced by the new knowledge and interpretations that have been created by scholars working in women's studies and in ethnic studies. However, mainstream academic knowledge is not only threatened from without but also from within. Postmodern scholars in organizations such as the American Historical Association, the American Sociological Association, and the American Political Science Association are challenging the dominant positivist interpretations and paradigms within their disciplines and creating alternative explanations and perspectives.

Transformative academic knowledge challenges the facts, concepts, paradigms, themes, and explanations routinely accepted in mainstream academic knowledge. Those who pursue transformative academic knowledge seek to expand and substantially revise established canons, theories, explanations, and research methods. The transformative research methods and theory that have been developed in women's studies and in ethnic studies since the 1970s constitute, in my view, the most important developments in social science theory and research in the last 20 years.

It is important for teachers and students to realize, however, that transformative academic scholarship has a long history in the United States and that the current ethnic studies movement is directly linked to an earlier ethnic studies movement that emerged in the late 1800s.[18] George Washington Williams published Volume 1 of the first history of African Americans in 1882 and the second volume in 1883. Other important works published by African American transformative scholars in times past included works by W. E. B. Du Bois, Carter Woodson, Horace Mann Bond, and Charles Wesley.[19]

The works of these early scholars in African American studies, which formed the academic roots of the current multicultural education movement when it emerged in the 1960s and 1970s, were linked by several important characteristics. Their works were transformative because they created data, interpretations, and perspectives that challenged those that were established by white, mainstream scholarship. The work of the transformative scholars presented positive images of African Americans and refuted stereotypes that were pervasive within the established scholarship of their time.

Although they strove for objectivity in their works and wanted to be considered scientific researchers, these transformative scholars viewed knowledge and action as tightly linked and became involved in social action and administration themselves. Du Bois was active in social protest and for many years was the editor of *Crisis,* an official publication of the National Association for the Advancement of Colored People. Woodson co-founded the Association for the Study of Negro (now Afro-American) Life and History, founded and edited the *Journal of Negro History,* edited the *Negro History Bulletin* for classroom teachers, wrote school and college textbooks on Negro history, and founded Negro History Week (now Afro-American History Month).

Transformative academic knowledge has experienced a renaissance since the 1970s. Only a few of the most important works can be mentioned here because of space. Martin Bernal, in an important two-volume work, *Black Athena,* has created new interpretations about the debt that Greece owes to Egypt and Phoenicia. Before Bernal, Ivan Van Sertima and Cheikh Anta Diop also created novel interpretations of the debt that Europe owes to Africa. In two books, *Indian Givers* and *Native Roots,* Jack Weatherford describes Native American contributions that have enriched the world.

Ronald Takaki, in several influential books, such as *Iron Cages: Race and Culture in 19th-Century America* and *Strangers from a Different Shore: A History of Asian Americans,* has given us new ways to think about the ethnic experience in America. The literary contribution to transformative scholarship has also been rich, as shown by *The Signifying Monkey: A Theory of African-American Literary Criticism,* by Henry Louis Gates, Jr.; *Long Black Song: Essays in Black American Literature and Culture,* by Houston Baker, Jr.; and *Breaking Ice: An Anthology of Contemporary African-American Fiction,* edited by Terry McMillan.

A number of important works in the transformative tradition that interrelate race and gender have also been published since the 1970s. Important works in this genre include *Unequal Sisters: A Multicultural Reader in U. S. Women's History,* edited by Carol Ellen DuBois and Vicki Ruiz; *Race, Gender, and Work: A Multicultural Economic History of Women in the United States,* by Teresa Amott and Julie Matthaei; *Labor of Love, Labor of Sorrow: Black Women, Work, and the Family from Slavery to the Present,* by Jacqueline Jones; and *The Forbidden Stitch: An Asian American Women's Anthology,* edited by Shirley Geok-lin Lim, Mayumi Tsutakawa, and Margarita Donnelly.

The Other Dimensions

The *prejudice reduction* dimension of multicultural education focuses on the characteristics of children's racial attitudes and on strategies that can be used to help students develop more positive racial and ethnic attitudes. Since the 1960s, social scientists have learned a great deal about how racial attitudes in children develop and about ways in which educators can design interventions to help children acquire more positive feelings toward other racial groups. I have reviewed that research in two recent publications and refer readers to them for a comprehensive discussion of this topic.[20]

This research tells us that by age four African American, white, and Mexican American children are aware of racial differences and show racial preferences favoring whites. Students can be helped to develop more positive racial attitudes if realistic images of ethnic and racial groups are included in teaching materials in a consistent, natural, and integrated fashion. Involving students in vicarious experiences and in cooperative learning activities with students of other racial groups will also help them to develop more positive racial attitudes and behaviors.

An *equity pedagogy* exists when teachers use techniques and teaching methods that facilitate the academic achievement of students from diverse racial and ethnic groups and from all social classes. Using teaching techniques that cater to the learning and cultural styles of diverse groups and using the techniques of cooperative learning are some of the ways that teachers have found effective with students from diverse racial, ethnic, and language groups.[21]

An *empowering school culture and social structure* will require the restructuring of the culture and organization of the school so that students from diverse racial, ethnic, and social-class groups will experience educational equality and a sense of empowerment. This dimension of multicultural education involves conceptualizing the school as the unit of change and making structural changes within the school environment. Adopting assessment techniques that are fair to all groups, doing away with tracking, and creating the belief among the staff members that all students can learn are important goals for schools that wish to create a school culture and social structure that are empowering and enhancing for a diverse student body.

Multicultural Education and the Future

The achievements of multicultural education since the late sixties and early seventies are noteworthy and should be acknowledged. Those who have shaped the movement during the intervening decades have been able to obtain wide agreement on the goals of and approaches to multicultural education. Most multiculturalists agree that the major goal of multicultural education is to restructure schools so all students will acquire the knowledge, attitudes, and skills needed to function in an ethnically and racially diverse nation and world. As is the case with other interdisciplinary areas of study, debates within the field continue. These debates are consistent with the philosophy of a field that values democracy and diversity. They are also a source of strength.

Multicultural education is being implemented widely in the nation's schools, colleges, and universities. The large number of national conferences, school district workshops, and teacher education courses in multicultural education is evidence of its success and perceived importance. Although the process of integration of content is slow and often contentious, multicultural content is increasingly becoming a part of core courses in schools and colleges. Textbook publishers are also integrating ethnic and cultural content into their books, and the pace of such integration is increasing.

Despite its impressive successes, however, multicultural education faces serious challenges as we move toward the next century. One of the most serious of these challenges is the highly organized, well-financed attack by the Western traditionalists who fear that multicultural education will transform America in ways that will result in their own disempowerment. Ironically, the successes that multicultural education has experienced during the last decade have played a major role in provoking the attacks.

The debate over the canon and the well-orchestrated attack on multicultural education reflect an identity crisis in American society. The American identity is being reshaped as groups on the margins of society begin to participate in the mainstream and to demand that their visions be reflected in a transformed America. In the future, the sharing of power and the transformation of identity required to achieve lasting racial peace in America may be valued rather than feared, for only in this way will we achieve national salvation.

ENDNOTES

[1]Glazer, N. (1991, Sept. 2). In defense of multiculturalism. *New Republic,* 1822; and D'Souza, D. (1991, March). Illiberal education. *Atlantic,* 51-79.

[2]Banks, J. A. (1994). *Multiethnic education: Theory and practice* (3rd ed.). Boston: Allyn and Bacon; Banks, J. A., & McGee, C. A. (Eds.). (1993). *Multicultural education: Issues and perspectives* (2nd ed.). Boston: Allyn and Bacon; and Sleeter, C. E., & Grant, C. A. (1988). *Making choices for multicultural education: Five approaches to race, class, and gender.* Columbus, OH: Merrill.

[3]Schlesinger, Jr., A. M. (1991). *The disuniting of America: Reflections on a multicultural society.* Knoxville, TN: Whittle Direct Books; Leo, J. (1990, Nov. 12). A fringe history of the world. U. S. *News & World Report,* 25-26; and Gray, P. (1991, July 8). Whose America? *Time,* 13-17.

[4]Taba, H. et al. (1952). *Intergroup education in public schools.* Washington, D.C.: American Council on Education.

[5]Graff, G. (1992). *Beyond the culture wars: How teaching the conflicts can revitalize American education.* New York: Norton; and Applebee, A. N. (1992, Sept.). Stability and change in the high school canon. *English Journal,* 27-32.

[6]Anzaldúa, G. (1987). *Borderlands: La Frontera: The new mestiza.* San Francisco: Spinsters/Aunt Lute, 3.

[7]Applebee, p. 30.

[8]*Standards for the accreditation of teacher education. (1977)*. Washington, D.C.: National Council for Accreditation of Teacher Education, 4.

[9]Pallas, A. M., Natriello, G., & McDill, E. L. (1989, June/July). The changing nature of the disadvantaged population: Current dimensions and future trends. *Educational Researcher,* 16-22.

[10]Banks, J. A. (1993). Multicultural education: Historical development, dimensions, and practice. In L. Darling-Hammond (Ed.), *Review of research in education,* (Vol. 19, pp. 3-49). Washington, D.C.: American Educational Research Association.

[11]Harding, S. (1991). *Whose science, whose knowledge? Thinking from women's lives.* Ithaca, NY: Cornell University Press; Code, L. (1991). *What can she know? Feminist theory and the construction of knowledge.* Ithaca, NY: Cornell University Press; and Collins, P. H. (1990). *Black feminist thought: Knowledge, consciousness, and the politics of empowerment.* New York Routledge.

[12]Collins, p. 11.

[13]Minnich, E. K. (1990). *Transforming knowledge.* Philadelphia: Temple University Press.

[14]Banks, J. A. (1993, June/July). The canon debate, knowledge construction and multicultural education. *Educational Researcher,* 4-14.

[15]Slavin, R. E. (1983). *Cooperative learning.* New York: Longman.

[16]Delpit, L. D. (1988). The silenced dialogue: Power and pedagogy in educating other people's children. *Harvard Educational Review, 58,* 280-98.

[17]Cortés, C. E. (1981). The societal curriculum: Implications for multiethnic education. In J. A. Banks (Ed.), *Education in the 80s: Multiethnic education* (pp. 2432). Washington, D.C.: National Education Association.

[18]Banks, J. A. (1992, Summer). African American scholarship and the evolution of multicultural education. *Journal of Negro Education,* 273-86.

[19]A bibliography that lists these and other more recent works of transformative scholarship appears at the end of this article.

[20]Banks, J. A. (1991). Multicultural education: Its effects on students' racial and gender role attitudes. In James P. Shaver (Ed.), *Handbook of research on social studies teaching and learning* (pp. 459-69). New York: Macmillan; and Banks, J. A., (1993). Multicultural education for young children: Racial and ethnic attitudes and their modification. In Bernard Spodek (Ed.), *Handbook of research on the education of young children* (pp. 236-50). New York: Macmillan.

[21]Shade, B. J. R. (Ed.). (1989). *Culture, style, and the educative process.* Springfield, IL: Charles C. Thomas.

BIBLIOGRAPHY

Amott, T. L., & Matthaei, J. A. (1991). *Race, gender, and work: A multicultural economic history of women in the United States.* Boston: South End Press.

Baker, H. A., Jr. (1990). *Long black song: Essays in black American literature and culture.* Charlottesville: University Press of Virginia.

Bernal, M. (1987, 1991). *Black Athena: The Afroasiatic roots of classical civilization,* 2 vols. New Brunswick, NJ: Rutgers University Press.

Bond, H. M. (1939). *Negro education in Alabama: A study in cotton and steel.* Washington, D.C.: Associate Publishers.

DuBois, C. E., & Ruiz, V. L. (Eds.). (1990). *Unequal sisters: A multicultural reader in U. S. women's history.* NewYork: Routledge.

Du Bois, W. E. B. (1896). *The suppression of the African slave trade to the United States of America, 1638-1870.* Millwood, NY: Kraus-Thomas.

Gates, H. L., Jr. (1988). *The signifying monkey: A theory of African-American literary criticism.* New York: Oxford University Press.

Geok-lin Lim, S., Mayumi, T., & Donnelly, M. (Eds.). (1989). *The forbidden stitch: An Asian American women's anthology.* Corvallis, OR: Calyx Books.

Jones, J. (1985). *Labor of love, labor of sorrow: Black women, work, and the family from slavery to the present.* New York: Vintage Books.

McMilllan, T. (Ed.). (1990). *Breaking ice: An anthology of contemporary African-American fiction.* New York: Penguin Books.

Takaki, R. T. (Ed). (1979). *Iron cages: Race and culture in 19th century America.* Seattle: University of Washington Press.

Takaki, R. T. (1989). *Strangers from a different shore: A history of Asian Americans.* Boston: Little, Brown.

Van Sertima, I. (Ed.). (1988). *Great black leaders: Ancient and modern.* New Brunswick, NJ: African Studies Department, Rutgers University.

Van Sertima, I. (Ed.). (1989). *Great African thinkers, Vol. 1: Cheikh Anta Diop.* New Brunswick, NJ: Transaction Books.

Weatherford, J. (1988). *Indian givers: How the Indians of the Americas transformed the world.* New York: Fawcett Columbine.

Weatherford, J. (1992). *Native roots: How the Indians enriched America.* New York: Faweett Columbine.

Wesley, C. H. (1935). *Richard Allen: Apostle of freedom.* Washington, D.C.: Associated Publishers.

Williams, G. W. (1989). *History of the negro race in America from 1619 to 1880: Negroes as slaves, as soldiers, and as citizens, 2 vols.* Salem, NH: Ayer. (Original works published 1882-1883)

Woodson, C. G. (1921). *The history of the Negro church.* Washington, D.C.: Associated Publishers.

THE MULTICULTURAL CAMPUS:
FACING THE CHALLENGES

by
Nancy "Rusty" Barceló

I would like to reflect upon a major fact in my life. Twenty-five years ago I left California and stepped off a bus in Iowa City to join the University of Iowa community as a student. If anyone would have told me that 25 years later I would be writing about the challenges of the multicultural curriculum, I would have told them they were crazy. When I arrived on campus in 1969, as I recall, there were about 48 African American students, one Asian American, three Chicanos, and one Native American participating in the Educational Opportunity Program. African American Studies and Women's Studies were in the embryonic stages of development and were not to come to full fruition until the mid-seventies.

I did not know at the time that being a Mexican American was important to my well-being. However, coming to Iowa was probably the best thing that ever happened to me because I had taken being a Chicana for granted in California. And why not? Mi familia, language, and all other aspects of my Chicano culture were around me, from the Mexican grocery store to the Mexican music flowing from my grandmother's radio. I was isolated from the broader society and the problems that forced many of my people to seek safety and identity within their respective barrios. It took my mother to remind me that my Mexican identity was critical to my growth and development, and ultimately, to my survival. It still does.

One evening during my first semester when I was feeling particularly blue and cold—I could not believe that the thermometer over the Iowa State Bank read -50—I called my mother to tell her I would be returning to California at the end of the term. I thought for sure she would tell me to pack my bags right then and there and come home. But she didn't. Instead, she replied: "Rust, where there is one Mexican there is probably another." Well, I did not have a clue what she was saying or what my Mexican heritage had to do with being cold. In fact, I was hurt that she was not more understanding. A week later I received a care package from her with some Mexican sweet bread and a couple of cultural icons for my room, but without a note. That scared me because she was trying to tell me something, and I just was not getting it.

The following day in the library her words and message were still haunting me when I suddenly found myself among the census data. Mom was right; I was not alone.

- I learned that Illinois, Wisconsin, Kansas, Minnesota, Missouri and even Iowa had significant Spanish-speaking populations
- I would learn later that the Chicago area had a Spanish surnamed population that was larger than the combined Chicano populations of Arizona and Colorado (Cardenas, 1976).
- I learned that the single largest employer of Mexican Labor in 1928 was not in El Paso, Texas, but on the southern shores of Lake Michigan (Cardenas, 1976).
- I learned that the first major Mexican American community in Iowa was established in Ft. Madison in 1898—just a hop, skip, and a jump from where I was (Garcia, 1974).
- I learned that the second language spoken in Iowa was not German but Spanish (Garcia, 1974).

Well, I asked, if all this is true, why am I the only Latina at my institution? As I became more aware of the status of Chicanos and other underrepresented groups, I began asking myself what courses were available to learn about the Mexican American experience. Not only were there no courses, there were no Mexican American professors or staff persons on campus to help me either. I began to understand the alienation I felt had nothing to do with the cold weather. That realization was all I needed to put me on my present path. I have never looked back. Sometimes we have to step outside of our environments to really see who we are and how we interact with the rest of the world. Iowa, in an important sense, put me in touch with the strength and importance of my identity in helping me survive the points of contestation in my life: my ethnicity, sexuality, and gender.

I share this story to illustrate that the work we do has its origins at the most personal level of our lives and to locate myself in the context of this essay. No vita can really do that! Too often we forget that where we position ourselves dictates our relationship to the broader world around us. Our positioning also provides the basis for how others interact with us, especially in terms of power dynamics: who has the power to assume or assert control. It is vital for each of us to understand this especially if we are viewed as "other," in order to empower ourselves to effect change. I believe knowing oneself in the most intimate way is critical for those of us working on multicultural curricula. How can we teach others if we do not first know ourselves and what we bring to an experience? At the same time, we have to understand where our students situate themselves to appreciate the experiences they bring to the classroom. We sometimes forget that we can learn from our students as much as they learn from us.

My teaching has been enriched because of this realization. When I taught the human relations course the first year it was required for students aspiring to be teachers, I asked on the first day of class how many were opposed to the requirement. I expected a few hands to go up, but when the entire class raised their hands, I promptly threw out the syllabus to find common ground. Together we reconstructed the class and succeeded in achieving the requirement goals because of our shared input. It was a lesson I shall never forget! Sharing power is at the heart of so much of what needs to be done in our changing society. This alone makes ours a very difficult task. We only need look to South Africa's struggle to know this is true.

When I was at my computer trying to pull these thoughts together in a cohesive manner, a couple of events that occurred this spring kept intruding on the task and served as a reminder that personal encounters continually serve to shape our work.

For example, recently I was at an institution to give two public presentations about the status of Latinos and Latinas in education. I also agreed to meet with the philosophy club for a roundtable discussion about diversity issues. I learned upon arrival, to my surprise and horror, that the discussion was titled "Affirmative Action Disadvantages White Males." Talk about walking into the lion's den! To make matters worse, the discussion was publicized all over the building with bright blue posters bearing this highly charged title and *my name!* I gathered all my strength and marched into a room full of people who, it quickly became apparent, were strongly divided. I outlined a ground rule for our discussion: each person would be allowed to speak without interruption. I added that when we come together as we had, we bring with us our differences: race, ethnicity, class, gender, sexuality, religion, and physical abilities. All of these, as well as many other factors, I said, affect the way we interact or choose not to interact with one another. Our differences often determine in large part how we respond to issues such as affirmative action, in terms of perceptions based upon personal experiences. We needed to listen to each other to appreciate where each of us was coming from even though we might never agree.

I concluded by saying that the process of working together to find solutions for difficult issues across multiple voices is never easy but not impossible, that each of us represented an individual who was prepared to place him or herself at risk by participating in the dialogue. Only then did I begin deconstructing the myth that white males were being penalized, pointing out the positive affirmative action effects white males enjoyed since the law had opened up the old boys network to everyone, including white males. What followed was a series of comments about affirmative action myths from employment quotas to curriculum integration. Some argued affirmative action should be eliminated because of preferential treatment; others debated the need for more aggressive affirmative action initiatives to meet the needs of an increasingly diverse society.

I had a second encounter during my public presentation that evening about racism in the academy. At the end of the talk I agreed to entertain questions. The first to rise was a senior English professor who began by asking for ten minutes since I had had 46 to spew propaganda and untruths. I told him I would gladly give him the ten minutes but reminded him that the 45 minutes I had spoken was minute in comparison to his voice which had been heard for over 300 years. Attacking me personally, he focused on how the propaganda I was spewing was the basis for special privileges, the destruction of the western canon, and the divisions among us. As he spoke, he unintentionally validated my points—much to his horror—and left in a rage.

The following day I met with administrators who asked how they could reassure members of their institution they were committed to affirmative action. In our discussion, when I used as examples the events of the previous day, they dismissed the encounter with the professor saying, "That's just the way he is." I pointed out that their attitude in effect condoned his behavior since no one at the presentation knew him and the perception could be that he represented the voice of the institution if those in charge did not publicly condemn such inappropriate attacks. I added that, given the personal nature of his attack and the volatile situation it had created, someone else might have filed a formal complaint based on racial harassment.

These events highlight how immediate and complex diversity issues are on every level. The May 11, 1994 issue of *The Chronicle of Higher Education* verifies this. Let me just quote the index notes to give you the breadth and complexity of the topics in this single issue:

- An official in an education department resigned amid allegations that he made repeated sexual advances to two college student-aid workers;
- Thousands of students rallied in Mississippi as a federal court prepared for trial of the state's long-standing desegregation case;
- A U. S. judge approved a plan by the VMI to maintain its all-male admissions policy;
- The Equal Employment Opportunity Commission sued Campbell University for firing an instructor because he had AIDS;
- The Education Department says two universities broke the law in their handling of sexual harassment complaints;
- Nine students sue Stanford to overturn a four-year-old speech code that bans verbal insults involving race, religion, or sexual orientation;
- Chicano students at Stanford demand the establishment of a Chicano Studies department and the rehiring of Cecilia Burciaga whose position was eliminated; and
- Students at UC-Santa Barbara are demanding more Chicano faculty.

When I combine these articles with the many e-mail items addressing diversity I receive daily and with the events of the last two months, the urgency of our work to transform the curricula and our teaching is evident to me. What has become most clear is that *institutions* must be transformed. The incidents I encountered last month illustrate how institutional culture serves to perpetuate myths about diversity, and the articles cited speak to how institutions respond to individual incidents but seldom connect the incidents with the broader campus culture. Too often institutions focus on individual incidents without acknowledging the role infrastructure plays in what is taught and how it is taught. The answer is not censorship. We need to explore strategies that provide space where multiple voices and views can be heard in open dialogue. Disagreements are healthy and encourage everyone to be clear about goals and objectives;

debate often expands our thinking and understanding regardless of the issue at hand.

Initiatives to curb individual incidents of racism as well as plans to diversify the curriculum must be analyzed within the context of the total institution from mission statement to student retention programs. Only by focusing on the total institution can real change be effected. Because of lack of attention to the infrastructure, progress to diversify the curriculum and develop new teaching methods has been limited. I have found this to be true, for instance, in working with the University of Iowa Lesbian, Gay, and Bisexual Staff and Faculty Association on developing a sexuality studies program. We have been teaching sexuality studies courses for over three years, but, because we do not have a senior professor teaching any of the courses, the program proposal remains in committee. One might legitimately ask, "Is this being stymied because of campus heterosexism?" That the proposal is coming from faculty and graduate students in the Association and not from the core faculty places it on the outside of accepted studies. Imagine the difference if the leadership came from the inner circle of the infrastructure. How much greater the possibility for change!

In spite of the difficulty in changing institutional infrastructure, colleges and universities across the country are introducing diversity requirements, often amid great debates about the canon. This happened on my campus when a cultural diversity requirement was proposed (It passed.) as part of the general education core. Debates included protests that the curriculum could not bear one more course and that the essential body of knowledge a student should acquire would be eliminated. These protests are problematic for many reasons and ignore some important realities.

As I have stated often, the protests are completely out of step with the changing demographics of our country. We know demographics project that at least 51% of the U. S. population will soon be what we today call "minorities," and most will come from a home where a language other than English is spoken (1990 U. S. Department of Education). "Much of this growth reflects the phenomenal rate by which the Asian American and Latino populations are increasing, and yet bilingual education programs are still considered unimportant and even controversial. The popular view concerning these two populations has been that they should assimilate as quickly as possible, forget their native languages and speak English only. Using language as a cultural battleground in the United States is not a new phenomenon nor limited to the Asian and Latino populations: many African Americans face discrimination for speaking 'non-standard' English, and American Indians have been subjected to centuries of cultural genocide, one aspect of which has been to enforce their abandonment of speaking and teaching their native languages. Yet bilingual education programs are critically important in preparing students for the coming century" (Barceló, 1991).

Actually, I believe the resistance to bilingual programs is related to my second concern: the preservation of the western canon and its role in the assimilation of western values and traditions. Everyday I hear or read the query, "Why can't 'these' people just assimilate to U. S. culture?" Little or no thought is given, however, to what that culture might be. The assimilation in this sense seems motivated by fear, fear of losing power, and fear that a diverse curriculum implies replacement not only of the canon but also of the individuals who have been in control. Fear makes it difficult, if not impossible, for individuals to believe that multicultural education is about expanding the canon, making it more inclusive of diverse works as well as of different modes of analysis. I can't imagine not including *Moby Dick* or the works of Shakespeare, Faulkner, or Mark Twain in a literature curriculum, but I would ask a class to critique them within the context of multiple theories that might include race, gender, and class.

The western canon issue has served to marginalize diversity courses and programs by refusing to recognize their legitimacy in developing new knowledge and preparing students to be good citizens. Faculty are also marginalized in some instances if they actively pursue ways to diversify the curriculum and explore new teaching methods to reach the diverse students in their classes. They experience great pressure to conform or assimilate to traditional teaching and research. This issue of legitimacy is complicated further by the fact people of color, women, gays, and lesbians are the ones primarily teaching multicultural courses. Individuals within these groups are often viewed, not for their skills or knowledge, but as "other," as affirmative action hires who are not quite legitimate themselves. Additionally, graduate students are often discouraged from pursuing topics focusing on race, class, sexuality, and gender because they are not valued as legitimate academic pursuits. Few institutional rewards are available to individuals who seek this line of study. A complete restructuring of the reward system is necessary before faculty will wholeheartedly come forward in this endeavor.

Marginality also results from the prevailing notion that diversity courses are only for students of color. I was at a recent meeting of administrators that confirmed the continuation of this myth when an academic affairs person spoke about how diversity courses were being designed for students of color so they could become familiar with their cultural identities. No mention was made about the value of such courses for all students if they are to function effectively within our increasingly pluralistic society.

The challenge of defining a multicultural curriculum is a major issue for many institutions. Traditionally the term tended to refer to five major groups: Native, African, and Asian Americans, Latinos, and women. However, since the 1980s groups such as gays and lesbians and persons with disabilities have been encompassed in a move to be more inclusive. While some institutions still struggle with any definition, many campuses have responded by expanding their human rights statement to be more inclusive. To hear individuals who have dedicated their lives to working on diversity issues fail to understand or reject outright an inclusive definition has been discouraging. Such failure or rejection serves to reinforce an institution's lack of action on behalf of all the disenfranchised. I have argued that the need for alliances has never been greater in the face of these and other challenges.

The term multicultural itself can also be problematic since it tends to obscure not only individual identity but also the identities of various cultural groups. I have often argued that such generic terms send the message that we are all the same. Consequently, a course might be designed with a single ethnic group as the referential core from which connections or comparisons to other groups are made. For example, a course could focus primarily on African American literature with only token references to other groups, or a course might focus on Latino issues with no clear recognition that the term Latino includes over 20 ethnic groups, each with its own stories, histories, and proud traditions. Some institutions subscribe to a color-blind philosophy without realizing color blindness limits the notion of difference and fails to explore how our experiences intersect, parallel, and diverge at various points.

All too often we believe we have achieved diversity in the curriculum when we have simply added material that reflects greater inclusivity and multiple perspectives. More is needed, however, than additions to course content. Fortunately, pedagogy is becoming a major concern among those researching and teaching from multicultural perspectives. Linda S. Marchesani and Maurianne Adams (Adams, 1992), in *Dynamics of Diversity in the Teaching-Learning Process: A Faculty Development Model for Analysis and Action,* describe four dimensions of teaching and learning in a diverse society. They include
1. Knowing one's students and understanding the ways that students from various social and cultural backgrounds experience the college classroom;
2. Knowing oneself as a person with a prior history of academic socialization interacting with a social and cultural background and learned beliefs;
3. Creating a curriculum that incorporates diverse social and cultural perspectives; and
4. Developing a broad repertoire of teaching methods to address learning styles of stu-

dents from different social backgrounds (pp. 10-11).

This last dimension includes the possibility of decentering traditional power structures in the classroom, exploring ways to make classes more participatory, and using field experiences in innovative ways.

I would like us to consider what constitutes a multicultural curriculum: New courses? Integration of traditional courses? Human relations courses in which everybody is included on a one-time basis? Ethnic Studies? Women's Studies? Sexuality Studies? Aging Studies? The list could go on. Personally, I would like to see them all. Bits and pieces of all of these may already exist on a single campus. The greatest need, however, is the integration of multicultural perspectives into traditional courses *while* these other options are also in place. Each has its strengths and limitations. As curricular reform occurs, we must be sure Ethnic Studies, Women's Studies, Gay and Lesbian Studies, and the like are not eliminated.

These programs are critical in bringing to the forefront of academia new paradigms and theories related to specific bodies of study. The programs serve as change agents in the institutions by bringing diverse faculty, students, and methodologies to the academy. Unfortunately, few of these programs have achieved departmental status. Often viewed as less than legitimate, they are kept at the borders of the institution. Consequently, they are frequently underfunded and understaffed. The interdisciplinary paradigm upon which they are based is viewed as a weakness by traditionalists within the institutions. A core body of knowledge such as that characteristic of a traditional discipline, they argue, is missing. However, the interdisciplinary approach is the heart and soul of these programs, and it is interesting to see how in recent years some validation of this approach has occurred even within the most established disciplines as the interrelatedness of bodies of knowledge is recognized and explored.

In spite of the numerous contributions they have made to new knowledge, to new paradigms of teaching and learning, many of these programs have come under close scrutiny because of their place on the margins; they are seen as expendable, especially when resources are scarce. If ever there was a time to have these programs, it is now. Changing demographics and the legitimacy of the groups being studied demand them.

However, some of these programs, while committed to transforming the academy, have become exclusive and resistant to continued growth and change. For example, Women's Studies has been closely critiqued by women of color who accuse the programs of being racist because of their reluctance to hire women of color or to incorporate the perspectives of women of color. African American and Chicano Studies have also come under fire for their failure to include a feminist perspective, and all are being challenged to address the issue of sexuality.

At a recent National Chicano Studies Conference I shared the following: Not long ago I attended a conference luncheon at which a Chicano teacher was sharing some thoughts about a Chicano history book he had written for high school students in Los Angeles. I had dutifully bought the text just prior to his presentation because I was pleased that such a book was finally available. As he began speaking, a Chicana student leaned across and asked me if Chicanas were represented in the book. I felt a pit develop in my stomach as I started flipping through the pages and could not find one photo of a Mexicana or Chicana, not even Dolores Huerta! I turned first to the index and then to the table of contents hoping for some reference, but there were none. In the first chapter a short paragraph was dedicated to Malinche as the traitor and, more symbolically, as the whore of Mexico, views that have been refuted by Chicana and Mexican scholars alike.

I listened patiently to the author hoping he would recognize the significant role that Mexicanas and Chicanas have had in our struggle as a people. He was proud to report that he was part of the National Association for Chicano Studies; I wondered if he knew NACS has recognized the importance of Chicana scholars through the Chicana Caucus. He spoke about how Chicanos needed to address their own racism toward others, but he never talked about sexism or, for that matter, classism or heterosexism. In closing remarks when he referred to the audience as "guy," I had to rise to challenge the limited view of Chicano history he was presenting.

- I reminded him that, indeed, fathers had marched off to WWII but mothers had marched off to the factories, and both served with distinction.
- I reminded him that, while the zoot suiters were being beaten on the streets of L.A., the pachucas were being raped.
- I reminded him that women worked in the fields right along with the men and were in fact the ones who provided so much of the impetus for union organizing.

Although my brief rebuke was well received by most of those present, I felt somewhat discouraged. It was difficult to comprehend that such an omission was possible given the proliferation of Chicanas documenting our experience in history, poetry, music, literature, education psychology, health, sociology. While I acknowledged his apology, I could find no excuse, nor could others. This made me realize we cannot assume that the "o" in Chicano or in Latino includes women. In fact the "a" is often muted, silenced, invisible when we talk about Chicano studies. We are taught that the "o" in Spanish is inclusive when referring to us collectively, but is it? Scholars have long addressed the issue of the power of language minimizing one's existence and reality. We must be vigilant in recognizing how easily language can situate us on the margins in society and in our community as women. The "o" places us on the margins of our communities and ultimately of the broader society; multicultural institutions might also assimilate us if we are not vigilant.

In spite of some of the issues I've raised, I remain optimistic about the future because of individuals who are already exploring diversity issues in new and meaningful ways. I also recognize the strides my own campus has made. Students of color now number 2000 and several multicultural courses are taught regularly. I work with faculty who are committed to making the curriculum more inclusive. The same can be said about most institutions. We can never go back because the momentum is too strong. Just reviewing the proliferation of texts and research on this topic gives me reason to be positive. But continued progress won't be easy.

As I so often reiterate, when we come together we bring with us our differences of gender, sexuality, ethnicity, race, and religion, as well as our own internalized oppressions and biases. No matter how good our intentions, we all fear difference. That is why we must continue to explore these issues. We have to create space in which our own identities flourish and are validated so we can work toward our common goals. We need to constantly ask ourselves: How does one system of oppression, such as racism, allow other forms of oppression, such as classism, sexism, heterosexism, to develop? Are they different models of oppression or are they the same? Do the different forms of oppression parallel and intersect? How can we as individuals respond to oppressive attitudes and behaviors when viewed through multilayered identities such as gender, race, class, sexuality, or ableism, or when oppression occurs at different levels such as at the personal, the social, or the institutional? Finally, what is the responsibility of individuals who themselves experience oppression but also oppress others? These are fundamental questions and the answers can only come when we come to know ourselves, our strengths, and our own fears:

- For some of us this means reclaiming our history and language;
- For some it means dealing with forms of emotional and physical abuse from sexism to racism;

- For some it means coming to terms with our privilege and power because of our class, age, the color of our skin, or sexuality.

It is sad but true that each of us has biases about others. I no longer believe that I am preaching to the choir in spite of individuals' commitment to diversity. I continually ask: What are my personal boundaries? What are yours? We need to continually work on these issues because so much is at stake. As Arturo Madrid, a colleague and friend, in "Writing on Missing People and Others: Joining Together to Expand the Circle" urges:

> Let us work together to assure that all American institutions, not just its precollegiate educational and penal institutions, reflect the diversity of our society. Not to do so is to risk greater alienation on the part of a growing segment of our society. It is to risk increased social tension in an already conflictive world. And ultimately it is to risk the survival of a range of institutions that, for all their defects and deficiencies, permit us the space, the opportunity, and the freedom to improve our individual and collective lot, to guide the course of our government, and to redress whatever grievances we have. Let us join together to expand, not to close the circle. (p. 9)

REFERENCES

Adams, M. (Ed.). (1992, Winter). *Innovative responses for the curriculum, faculty and institution.* San Francisco: Jossey-Bass.

Barceló, R. (Speaker). (1994, March 26). *Chicanos in the midwest: The struggle to gain space and identity.* 1994 National Association for Chicano Studies Midwest Regional Conference.

Barceló, R. (Speaker). (1991). *The importance of exploring racism in our educational institutions while working toward a multicultural ideal.* Springfield, IL.

Cardenas, G. (1976, Summer). Los Desarraigados: Chicanos in the midwestern region of the United States. In G. Cardenas (Ed.), [Special issue: Chicanos in the Midwest]. *Aztlan International Journal of Chicano Studies Research.* Los Angeles: UCLA Chicano Studies Center.

Garcia, J. F. (1974). "Chicanos in Iowa." *In Conoceme in Iowa.* The Official Report of the Governor's Spanish Speaking Task Force Submitted to Governor Robert D. Ray and the 66th General Assembly.

Madrid, A. (1992). Missing people and others: Joining together to expand the circle. In M. L. Andersen & P. H. Collins (Eds.), *Race, class and gender: An anthology* (pp. 611). Belmont, CA: Wadsworth.

MULTICULTURAL TRANSFORMATION
OF THE ACADEMY

by
James B. Boyer

In the United States, all post-secondary education seems to have borrowed its format and substance from the 1636 Harvard University model. We in the United States still think of that model as providing the classic definition of higher education despite the major changes in our demographic mosaic, in the way information is produced, stored, and transmitted, and in the emphasis and power of information in our **information society.** I want to make a case for the total multicultural transformation of the academy that includes the state, university, the liberal arts college, the technical college, the community college, graduate schools, and the full array of adult post-secondary efforts to educate the United State's populace. We must all raise new questions about the appropriateness of the substantive content we consider essential in higher education.

The multicultural transformation of the academy is necessary because graduates of post-secondary education participate not only in shaping the future, but in also **executing** the future, and in the United States, that future will be characterized by diversity in all its forms. While there are those who are in denial of this reality and others who are in opposition to it, the academy has a responsibility to foster the new competencies for full participation in the diverse life of our nation. To succeed, the traditional academy must be transformed.

Leadership for Curriculum Transformation

Persons whose careers place them in curriculum leadership roles in the academy must become culturally competent in curriculum design, instructional services, program policy making, assessment measures, and the capacity to envision schools of the future. We must seek to make connections across cultures in ways that enhance the academic experience for all collegiate learners. As we communicate across cultures, we must humanize the experience while working to accommodate psychologically all the clients and potential clients of the academy.

Since our work is pivotal in determining and communicating the substance of the academic curriculum, the multicultural transformation of the academy must begin with us. What is our multicultural literacy level? What is our level of multicultural comfort in the academy? How do we see curriculum and instructional power? How do we engage our diverse students in the academic enterprise?

The transformation of the academy means the transformation of our perspectives, practices, programs, and provisions whether we work in collegiate classrooms, counseling offices, administrative offices, libraries, cultural centers, or residence facilities. Given the rapid ethnic and linguistic transformation of our society, our own levels of ethnic awareness and competency in cross-ethnic teaching and learning will be tested in the future. Self-assessment of our lives, our careers, and the essence of our services in the academy becomes a necessity. Are we ready for this level of change in the academy? Are we committed to serving clients of all descriptions? Can we survive? Can they?

The work involved in transformation must deal with curriculum content, instructional delivery systems, and structures and strategies for pluralizing the post-secondary curriculum in quest of greater ethnic diversity. It goes without saying that gender equity is also a major component of such transformation and that multicultural, multilingual understandings are essential as we embrace nontraditional populations of collegiate students. Nontraditional undergraduate populations include persons who are not in the age category of 19 to 26 years, while graduate students range in age from the early 20s to over 80; collegiate services, particularly instructional services, can no longer assume that clients will represent young minds that are presently unfolding.

Explorations of degree programs, ideas for program overlays, and analysis of essential content in all disciplines are part of the multicultural transformation of which we speak. We must be aware that the transformation of the post-secondary academy in the United States is a new idea since, historically, many persons have felt all transformation must be done by the clients-students since they chose to come to the institution to be, supposedly, changed. It may be true that clients have come to be changed but the process of change is now under social, political, economic, and technological scrutiny. As Leon Botstein (1991) points out:

> The relative homogeneity...of the professoriate and student body in America and the undisturbed allegiance to nineteenth century epistemological foundations are connected historically. Complementary relationships existed among (1) stable intellectual ideology of knowledge and inquiry; (2) the structure of the university; and (3) the elite population the university served. The symmetry and symbiosis among these three elements has gone down since the early 1960s. (p. 93)

The changes in the population, the advances in the use of the academy, and the expanding sources of post-secondary learning in our information society all demand a multicultural transformation. The social and economic democratization of access to the academy now demands that programmatic diversity become the norm rather than the exception in what is learned as well as what is taught. Since what is learned is often shaped in emphasis by who is doing the teaching, transformation involves personnel as well as personal decisions.

Why a Multicultural Transformation?

What are the goals of a multicultural education? Why should the academy embrace multicultural programming for college learners who are not ethnically or linguistically different from the masses who have benefitted from college in earlier times? In other words, why multicultural education? A multicultural perspective and overview characterizing collegiate curriculum programs as well as human service delivery are intended to result in a society that is nonviolent, open, and diverse in its framework and supportive of all humanity, especially participants in the academic marketplace.

Multicultural, multiethnic curriculum can only be effective when it is accompanied by culturally sensitive instruction, appropriately diverse curriculum materials, and an understanding of culturally influenced learning styles. The ultimate outcomes of a multicultural transformation of college learning should include a **celebration** of ethnic identity, a recognition of gender adequacy, and an understanding of the necessity for economic sufficiency. Gender adequacy involves understanding that neither gender is better than the other and that equality does not mean sameness. No one should ever have to apologize for his or her gender, personal ethnic, linguistic, or economic profile as a college participant. As college professionals we are human service providers and function in a profession devoted to the enhancement of the **quality of life** for all learners who come for our services. As such, the professoriate must now undergo serious analysis, with due respect for academic freedom, but with clear understanding that clients also have freedoms. As college professionals we never have the right to embarrass, exclude, psychologically assault, or intellectually downgrade a student who comes for our services. The transformation of the academy, then, involves a friendly confrontation

24

with professional perspectives that fail to embrace such responsibility.

The following five factors are critical to college training in an information-based society.

College Learning in the Age of Information

Today five times the quantity of information is available for college learning as was available just 40 years ago. Information selectivity is, therefore, a new competence needed within the academy, whether one is primarily engaged in research or in direct instruction. Secondly, in an age of information, a new consciousness of *who is included* in such information is critical since information is power. New analyses of power and power brokering are needed. What is truth? How is it determined? How is it transmitted? Why are certain truths emphasized more than others?

College Learning in the Age of the Consumer

After the academy's position on access changed, the clientele also changed, with the academy the center of an academic marketplace where ideas are created, refined, stored, retrieved, and **sold**. Because the consumers have changed and they insist on the production and utilization of knowledge deemed most functional, their **rights** must be addressed. Who are our consumers? What do we know about them? What is our cultural competence regarding these students who come for collegiate curriculum services? What do they respect? How do they feel? How do they vote on our courses, classes, internships, assignments, and instructional performances?

College Learning in the Age of Intelligence Redefined

Never before has the issue of intelligence been such a matter of interest and discussion in the academy as now. Intelligence is being more broadly defined and channels of learning are no longer limited to the impact of an information society. Who knows what? How do they know? What knowledge is worth knowing—as determined by whom? Howard Gardner's work in *Frames of Mind* (1983) has alerted us that diversity extends to more than telephone companies. No longer is it appropriate to ask if a college applicant or student is intelligent. Rather, one must ask in what ways he or she is intelligent. Cultural differences in how information, knowledge, and skills are acquired need to be studied by more college professionals than ever before.

College Learning in the Age of Self-Definition

Historically, in collegiate learning instructional perspective defined learners both intellectually and sociologically. Generally, those definitions attempted to be ethnically neutral, but diverse learners viewed them as disturbing. College populations now define themselves, and professionals in the academy have the responsibility of discovering these new definitions even though they are not static or conveniently announced in all instances. Ruth Burgoss-Sasscer (1987) suggests the task of empowering Hispanic students poses a special challenge, with many academics studying Hispanics as if they were one ethnic group and failing to take into account that Puerto Ricans in New York are quite different from Cubans in Miami or Mexican Americans in California. Collegiate services need to explore the more intricate details of culturally diverse populations. Almost all professionally conscious college teachers know the impact of labeling in instances of gender concern; they also need to understand the impact of ethnically related definitions.

College Learning in the Age of Options and Alternatives

Post-secondary learning centers need to become centers for options and alternatives for both learners and professors where present concepts of college learning can be significantly changed and upgraded. In more than 75% of U.S. homes today, cable television is a reality. Most people acquired cable because they wanted more options than those provided by the three traditional television networks. At one time the networks commanded some 90% of television viewership, but today they command less than 60% of that total viewership. In our age of information and diversity, providing options in completing tasks for collegiate credit must become part of the normal operations of colleges and universities. Even the definition of degree programs and the processes through which degrees are earned must be critically examined.

The multicultural transformation of the post-secondary institution must begin to address numerous environmental and procedural areas of its structure. Even *Time Magazine* (1990) referred to the inadequacies of a monocultural curriculum that failed to address diversity when stating, "If you create a curriculum that lauds the achievements of one group and omits and distorts the achievements of another, it has its effect" (p. 89).

What Is Multicultural Education?

Multicultural education is a comprehensive curriculum program that embraces cultural differences as basic foundational components of collegiate learning. It enhances the presence of ethnic, linguistic, gender, age, ability, and economic variations through curriculum content, especially in the social sciences, natural sciences, and humanities, in collegiate curricular policies, procedures, and practices, including practices of recognition, reward, and endorsement. The curriculum reflects the experiences, perspectives, cultural orientation, and mannerisms of culturally different populations. Instruction, counseling, administration, coaching, mentoring, and communication all reflect diversity in implementation and assessment.

Collegiate multicultural education encompasses the six Cs: consciousness, commitment, cohesiveness, collaboration, cultural competence, and courage.

1. Consciousness of diversity by all parties engaged in higher education.
2. Commitment to equity by those responsible for designing collegiate experiences for learners.
3. Cohesiveness of collegiate curriculum through carefully planned programs, including ethnic and women's studies programs, and the integration of ethnic and women's studies scholarship into traditional disciplines to enrich the learning experiences of all students.
4. Collaboration of persons from different academic programs to insure the full transformation of the academy.
5. Cultural Competence of collegiate curriculum workers to include our understanding of the differences in the way members of different cultural groups **prefer** to learn.
6. Courage to confront tradition that is deeply entrenched institutionally and personally. **Leaders** of the transformation must be personally **strong.** Leadership is essential to any transformation of any institution. The academy is a powerful institution in society, transforming raw intelligence into sophisticated thinking and organized direction. It impacts the quality of life, the quality of institutional practice, and the destiny of citizens. Strong leadership for the multicultural transformation must include all those

whose work provides direction for learning whether as instructors, administrators, or support service workers.

Institutional Commitment to Diversity

James Montford, Jr. (1990), writing in *Black Issues in Higher Education,* asserts that institutions must make a commitment to diversity at every level, particularly at the support programs level. He writes, "The mission of cultural diversity means the institutionalization of a cross-cultural perspective into curriculum, programs and services at any institution" (p. 64). Further, he insists, "It is incumbent upon all institutions of higher education to move forward with deliberate speed to develop draft proposals designed to address infusion of cross-cultural education into the very fabric of higher learning" (p. 64).

Once commitment is made for all areas of the academy to recognize and institutionalize diversity, the following dimensions need specific study and reorganization.

Cultural Diversity in Student Affairs

This would involve a service orientation for all staff and a constant review by leadership teams to monitor the program's focus, the students' involvement level, and the extent the programming meets the needs of all clients. For example, does the lyceum program include speakers and resource persons from diverse populations? Is there planned, active inclusion of all the cultural profiles enrolled in the academy? Is anyone being left out? Have efforts been made to attract all groups to the full resources of the student services programs? Is the academy perceived as providing diverse cultural experiences for the campus community?

Race Relations

Because of the seeming deterioration of healthy race relations in the United States over the past decade, colleges and all post-secondary programs must become deliberate and comprehensive in their efforts to upgrade race and ethnic relations. The postsecondary institution is a public academic marketplace, and all cultural and ethnic groups are to be comfortably included at a meaningful level. Improved race relations will involve intellectual interaction within the social context of higher education. Respect for differences and respect for differences of opinion must be developed so leadership can emerge and enhance healthy exchanges between ethnic groups. The institution is a nonprofit workplace, an academic corporation, and the ideas, the concepts, the perspectives developed there should have a substantive support stance for a **better United States,** not a more divisive one.

Cultural Competence

Cultural competence involves the ability of an individual or agency to give assistance to clients in ways acceptable and useful to the clients; it must make sense in terms of clients' backgrounds and expectations. All members of the academy's workforce must seek to understand not only the power of ethnic identity but also what it means to diffuse hostility and resentment even when they are not directly caused by the service provider him- or herself. A professional commitment to all, whatever their cultural framework, is needed without regard for differences. Workers must understand ethnic values and the extent of significance placed on non-harmful behavior by those whose cultural comfort zones differ from traditional behavior within the academy.

All human relationships are affected by the biographical frameworks, the life experiences, of the individuals involved. If someone does not have multicultural experiences during the first 18 years of life, some training will likely need to occur to develop strong levels of psychological comfort in such relationships, whether they are student-teacher relationships, worker-to-worker relationships, supervisor to supervisee relationships, or others. In all of these, the academy must embrace a commitment to the preservation of the mental health of individuals, to the urgency of diversity, and to comfortable multicultural working environments.

To insure healthy human relationships, we must analyze whether we are essentially isolated or essentially connected to others in the academy. We must constantly appraise whether we display negative interactors or positive interactors across culture. Our decisions must be balanced between traditional concepts of objectivity and compassion for the reality of our clients' worlds. We must, within the context of the diverse academy, remind ourselves we are competent and comfortable in the delivery of human services, that we are committed to growing on the job and to becoming better activists in an academy that is better because of its diversity.

Areas and Stages of the Multicultural Transformation

To effect the multicultural transformation of collegiate curriculum and instruction we must develop the following:

1. Insight into the disciplines, into ourselves, into others;
2. Perceptions about change, about people, about systems, about programs, practices, and policies;
3. Knowledge about scores of topics and events as the United States becomes increasingly a society of information and the academy accepts more responsibility in brokering that information;
4. Skills of all kinds, including verbal, social, political, writing, analytical, and practical skills, from traditional agricultural skills to computer skills, but perhaps most significantly, cross-cultural skills;
5. Concepts that go beyond definitions, beyond limited, perhaps isolated notions about phenomena, to include understanding of contextual frameworks—among the more urgent being the concept of multicultural, rather than monocultural, comprehension;
6. Theories that embrace the diversity in the academy and that can be tested and researched effectively; and
7. A more open system of reviewing and analyzing relationships and cause-effect outcomes: how, for instance, can an institution that functions on the intellectual level of existence ignore the causes of violence within our society?

Curriculum Realities in Higher Education

Three dimensions of higher education curriculum are critical to understanding the totality of the multicultural transformations of the academy: the psychological, the cognitive, and the political.

The **psychological dimension** of collegiate curriculum involves the way both clients and service providers **feel** about their presence in the academy, their assigned responsibilities, and the ongoing assessment of their participation. Obviously, this involves perspectives on who should enjoy access and who should be privileged to pursue successfully goals in this arena. For many years, the academy did not embrace the culturally different, including women, in our society. Today, that is changed and the psychological inclusion must be reflected in text-books, assignments, staff, resources, lyceum programs, residential considerations, and cele-brations. This can only occur with deliberate training and attention to this dimension.

The **cognitive dimension** of curriculum involves the art and science of **knowing** and the decisions surrounding **what** is to be known and **how** that knowing is to occur. We now recog-nize that there are many ways of knowing. In an information society, major selections must be made about what is to be known. What knowledge is of most worth? And of most worth to whom? Over the last 40 or 50 years, Benjamin Bloom's taxonomy of the cognitive domain has been the basis for analyzing much about cognition and has served a useful purpose. Our concern today, however, is the patterns of **selection** of the information to be known and how **inclusive** that information is for all clients in the academy.

The **political dimension** of curriculum involves the forces driving program emphasis, degree requirements, course syllabi, textbook selection, library acquisitions, and the scores of other factors that impact the academy. The U. S. has done a relatively decent job in keeping up with technological advancements but we have failed in our progress with multicultural, multiethnic, multilingual competencies in the academy. This is partially because legislators, administrators, and citizens at large, as well as faculty and students, have not been informed that such transformation **should** occur. Multicultural issues grew out of our effort to desegre-gate our major institutions and, for many, desegregation has always been viewed negatively. To transform the academy multiculturally is still a bitter pill for many practitioners and citi-zens. Our political agenda, however, suggests it will occur despite the efforts of those who would like to ignore its meaning and its evolving power. A multicultural transformation brings reality and the Constitution of the United States into closer alignment: we are a nation committed to democracy for **all the people.** The curriculum of the academy must embrace this dimension and implement it in all programming.

The politics of the curriculum involves collegiate learning priorities, academic language adoption, collegiate program requirements, and much more. However, one must remember **learner vulnerability** as well as **professional prerogative.** Herein lies the political agenda. If the academy is not committed to diversity, it will fight to save the monocultural curriculum and perspective. Only when it commits to an **inclusive** way of programming and serving will it truly upgrade itself for the year 2000 and beyond.

The Two-Year Academy and Diversity

Perhaps more than the four-year institutions, the two-year academy tends to attract clients who are **more** interested in immediate workplace competency than in the liberal education traditions. Consequently, the clients in such programs have even more urgent need for envi-ronments that embrace diversity than some others. Given this, the two-year academy must seek to create policies, programs, and procedures for every unit within its purview that delib-erately respect the dynamics of diversity in the schooling process. Not only will clients hold us responsible for such provisions once they are alumni, but the corporate agencies, whose workforce participants come primarily from these programs, will charge the academy with inadequacy unless their graduates bring pluralistic perspectives to the entry-level workforce.

Diversity Issues in the Research Paradigm of the Academy

Perhaps no area of the academy's function is more complex than research, its agenda, scope, and implications. In the United States we depend on the academic research community for information about national policy and priorities in addition to academic policy and priorities. **Diversity** must become part of the foundational base on which research endeavors and discussions are built.

Expanding the Definition of Academy Research

What constitutes research? How will it be used? Which research functions and projects are worthy of the academy's seal and image? Who shall make these decisions? On what basis? Despite a tendency to favor research parameters of the past, a stronger level of **inclusion** must be part of our research definitions. What is the prevailing definition and who created or offered it? Should research be designed to improve the quality of life for the people? If so, which people? All the people—including those who are culturally different from the masses? This will involve greater comprehensiveness in definition and scope.

Choice of Research Topics

As research topics are chosen by students and faculty, what types of topics are encouraged? Which are discouraged? To what extent are candidates encouraged to engage in research on issues of race, gender, ethnicity, bilingualism, and economic exploitation? In the natural sciences, to what extent are concerns about ethical issues investigated? How, for example, are decisions made about where toxic waste dumps are placed? Or which patients shall get organ replacements in medical facilities? Academic research must be deliberate in its concern for the diversity such questions imply. How are research topics chosen? With which populations in mind? Much technical research is conducted to enhance the life of all human beings, regardless of ethnic-racial-gender profiles, but much research in the academy is related specifically to culturally identified groups. This research must become more responsive to the differences that help define us.

Research Production and Consumption

Research production is both a science and an art. To what extent do researchers feel that all clients and potential researchers must **duplicate** the patterns and techniques of past research? Why must research in one area be acceptable to academicians who are engaged in other categories of research activity? Researchers must expand the range of research topics, methods, and outcomes to reflect their own cultural diversity. The academy's research specialists need not be threatened or alarmed by this. Diversity implies that some traditions and customs will be challenged within the research community.

Research consumption is an ever expanding endeavor. Since the invention of the printing press, the academy has assumed that the only way to expand consumption was through the printed word. While that is still the most common form of dissemination, it is certainly not the **only** way to share. The electronic media, with its advances in educational technology and other forms of publishing and communication, are equally valid and valuable. Transformation demands respect for these additional channels of communication.

Summary

Much of the academic research activity, particularly educational and social science research, has assumed a monocultural audience and a monolingual readership. Such a limited western civilization, English-speaking, middle-class Eurocentric perspective is no longer adequate for our comprehensive definition of academic research or of the academy itself. The quest for diversity within the community of scholars and educators who comprise the academy cannot be overemphasized. Whatever way one defines diversity, the bottom line is its expansion of tradition and its **inclusiveness.** To insure progress toward greater expansion and inclusiveness in the curriculum, in staff and students, in instruction styles, in research, in every aspect of the academy, we must continuously ask the hard questions of what, why, who, and how. What is the academy? Why does it exist now? Who is it to serve now? How is it to do so effectively? Given the demographic profile of our nation and the information explosion of our era, a transformation of the academy must respect our diversity, our multicultural reality.

REFERENCES

Botstein, L. (1991). The undergraduate curriculum and the issue of race? Opportunities and obligations. In P. G. Altbach & K. Lomotey (Eds.), *The racial crisis in American higher education.* Albany, NY: Suny Press.

Boyer, J. (1989). *Collegiate instructional discrimination index.* (Multiethnic, multilingual, cross-racial, non-sexist). Manhattan, KS: College of Education, Kansas State University.

Boyer, J. (1992, Spring). Multicultural concerns in educational research, *Midwestern Educational Researcher, 9*(2), 7-8.

Burgos-Sasscer, R. (1987, Spring). Empowering Hispanic students: A prerequisite is adequate data. *Journal of Education Equity and Leadership, 7*(1).

Cox, Jr., T. (1993). *Cultural diversity in organizations: Theory, research and practice.* San Francisco: Berrett-Moehler Publishers.

Gardner, H. (1983). *Frames of Mind: The Theory of multiple intelligences.* New York: Basic Books.

Montford, Jr., J. W. (1990, May 10). Institutions must make commitment to diversity at every level. *Black Issues in Higher Education*, p. 64.

Time Magazine (1990, September 24), 89.

CREATING INCLUSIVE AND MULTICULTURAL COMMUNITIES: WORKING THROUGH ASSUMPTIONS OF CULTURE, POWER, DIVERSITY, AND EQUITY

by
Brenda M. Rodriguez

What does it mean to create inclusive, multicultural communities, especially in our class-rooms and institutions? For multicultural and inclusive education to move beyond its current rudimentary stage, we must examine our institutional and personal assumptions about culture, power, diversity, equity, and community. Without further reflection and understanding of these concepts, we will not be able to understand the strength multicultural, inclusive education brings to our pluralistic nation and world, nor will we be able to avoid the pitfalls of implementing multiculturalism in education and creating more inclusive school communities.

Culture

I like to define culture as the framework that guides and bounds life practices: it shapes everything we do. All of us are cultural beings, with culture influencing the development of our beliefs, perspectives, and behavior. According to Anderson and Fenichel (1989), our "cultural framework must be viewed as a set of tendencies or possibilities from which to choose" (p. 8), not a rigidly prescribed set of assumptions. Cultural frameworks are constantly evolving and being reworked, and we are continuously observing and participating in events that shape our individual experience within those frameworks. Thus, although persons of the same cultural background share a readiness to act or think similarly, not all members of the group will behave in the same manner. Individuals may differ in the degree to which they choose to adhere to a set of cultural patterns. For instance, some individuals identify strongly with one particular group; others combine practices from several cultural groups. Either way, the multiple dimensions of culture help form an individual's identity. Because of variations within cultures and the multiple cultural groups within society, as well as individuals' different experiences of cultural events and responses to cultural influences, an appreciation and respect for both individual and cultural diversity is crucial for educators.

Self-Awareness

Everyone has a culture and belongs to multiple communities, but often individuals are not aware of the behaviors, habits, and customs that are culturally based (Athen, 1988). Becoming aware of our own cultures facilitates our capacity to:
1. explore, understand, appreciate, and assess the many aspects of culture that make up our social background, including our ethnicity, social class, gender, geographic region, sexual orientation, exceptionality, age, and religion or mode of spirituality;
2. increase our awareness and insight into our own learning processes, strengths, weaknesses, successes, failures, biases, values, goals, and emotions;
3. experience our own cultures in relation to others as they are illuminated through cross-cultural interactions;
4. understand and confront areas of conflict and tension when we encounter individuals from unfamiliar cultures and learn to become more comfortable with being uncomfortable;

5. explore and appreciate thought processes that occur across cultures but may also take on different shapes and meanings for different cultural groups and for individual group members; and

6. understand more deeply the cultural values and beliefs of those with whom we come in contact.

According to Hall (1976):

There is not one aspect of human life that is not touched and altered by culture. This means personality, how people express themselves (including shows of emotion), the way they think, how they move, how problems are solved, how their cities are planned and laid out, how transportation systems function and are organized, as well as how economic and government systems are put together and function. (pp. 16-17)

Although this is true for all people, Anglo Europeans and some other European Americans who are part of the dominant or mainstream United States culture may have the least awareness of the ways their culture influences their behavior and interactions. They have predominated in this country, and their culture, customs, and habits have shaped and been acknowledged by themselves, as well as other ethnic groups, as shaping the society more than any other single group. In addition, the "melting pot" to which the United States aspired during the early waves of immigration took its toll on the diversity among European American groups, diminishing the distinctiveness of early immigrants' roots as they became mainstream members of the United States and deemphasizing their separate ethnic cultural heritages without noting that the process of joining the mainstream involved adopting or adapting to a new culture. This process results in an ethnocentrism and a notion of monoculturalism that is often not even recognized because it has been identified as the norm.

To understand and appreciate fully the diversity that exists among us, we must first understand and appreciate our own culture. Self-awareness (Tiedt & Tiedt, 1990) is the first step toward cross-cultural competence or capacity.[1] But how does cultural self-awareness begin? What are the steps we can take to achieve it? How does cultural self-awareness lead to improved understanding of other cultures? And what does this understanding have to do with multicultural education?

Cultural self-awareness begins with an exploration of our own heritage, encounters, and experiences. Place of origin, language(s) spoken, time and reasons for immigration, relocation, or colonization, and the place of the family's first settlement, as well as geographic relocations and movement within the United States, all help to define one's cultural heritage. The political leanings, jobs, status, beliefs, religions, and values of one's first peoples, as well as whether they were voluntary or involuntary immigrants, help portray a cultural picture of one's family. Also contributing to this portrait are the economic, ethnic, political, religious, social, and vocational changes that subsequent generations have undergone. Another important factor is a recognition of how one's cultural group relates to the mainstream culture of the United States and how it is or has been reflected through history.

Perhaps the most enriching way to gather this information is through the recollections of the oldest family members as they tell stories of their early lives and the lives of their grandparents and great grandparents. When it is possible, oral history provides a wonderful bridge between generations and can be supplemented by photographs, journals, family albums, or notes and letters about important events.

Learning about one's own roots is the first step in determining how one's values, beliefs, group or collective consciousness, customs, and behaviors have been shaped by culture. Frequently, we learn the shaping reflects not one culture but multiple cultures since we belong to multiple communities, communities identified by, for example, our ethnicity, religion, region, socioeconomic status, or gender. This knowledge helps us realize the ways of thinking, believing, and behaving we may have assumed to be universal, rigid, and static are actually based upon cultural beliefs and biases. When one has explored one's own cultural heritage, the second step of discovery can begin.

The second step is to examine in depth some of the values, behaviors, beliefs, and customs that are identified with one's own cultural heritage (in its broadest sense). Educators and students will be better prepared to learn about diverse cultures if they are first certain of the significance of their own identity. It is also important, particularly for educators, to understand how their own cultural assumptions about education and educational institutions, and about teaching and learning influence what they teach, how they teach it, and how they relate to students. Cultural self-awareness is the bridge to other cultures. To be truly sensitive to someone else's culture, we must be sensitive to our own and to the impact cultural frameworks, customs, values, beliefs, and behaviors have on education.

Cross-Cultural Sensitivity/Awareness

Because the reality of a pluralistic society and world is confronting us so much more quickly and tangibly than previously, many individuals are converging to classes, in-services, and special programs to learn all there is to know about other cultures. We approach cultural learning and related issues in the tradition of our U. S./Western educational culture and history: with the notion that we can attend a class or seminar and digest all we need to know in a few sessions to achieve cross-cultural knowledge. In the workshops and training I conduct, I am continually reminding and cautioning participants against overgeneralizing or characterizing cultural groups in a rigid, unidimensional, and static way.

Earlier, we discussed what culture is, but it is equally important to understand what it is not. Culture **is not:**

1. mere artifacts or materials used by people;
2. a laundry list of behaviors, values, and facts;
3. the pseudo-biological or pseudo-scientific trait of "race";
4. the ideal and romantic heritage or experience of a people as seen through music, myths, dance, holidays, and folklore;
5. stereotypic depictions of groups as seen in television, movies, newspapers, and other media;
6. objects to be bought, sold, and distributed;
7. generalized explanations about the behavior, emotions, or values of groups of people applied to individuals; or
8. higher class status derived from a knowledge of arts, manners, literature.

Consequently, cultural capacity or awareness **is not** becoming a member of another culture by a superficial, wholesale adoption of elements, such as customs, language, dress, or behavior, of that group's culture. Such shallow identification could "be manipulative and patronizing" (Green, 1982, p. 52) and could suggest that changing one's own cultural identity is easy. Culture encompasses values, attitudes, and beliefs as well as customs and behaviors. While the latter can be readily adopted, the former requires deeper and more fundamental awareness and changes. Additionally, cultural capacity recognizes that individuals cannot be categorized into totally discrete groups and that much variability within cultural groups exists. Cultural identification is a complex network of intertwining cultural influences that frames individuals' identities and values and influences their choices and behavior in continually evolving and dynamic ways.

Being culturally competent or aware does not mean knowing everything about every culture. It is, instead, respect for difference, eagerness to learn, and a willingness to accept that there are many ways of viewing the world. As Anderson and Fenichel (1989) relate:

Cultural sensitivity cannot mean knowing everything there is to know about every culture that is represented in a population to be served. At its most basic level, cultural sensitivity implies, rather, knowledge that cultural differences as well as similarities exist... Cultural sensitivity further means being aware of the cultures represented in one's state or region and learning about some of the general parameters of those cultures... Cultural knowledge helps a professional to be aware of possibilities and to be ready to respond appropriately. (pp. 8-9)

Culture is akin to being the observer through a one-way mirror; everything we see is from our own perspective. It is only when we join the observed on the other side that it is possible to see ourselves and others clearly, but getting to the other side of the glass presents many challenges. As Storti (1989) so aptly stated in *The Art of Crossing Cultures:* "The old proverb notwithstanding, we cannot put ourselves in someone else's shoes; or, rather, we can, but it's still our own feet we will feel" (p. 51). Although it may be impossible to feel or experience what someone else is feeling, becoming more culturally sensitive can help us as educators understand, appreciate, and support our students and colleagues more effectively.

Achieving cultural sensitivity or cross-cultural capacity requires that we lower our defenses, take risks, and practice behaviors that may feel unfamiliar and uncomfortable. It requires a flexible mind, an open heart, and a willingness to accept alternative perspectives. It may mean setting aside some cherished beliefs to make room for others whose value is unknown. It may mean changing what we think, what we say, and how we behave, even acknowledging that we have learned and taught untruths, myths, and misinformation about ourselves and others that affect our own and their beliefs and identities. The rewards, however, are significant: bridging disparate cultures, knowing more about ourselves, and becoming more effective interpersonally .

Power, Privilege, and Diversity

Diversity is about difference. But how does difference impact our daily lives as educators and members of communities? Audre Lorde (1984) poignantly describes difference as something that is feared in our society.

Institutionalized rejection of **difference** is an absolute necessity in a profit economy which needs outsiders as surplus people. As members of such an economy, we have all been programmed to respond to human differences between us with fear and loathing and to handle that difference in one of three ways: ignore it, and if that is not possible, copy it if we think it is dominant, or destroy it if we think it is subordinate. But we have no patterns for relating across our human differences as equals. As a result, those differences have been misnamed and misused in the service of separation and confusion. (p. 115)

Frequently, educators have taken a safer and simpler approach to diversity than Lorde's call to relate "across our human differences as equals." We have chosen instead to celebrate discrete aspects of different cultures, i.e. holidays and individuals who excel in some way. Although this is not wrong, it is inadequate in a society that is stratified on the basis of conceptions of race, ethnicity, gender, and socioeconomic class. We need to look at diversity issues as they relate to issues of power and oppression. In the classroom with young people and in workshops among adults, differences exist--differences in gender, ethnic heritage, age, physical ability, economic class, and sexual orientation, among others. Some differences are visible, some we look for automatically, some we may pretend not to see. But all of them are used to separate us along lines of power. This power takes the form of access to resources, work, housing, education, physical security, protection by law, and representation in government. This power is institutionalized discrimination. And while some groups are socially sanctioned to be powerful, they are permitted to have their power at the expense of other groups whose access to resources is correspondingly limited or denied. Examples of such unequal power relationships are evident between landowners and migrant workers, males and females, and students in well-financed suburban school districts and those in underfunded inner city schools.

The social perspective from which I conduct my training and teaching is that the primary root of violence in the United States is the systematic, institutionalized day-to-day imbalance of power. This means that social groups--most recognizably women, children, people of color, workers, and others who do not have power equal to that enjoyed by those wielding the greatest amount of power in our society--have less control over their lives and are often targets of physical and sexual violence, discrimination, harassment, and poverty at home, in the workplace, and in the wider community.

The reason issues of power have to be addressed by educators is that patterns of power imbalances are continually renewed through the socialization of each generation of young people. When children in this country learn about the groups of people different from themselves through misinformation, distortions, jokes, stereotypes, history, and biased research and textbooks, they are being taught to justify, enforce, and continue the power differences. Frequently, they are learning to hate. This is how our society, including our educational institutions, creates "-isms" such as, racism, classism, sexism, heterosexism, enthnocentrism, and ableism. These "-isms" refer to prejudice, stereotypes, and discriminatory actions that are systematically perpetuated or enforced by those with more power, authority, and resources to their advantage. Supported by institutions, cultural attitudes, and values, these "-isms" have far-reaching effects on people's lives.

Systemic power is one critical element that makes "isms" much different and more complex than prejudice, stereotypes, and discrimination alone. Because the institutions of family, education, work, business, religion, housing, law, and government in which we are raised sustain these "-isms," the inequality they sanction is accepted as normal, goes unnoticed, or is easily denied. But it is precisely because inequality is institutionalized that the mistreatment of nonpower groups is so complete. And since the institutional imbalance is in one direction—power over nonpower—it is counterproductive to use concepts like "reverse racism" or "reverse sexism." Individuals in a nonpower group can stereotype or have prejudices about people in a power group. They can act aggressively toward them, but the power imbalance between them nonetheless targets nonpower groups. Nonpower groups do not have the social power and command of resources to limit the powerful or protect themselves from system-wide violence and discrimination.

We cannot expect to support each other and young people in unlearning the myths of inequality unless we are prepared to assist them and ourselves in unlearning all the isms while modeling other examples of behavior and value. We must understand that our differences do not cause the institutional power imbalances; they are used to **justify** already existing imbalances. People do not earn mistreatment because they are darker skinned, Latino, women, or have disabilities. Nothing natural or biological about these differences causes oppression.

Once we begin addressing the issues of power and social inequities, the concomitant aspect of privilege must also be explored. Privilege is an unearned right or resource that one group has access to that other groups are denied. Because it is unearned, we are often unaware of the privileges that we might have. And since we apparently have always had them, they seem normal (See McIntosh, 1988). Consider the privileges we exercise as adults, as educators, as able-bodied persons, as men, as persons with light skin, as gentiles, or as heterosexuals. How are these privileges connected to our fears of loss of control or our notions of power? These questions have no set answers; they are contested as people in our society struggle to decide how to treat each other.

Equity

What is equity? How should it be defined within a democratic, pluralistic society? Issues of power and privilege impact our construction of equity and compel us to question how they are related to multicultural education and inclusive schools. Secada (1992) characterizes equity in the following way:

> The heart of equity lies in our ability to acknowledge that, even though our actions might be in accord with a set of rules, their **results** may be unjust. Equity goes beyond following the rules, even if we have agreed that they are intended to achieve justice... Educational equity...should be construed as a check on the justice of specific actions that are carried out within the educational arena and the arrangements that result from those actions. (quoted in Pignatelli and Pflaum, 1992, p. ix)

To struggle for equity sometimes means to struggle against the rules or the common assumptions of a community. When these struggles focus on multicultural issues, they raise community as well as individual passions and often prompt advocates and opponents alike to claim the moral high ground and mobilize the rhetoric of democracy. Such moves demand we be particularly sensitive to the personal and sometimes religious and moral values that drive persons to action. We must also be ready to assume a position of opposition, particularly to the negative and destructive practices within our own cultures. Logic, reason, theoretical commitments are not enough. Equity is a passionate issue and it must engage the passions of people who struggle for it, just as it releases the passions and fears of those who resist it. Struggles for equity often entail conflict and pain as power and privilege are rethought and redistributed, but the resistance and discomfort should lead to the greater recognition of basic human rights and to empowerment of individuals and the growth of community.

Envisioning Educational Communities

Theories of power and equity are implicitly theories of community. Acknowledging this encourages us to begin envisioning a new definition of power, one that focuses on empowerment and embraces the concept of power as energy, capacity, and potential rather than as domination. This is an image of power as the glue holding a community together, giving the people the opportunity "to act, to move, to change conditions, for the benefit of the whole population" (Lane, 1983). Under traditional conceptions of power as domination, justice requires that limits be placed on power and that a balance of power be achieved to mitigate the results of domination. Under conceptions of power as capacity, the goal is not to limit the power of some but to increase the power of all actors. To do this we need to develop strategies to counteract unequal power arrangements, strategies that recognize the potentiality for creating equal relations.

This conception of power as creative community energy recognizes that people need power, both as a way to maintain a strong and positive sense of self and as a way to accomplish ends (Janeway, 1980). Power can be used to enhance both autonomy and mutuality. To be empowered is to be able to "claim an education" as Adrienne Rich (1979) urges us. To be empowered is to act to create a more humane social order. To be empowered is to engage in significant learning. To be empowered is to connect with others in mutually productive ways.

A walk through a garden reveals a panoply of lovely plants—all varied in form, blossoms, and size. All share such basic needs as soil, water, and sunlight; yet each plant may have different needs as to the type of soil, amount of water, and the degree of sunlight required for life and growth. Each type of plant is of interest to the observer and offers its own beauty and special characteristics. However, seen together, as a whole, the plants form a wondrous garden to behold. (Hanson, 1992, p. 3)

Like the garden, communities are made up of individuals—all of whom contribute their own unique characteristics to the sense of place in which they live. However, communities are also highly interactive, dynamic settings where individuals are constantly interacting and responding to one another and where the characteristics of those individuals are being modified through those interactions.

Although communities are not static and generally are not planned, societies do have cultural mores and practices that guide human behavior and provide a socialization framework that shapes and directs interactions. In an educational community this framework is often described in the mission statement, a statement of purpose that should be driving the institution's decisions. That the mission statement addresses issues of diversity and equity is critical. Evidence suggests schools act as systems that continue to perpetuate patterns of hierarchy and an oppressive "power over" approach with their implicit valuing of certain groups of people over others. As educators and members of multiple communities, we need to dismantle these notions of *up/down, them/us,* and *power over* and to transform our relationships into partnerships where *power with* is the norm for our interactions.

Conclusion

Creating inclusive schools is an evolutionary process. What we are undoing did not happen overnight. These systems and ways of thinking have been deeply embedded in our societal psyche for a long time. Our society faces many legitimate concerns and profound challenges, challenges reminding us that schools exist and need to be understood within their sociopolitical contexts. Our schools exist in a society in which societal and economic stratification is a fact of life, where competition is taught over caring, and where the early sorting (tracking) that takes place in our educational settings often lasts a lifetime. Supporting multicultural education and inclusive communities requires a very active process and a commitment to change that incorporates social justice as a major consideration of this process.

Single courses or step-by-step checklists to create this change do not exist. Understanding this can free us from frustration when we do not see a quick fix for the imbalances of power and privilege, the inequities we observe and experience as members of a less-than-perfect world. As educators, we have to prepare ourselves for the long haul. Creating inclusive schools and fostering multiculturalism in education involves an awareness that the very process of relating to one another is moving us toward more inclusive institutions, ones that encourage all members to succeed. We do not have to embark on this great mission by ourselves, but we must take individual responsibility in learning to teach in new ways and with new perspectives. We must enter other worlds of imagination, culture, and justice, of literacy, history, and communication, of science, psychology, and art to enrich ourselves and our teaching and to serve as models for others. This enrichment is at the heart of pluralism and excellence and at the core of equity and social justice. To further equity and social justice is our only responsible choice.

The challenge for the years ahead is to conquer our fear of change and difference and imagine how we might create and realize the exciting possibilities of equity for ourselves, our students, and our communities—one by one, step by step, voice by voice.

ENDNOTE

[1] I prefer cultural capacity to cultural competence since competence suggests to me something that can be measured or evaluated.

REFERENCES

Anderson, P. P., & Fenichel, E. S. (1989). *Serving culturally diverse families of infants and toddlers with disabilities.* Washington, D.C.: National Center for Clinical Infant Programs.

Athen, G. (1988). *American ways—A guide for foreigners in the United States.* Yarmouth, ME: Intercultural Press.

Green, J. W. (1982). *Cultural awareness in the human services.* Englewood Cliffs, NJ: Prentice-Hall.

Hall, E. T. (1976). *Beyond culture.* Garden City, NY: Anchor Books.

Hanson, M. (1992). Ethnic, cultural and language diversity in intervention settings. In Lynch, E., & Hanson, M. (Eds.), *Developing cross-cultural competence: A guide for working with young children and their families* (pp. 3-18). Baltimore, MD: Brookes Publishing.

Janeway, E. (1980). *Powers of the weak.* New York: Knopf.

Lane, A. M. (1983). The feminism of Hannah Arendt. *Democracy 3,* 107-17.

Lorde, A. (1984). *Sister outside: Essays and speeches by Andre Lorde.* Trumansburg, NY: The Crossing Press.

McIntosh, P. (1988). White privilege and male privilege: A personal account of coming to see correspondences through work in women studies. Wellesley, MA: Wellesley College Center for Research on Women.

Pignatelli, F., & Pflaum, S. (Eds.). (1992). *Celebrating diverse voices: Progressive education and equity.* Newbury Park, CA: Corwin.

Rich, A. (1979). *On lies, secrets, and silence.* New York: W. W. Norton.

Storti, C. (1989). *The art of crossing cultures.* Yarmouth, ME: Intercultural Press.

Tiedt, P. L., & Tiedt, I. M. (1990). *Multicultural teaching—A handbook of activities, information, and resources* (3rd Ed.). Boston: Allyn & Bacon.

PERSONALITY AND PREJUDICE

by
Bem P. Allen

There are three reasons why Gordon W. Allport's book *The Nature of Prejudice* (1954) is perhaps the single most important work ever done on the subject of prejudice. First, it was the earliest comprehensive discussion of prejudice that was based on a significant body of scientific research. Second, it was extremely influential in shaping social scientists' thinking concerning prejudice. Third, because Allport has had so much influence on prejudice research done since 1954, it is relatively easy to fit some of today's findings regarding prejudice into his theoretical framework.

Prejudice Defined

According to Allport (1954), *prejudice* is felt or expressed antipathy based upon a faulty and inflexible generalization and may be directed toward a group as a whole, or toward an individual because he is a member of the group. Thus, prejudice is negative feelings regarding members of some group that are sometimes just felt internally and sometimes expressed openly. It is based on the faulty generalization that all, or almost all, members of some group, such as Native Americans, possess certain negative traits, such as drunkenness. Obviously such a generalization is always inflexible, because no trait will apply to almost all, much less all, members of a large group (even skin color varies greatly among people who are called "black").

While prejudice involves feelings, discrimination refers to behavior directed against a group or its members. Allport thought of discrimination as acting out prejudice. Many measures of prejudice amount to asking people—usually via questionnaire—how much they discriminate so their level of prejudice can be inferred. For this reason, it is possible to offer a more empirical definition of prejudice that is consistent with Allport's theoretical definition. Because *prejudice* measures often ask about self-perceptions of discrimination, it may be seen as "the degree to which people believe that they discriminate against members of some group, as indicated by what they say or write" (Allen, 1990, p. 325). As prejudice is most often assessed with the use of questionnaires completed anonymously, people's pronouncements about their level of discrimination probably represent what they really believe.

Social Distance

Given this empirical definition of prejudice, it is immediately obvious that what people *believe* about their level of discrimination may not be accurate. Because nobody has total insight, some people who honestly claim not to discriminate against others may do so anyway. To explore this logical conclusion, it is necessary to consider Social Distance (SD), a measure of discrimination that requires individuals to indicate how close to themselves they would allow members of some group to come. Allport (1954, p. 39) listed the items of the SD scale as follows.

I would admit (members of some group):
1. To close kin by marriage
2. To my club as personal chums
3. To my street as neighbors

4. To employment in my occupation
5. To citizenship in my country
6. As visitors only to my country
7. Would exclude from my country

Notice that the social relations to which the members of some group can be admitted vary from those involving a great deal of intimacy with group members, commitment to them, and permanency of relationships involving them (top of list) to those involving no intimacy, commitment, and permanency (bottom of list) (Allen, 1975).

Not only do people who strongly claim not to discriminate against some often-disparaged group really believe themselves, these self-proclaimed "unprejudiced" people probably do not discriminate under most circumstances. Nevertheless, would they discriminate when asked to accept that same group for social relations that entail high intimacy, commitment, and permanency? An answer to the question may tell us whether what people believe about their level of discrimination is accurate.

A number of years ago, I gave some European American college students a test to determine the degree to which they were prejudiced against African Americans (Allen, 1975). Based on their scores, some students were classified as unprejudiced, some as prejudiced, and some as ambivalent with regard to prejudice (gave mixed signals about their level of discrimination). All of these subjects were then asked to indicate the degree of closeness they would allow African Americans by use of an SD scale composed of items 1 and 3 (Triandis, Loh, & Levine, 1966). Results showed that all categories of these students, even those who claimed they did not discriminate according to race, in fact did so. When it comes to relations involving intimacy, commitment, and permanency, even "unprejudiced" subjects show racial discrimination.

Although unprejudiced European American subjects did discriminate on the SD scale, when it came to indicating who they admire, another part of my same study showed that they did not discriminate by race. In fact, they actually expressed more admiration for African Americans than for European Americans. This so-called reverse discrimination effect reverted to no discrimination when subjects thought they were hooked up to a lie detector machine. But why do self-proclaimed nondiscriminators in fact discriminate when it comes to choices for intimate, committed, permanent social relations? Results of the administration of prejudice measures indicate that there are great individual differences in prejudice. Perhaps some underlying dimension for which individual differences are not great explains why most people sometimes discriminate by race, even those who claim not to.

In the case of discrimination against African Americans, such a dimension appears to exist. *Racism* is widespread negative sentiment directed toward African Americans as well as other people of color (Allen, 1975; 1990). It has been argued that racism is a part of the mainstream culture in this country. When people incorporate their culture into their lives, largely through the process of identification, they swallow it whole. They ingest not only the good aspects of their culture, of which there are many; they also consume the bad, racism. Because most people adopt their culture, most people in the majority would incorporate racism within themselves. This may be the reason that even unprejudiced people show discrimination in some areas: racism rears it ugly head when it comes to choices of others for intimate, committed, permanent relations, although it fails to show up in other realms (deciding who to admire). By contrast, racism is reflected often in a wide spectrum of prejudiced people's expressions and behaviors.

Consistent with this consideration of racism, Allport found that racial animosity is very widespread. After examining the polls assessing antagonism toward various groups—most frequently African Americans—Allport concluded, "These...studies tempt us to estimate that four-fifths of the American population harbors enough antagonism toward minority groups to influence their daily conduct" (p. 78). Although his statement was based on polls taken many years ago, there is reason to believe that it is still accurate today. While animosity was very open in the early fifties, today, for most of us, it has become limited to a relatively few social relations and it has evolved to be more underground and subtle. The reluctance of European Americans to engage in intimate, committed, permanent relations with African Americans is reflected in the still exceedingly low interracial marital rate (Allen, 1990). Also, many studies over the years have shown that careful investigation of subtle behaviors reveals definite traces of racial animosity (Allen, 1978; 1990).

"Race" Differences

Allport (1954) traces continued interest in alleged racial differences to arguments that sub-categories of humans exist and can be arranged in a hierarchy from best to worst. It made thinking and living itself simpler to believe that there are big differences between one race and the next, and few differences among people of a given racial designation. It was also grat-ifying: one could declare one's own race "best" and view the members of other races as uni-formly inferior.

Allport asserted that gender bias mirrors how we react to the races. "Only a small part of our human nature is differentiated by sex.... The vast proportion of human physical, physio-logical, psychological traits are not sex linked" (p. 109). Yet, despite the evidence of no dif-ference on critical traits such as I.Q., "women are regarded as inferior, kept in the home... [and] denied many of the rights and privileges of men. The special roles assigned to them are far in excess of what sexual genetic difference would justify. So it is with race" (p. 109).

Allport, a pioneer in questioning race, makes two important points about the concept. First, most of the world's people are of mixed heritage; thus most do not fit any racial catego-ry. Second, "Most human characteristics ascribed to race are...[actually] ethnic, not racial" (p. 113). Today, the validity of race is again being challenged (Allen & Adams, 1992; Weizmann, Wiener, Wiesenthal, & Ziegler, 1990; Yee, Fairchild, Weizmann, & Wyatt, 1993; Zuckerman, 1990). It now appears that three criteria must be met before race is applicable to humans:

1. Consensually accepted criteria for differentiation among races must be developed and shown to actually erect clear boundaries between one race and the next;
2. Variability within races must be adequately reconciled with assumptions of intraracial uniformity; and
3. Overlap among races must be reconciled with the assumption that races are meaning-fully distinct (Allen & Adams, 1992).

Stereotypes

According to Allport, prejudice affects our thinking as well as our feelings. It is associated with the development of beliefs concerning the traits supposedly possessed by all or most members of a group. A belief of this sort is called a **stereotype,** an exaggerated belief that members of a group possess a certain trait; "Its function is to justify (rationalize) our conduct in relation to that [group]" (p. 191).

Such beliefs may have a grain of truth to them. In centuries past, Jews were money han-dlers in Europe, simply because they were allowed few alternatives for making a living. The problem is that this veridical observation evolved to become "most [or all] Jews are obsessed with making money." Though there may be a grain of truth to a stereotype, it is almost always false to assume that most of any large group possess any trait one can conjure up.

Stereotypes do tend to change in content over time, although the overall valence of their emotional tone may be relatively constant. Before World War II, the tone of our stereotypes of the Japanese was negative, but not strongly so. As soon as Pearl Harbor was bombed, stereotypes of the Japanese became viciously negative. As the Japanese wrought their economic miracle following the war, stereotypes became more positive. Currently, because they are viewed as beating us economically and "buying up America," stereotypes of the Japanese have become more negative.

What of the tone and content of stereotypes about African Americans? Allport lists the following stereotypes of African Americans that were held by European Americans at the time he was writing his 1954 book: unintelligent, morally primitive, emotionally unstable, overassertive, lazy, boisterous, fanatically religious, gamblers, flashy dressers, criminal, violent, reproductively prolific, occupationally unstable, superstitious, happy-go-lucky, ignorant, musical. To find out how these stereotypes might have changed, I asked each of 81 European American undergraduate students to write down five words to describe African Americans (using the Adjective Generation Technique, Allen & Potkay, 1983). Sixty-three African American students were given the same instruction. Next I tallied the words most frequently used to describe African Americans. The results are presented in Table 1.

Table 1   African Americans Described by Themselves and by European Americans (% of each sample using each word)

By Themselves		By European Americans	
6	misunderstood	6	boastful
6	emotional	6	moody
6	poor	6	poor
6	funny	6	strong
6	humorous	7	musical
6	inventive	7	obnoxious
6	powerful	7	prejudiced
8	corrupt	9	black
8	determined	9	mean
8	educated	9	smart
10	independent	10	arrogant
10	friendly	10	funny
11	athletic	10	independent
13	intelligent	11	corrupt
14	beautiful	11	friendly
14	oppressed	21	humorous
27	strong	25	loud
27	smart	40	athletic

You can see that European Americans' stereotypes of African Americans are still negative. Though some content remains the same—"musical" and "loud" (boisterous)—there have been some changes. African Americans are now seen as "humorous" and "athletic." Notice also that African Americans' self-descriptions agree with those of European Americans on "independent," but include "athletic" much less often and include "intelligent," omitted by European Americans.

Unlike the vast majority of other stereotype studies, I asked African Americans to indicate stereotypes of whites. (Usually African Americans are not asked, or stereotypes of various

European American ethnic groups are assessed, not whites in general.) Table 2 displays the stereotypes of whites.

Table 2   European Americans Described by Themselves and by African Americans (% of each sample using each word)

By Themselves		By African Americans	
6	corrupt	6	inventive
6	free	6	competitive
6	happy	6	powerful
6	kind	6	wealthy
7	conceited	8	educated
7	educated	10	racist
7	egotistical	11	selfish
10	intelligent	11	greedy
10	prejudiced	13	rich
10	rich	16	mean
12	humorous	19	smart
12	independent	24	prejudiced
12	inventive	41	corrupt
12	lazy		
15	arrogant		
15	friendly		
19	competitive		
19	greedy		
32	smart		

Again, African Americans and European Americans show limited agreement. African Americans are more negative about whites than whites are about themselves. Though both agree that whites are "greedy" and "smart," European Americans see themselves as "lazy" and "intelligent," but African Americans do not. European Americans now ascribe "lazy" to themselves, not African Americans.

Neither these results nor those reported by Allport were produced by large, representative samples of U. S. citizens. My survey, however, does have some advantages. One plus is that subjects produced the words from their own vocabularies, rather than being forced to choose from some limited, possibly biased list. This fact probably accounts for results not predicted by previous surveys, like whites being seen as "corrupt," "prejudiced," and "greedy" and African Americans as "friendly," "funny," and "humorous."

Painting the Picture of the Prejudiced Personality

The traits that highly prejudiced people share can be summarized in the phrase "threat oriented." The reference is partly due to viewing the world as a threatening place. However, some of the threat comes from within. The prejudiced person "seems fearful of himself, of his own instincts, of his own consciousness, of change, and of his social environment" (Allport, 1954, p. 396). To put it another way, very prejudiced people suffer from crippled egos. By promoting oppression of other groups, they can ensure that their own status in society is not threatened.

Beyond this general description, Allport offers some specific traits that prejudiced people tend to have in common.

Ambivalence about Parents

In a study of anti-Semitic white women students that Allport relies on repeatedly, ambivalence toward parents is clearly evident. While they openly praised their parents, on projective tests these women showed hostility toward their parents. Tolerant subjects were the opposite: they were openly critical of their parents, but the projective tests revealed no underlying hostility toward parents. Prejudiced students' hostility toward their parents may stem from child-rearing themes of obedience, punishment, and actual or threatened rejection.

Moralism

Allport reports that very prejudiced people tend to be highly moralistic as reflected in high attention to cleanliness and good manners. When the anti-Semitic students were asked what would embarrass them the most, they "responded in terms of violations of mores and conventions in public. Whereas [the] non-prejudiced spoke more often of inadequacy in personal relations" (p. 398). Again, child-rearing practices are implicated. The prejudiced had parents who punished them severely for any show of interest in their genitals and for aggression against the parents. The result was children who were guilt-ridden and full of self-hatred due to repeatedly being reminded of their wickedness. As adults, their repressed hostility exploded onto members of other groups, and their rigid morality was the source of a rationale for rejecting those individuals.

Dichotomization

Highly prejudiced people literally see in black and white. There is good and there is bad; there is right and there is wrong. This orientation was forced on them by parents who dished out approval and disapproval categorically: everything the child did was either right or it was wrong; there was no middle ground. Little wonder that as adults they see only two classes of people: those who are acceptable and those who are not.

Need for Definiteness

Allport believed that very prejudiced people are distinguished by their unique cognitive processes. Consistent with their tendency to classify everything into two categories, they show another critical characteristic. They have little tolerance for ambiguity: their cognitive orientation requires that everything be clearly distinguished from everything else, questions have definite answers, and problems have simple solutions. In short, prejudiced people want everything to be clear-cut, no gray areas. Shown an illusion involving a stationary point of light presented in darkness that appears to move, prejudiced people "reported the light as moving in a constant direction from trial to trial and to [move] a constant number of inches" (p. 401). By contrast, unprejudiced people saw movement in all directions and to a variable extent. Prejudiced people imposed clarity and order on an inherently ambiguous situation, while unprejudiced people tolerated the ambiguity.

Externalization

Allport saw very prejudiced people as lacking in self-insight. They do not see their own faults; they project them onto other people. Further, "things seem to happen 'out there'" (p. 404). Rather than believing that they control what happens to them by use of their own resources, they believe that fate controls them. Allport explained, "It is better and safer for a person in inner conflict to avoid self-reference. It is better to think of things happening to him rather than as caused by him" (p. 404). Also, prejudiced people externalize punishment: "It is not I who hates and injures others; it is *they* who hate and injure me" (p. 404).

Institutionalization

Allport believed the highly prejudiced person prefers order, especially social order. He finds safety and definiteness in his institutional memberships. "Lodges schools, churches, the nation, may serve as a defense against disquiet in his personal life. To lean on them saves him from leaning on himself" (p. 404). Also, the prejudiced are more devoted to institutions than the unprejudiced. The anti-Semitic college women were more wrapped up in their sororities and more patriotic. While patriotic people are not necessarily prejudiced, Allport referred to evidence that very prejudiced people are almost always super patriots. He cites an investigation in which club members completed a lengthy belief questionnaire in return for a monetary contribution to their clubs. The large number of variables examined were reduced to only one trait held in common: nationalism. Allport is quick to point out that "the nation" to these people is not what it is to most people. When most people think of the nation, it is the people, the principles of the constitution, and the land that come to mind. Instead, prejudiced people view the nation as something that will protect them from people seen as unlike themselves and that will preserve the *status quo.*

Authoritarianism

Allport believed that very prejudiced people are uncomfortable with democracy. "The consequences of personal freedom they find unpredictable. Individuality makes for indefiniteness, disorderliness, and change" (p. 406). It is easier to live in a power hierarchy where everyone has a place and the top spot is occupied by an all-powerful person. In a word, prejudiced people are authoritarian, they show high deference for authority figures, submission to the power of authority, and a need to command those seen as lower in power than themselves. Allport cites a study in which prejudiced people listed dictators like Napoleon when asked who they admired most, while unprejudiced people listed figures such as Lincoln.

Authoritarianism is seen in prejudiced people's mistrust of others. Authority embedded in a strong nation can save oneself from suspected others. "To the prejudiced person the best way to control these suspicions is to have an orderly, authoritative, powerful society. Strong nationalism is a good thing. Hitler [wasn't] so wrong.... America needs...a strong leader" (p. 407). This crucial concept is still receiving attention from researchers (Peterson, Doty, & Winter, 1993).

Classroom Discussion and Exercises

When teaching about diversity issues, we can help move our students toward a greater awareness of prejudice as a concept and as an influence in their own and other people's lives. Some of the exercises found useful include the following.

Discussion

Why does contact between European Americans and African, Asian, Latino, or Native Americans sometimes improve relations between the two groups and sometimes make relations worse? Some people, even some social scientists, naively criticize the psychologists who testified before the Supreme Court prior to the 1954 desegregation decision, because these academics argued that contact between African and European Americans in the schools would improve relations between them. That is exactly what they argued, but that is not all of the argument. Clearly, these psychological professionals felt that contact would have positive effects only under certain conditions. Put in summary form, the contact had to be under conditions of equal status, have the support of the powers that be, and occur in a cooperative atmosphere. Obviously, those conditions are all too rarely met in the school and elsewhere.

Let me suggest that you start with a question phrased something like this: "Does contact between African, Asian, Latino, or Native Americans and European Americans promote liking and understanding one another better?" You are likely to get arguments on either side, with neither side saying much about the circumstances of contact. Some will refer to their high school experiences of perpetual conflict between the groups while others will tell how they experienced a decline in personal prejudice once they got to know members of the other group. Guide them to a consensus by pointing to the conditions that must prevail if friendly, as opposed to hostile, interactions are to occur.

Classroom Exercises

1. Have the students use the Adjective Generation Technique (AGT) to describe their own group and another group (e.g. "write down five words to describe your own [the other] group"). You may want them to describe a group that is not represented in class or, if the class is composed of two groups in approximately equal numbers, you may want them to describe each other. The first alternate is safer and less fraught with social desirability problems: students won't be offended by descriptions and they will be more candid. The second alternative involves the problems avoided by the first, but may generate considerable insight.

You can score these descriptons by using the actual FAVorability values (and ANXiety values and FEMininity values) of Allen and Potkay (1983). A quicker way is just to assign a valance (+ or -) to each word depending on whether its connotation is positive or negative. In this case a whole description of five words is positive if at least three of the words are assigned pluses, and negative if three minuses are assigned (zeros could be assigned to "iffy" words and a neutral score recorded if there is not a majority of either pluses or minuses, but this option will give students license to hide bias). You could do the assignment of the valances or have students exchange descriptions and do it themselves. In the latter case, descriptions would be done anonymously, with only the describer's own group name coded somewhere on the sheet, perhaps the back (initials or "the last four digits of Grandmother's phone number" could serve as individual codes, so that students could find their descriptions later, if that is needed).

Did students favor their own group? It is entirely possible that the members of a particular group will not show the ingroup bias effect (favoring their own group), while the members of another group will show bias. Also, it is possible, as I found in comparing African Americans' and European Americans' descriptions, that one group will show a greater bias than the other. After this consideration, the remaining time on the exercise might be spent comparing descriptions of groups, using some sample stereotypic words frequently found on a group's lists of descripters of another group. For example, I found that European Americans frequently described African Americans as "athletic" and the latter described the former as "prejudiced." Should you have African American and European American students describe each other, you can expect some interesting comments upon comparing your students' descriptions with those of my subjects.

2. After the "prejudiced personality" has been considered, it would be interesting to discuss the "unprejudiced personality" (or more realistically, the "low-prejudiced personality"). What are people like who tend to be open-minded, tolerant, and egalitarian? Have participants list traits of the "low-prejudiced" person. How are the traits of such a person different from those of "prejudiced personality" types? Participants may also wish to consider how egalitarian persons are likely to be reared: What child-rearing practices are they likely to be exposed to? What life experiences have they had? How do they view their parents?

3. Have students respond to the Social Distance Scale (SD scale) in this essay. The seven items could be responded to with the use of seven-point scales anchored by "yes, I would" and "no, I wouldn't." Let the target of responses be some group that is not represented in class and is likely to be held in contempt at the time of the exercise. Alternatives are a fictitious group with an evil sounding name (Vulturians?) or some group whose oppression is just now coming to our consciousness (e.g., Haitians or, more generally, "boat people"). Your choice of a target group will greatly shape results and affect the direction of class discussion.

This exercise should be done anonymously. Even with identities hidden, my research experience (see Allen, 1975) tells me that with use of the SD scale, which entails high degrees of intimacy, commitment, and permanency, students will show a tendency to reject closeness to the target. You need not score the scale formally, but looking over the responses will probably allow you to state that few people would accept the target in close relationships. If so, ask students why they think the class rejected the target. Some answers will take the form: "What will my friends (or neighbors or relatives) think if I married one of these people?" I believe this discussion will not have to go very far before participants get the message: almost everyone shows some discrimination when it comes to choices for intimate, committed, permanent relationships.

REFERENCES

Allen, B. P., & Adams, J. Q. (1992). The concept "race": Let's go back to the beginning. *Journal of Social Behavior and Personality, 7,* 163-168.

Allen, B. P., & Potkay, C. R. (1983). *Adjective generation technique: Research and applications.* New York: Irvington Publishers.

Allen, B. P. (1990). *Personal adjustment.* Pacific Grove, CA: Brooks/Cole.

Allen, B. P. (1978). *Social behavior: Fact and falsehood.* Chicago: Nelson-Hall.

Allen, B. P. (1975). Social distance and admiration reactions of "unprejudiced whites." *Journal of Personality, 43,* 709-726.

Allport, G. W. (1954). *The nature of prejudice.* Reading, MA: Addison-Wesley.

Finchilescu, G. (1988). Interracial contact in South Africa within the nursing context. *Journal of Applied Social Psychology, 18,* 1207-1221.

Green, C. W. (1981, August). Operationalizing contact theory: Measuring student attributes toward desegration. Paper presented at the Annual Convention of the American Psychological Association, Los Angeles.

Triandis, H., Loh, W., & Levine, L. (1966). Race, status, quality of spoken English, and opinion about civil rights as determinants of interpersonal attitudes. *Journal of Personality and Social Psychology, 3,* 468-472.

Weizmann, F., Wiener, N. I., Wiesenthal, D. L., & Ziegler, M. (1990). Differential K theory and racial hierarchies. *Canadian Psychology, 31,* 1-13.

Yee, A. H., Fairchild, H. H., Weizmann, F., & Wyatt, G. E. (1993). Addressing psychology's problems with race. *American Psychologist, 48,* 1132-1140.

Zuckerman, M. (1990). Some dubious premises in research and theory on racial differences: Scientific, social, and ethical issues. *American Psychologist, 12,* 1297-1303.

DIVERSITY READING CLUBS

by
Samuel Betances

A very clever, humorous, oxymoronic sign in a merchant's window greets visitors to Ithaca, New York's airport: "Welcome to Ithaca, Our Community Is Centrally Isolated." I smiled and reflected on the message embodied in the sign. I was in Ithaca to deliver a lecture on diversity and on the forces at work in the global economy, on the demographic changes in the U. S., as well as the rise of interest-group marketing in society. I spoke at Cornell University, the pride of Ithaca. In view of the sign and my reasons for being in Ithaca, I reflected on both the good and bad aspects of residing in a "centrally isolated" place. The bad news, of course, has to do with the fact that isolation can impoverish the human spirit. The quest for a global vision can be easily frustrated in such places. The good news, on the other hand, is that even in such an environment one can build and have access to a university that supports the quest for global visions and counters the isolation.

It is possible to be both in an isolated community and to have access to a great institutional resource, a university process, right in the midst of that isolation. The reverse is also possible. One can reside in a centrally located community, with access to every universalizing resource, yet be personally—tragically—isolated. While thousands of people might be engaged in universalizing their spirits, others may not be benefitting from the opportunities to do so. Worse, some who live in isolation might lack the knowledge or the literacy to break the cycle of isolation even while employed in institutional settings whose mission is to educate and to expand the human vision.

We are all isolated in many ways from certain experiences, perspectives, and points of views in cultural matters. We are stymied in our quest for diverse groups in which we can share our interest in social justice and in the elimination of barriers to heterogeneous communication and interaction. In order to promote multicultural understanding we must break the cycle of our own isolation. It matters not whether we live in a homogeneous community or a heterogeneous one, in a small town or a large metropolitan area. Our spirits need to be universalized lest we become "centrally isolated." It would be awful indeed, if those of us who talk a great deal about global and multicultural education fail the ultimate test of consistency in "walking the walk," of doing what is necessary to enter into meaningful relationships with the residents of our pluralist society.

We simply must avail ourselves of contacts with members of different cultural heritages and interest groups. Breaking the cycle of our isolation must take us beyond the workplace and coincidental meetings in marketplace encounters. We can benefit greatly, of course, through literate video watching that enhances our views about people and cultures different from our own. But the ultimate challenge to our isolation and our breaking through it is personal dialogue, honest exchanges of ideas, and face-to-face communication with members of diverse groups in each other's homes. How can this be possible, in view of our housing patterns in both small and large communities? One simple, practical way of getting people together in order that, as a small, highly interactive group we may learn about each other, is to form a reading club.

We can create what I call diversity reading clubs. We have had such interest groups in our society for a long time. Study groups have, for example, been founded around "Great Books," around political issues, and around the reading and discussion of literature. Why not use this traditional form of exchange to further our understanding of different cultures? Even a cursory look at socialization patterns in our country suggests that we live in a very diverse and dispersed society, yet members of one cultural heritage group or identity group bond with like-minded people in terms of values, orientation, or experiences. We tend to socialize only among ourselves and to learn only about ourselves.

It is not unusual during staff development events that focus on diversity issues to hear speakers, seminar leaders, or trainers focusing only on the struggles, pains, and achievements of the particular group they represent. In order to gain a wider perspective, we need to change that. As individuals we can collaborate with people of diverse backgrounds to create a diversity reading club in which we can compare and contrast different cultural experiences and perspectives through the reading and discussion of a variety of books.

Ideally, eight to ten people would agree to get together to discuss a particular book once a month for a period of an academic year. The event host would prepare some light refreshments and open his or her home to club members for an intense, frank, and honest exchange of perspectives on a book every member of the club has read during the preceding weeks. The host would be a person who has powerful connections to the topic or theme of the particular book being discussed and would prepare a three-page statement or critique of the book to guide the discussion. The statement could include the author's qualifications to write on the subject; five significant lessons the book taught the discussion leader and host; five to ten concepts made sharper and clearer as a result of the reading; the persons most likely to benefit from the work; and lastly, the impact the book is likely to have on the professional, communal, and personal life of the host.

The meetings ought to take place on a week night at a time agreed upon by the participants. The first twenty minutes could include reading the host's critique. This would be followed by a freewheeling discussion that includes input from all the members. The last ten minutes would be reserved for setting up the next meeting, with the host of that meeting explaining the next book's importance and handling logistical questions.

Every member of the club must agree to read the whole book before coming to the meeting. Even if the book is familiar to a member or two or was read at some point in the past, it is imperative that each participant read the book again. People grow in perspective, maturity, and experiences. Re-reading the book within a new context may reveal a surprising change of opinion or have an impact that would not have been possible if we relied only on the vague memories of a previous reading. Every participant must be empowered to contribute to the exchange of ideas related to the reading. A fresh reading will contribute greatly to that empowerment.

The themes of diversity in such areas as educational change, race and ethnic relations, gender, and sexual orientation are broad and can serve as parameters when choosing books for the club. Recommendations from the people close to the communities, groups, and/or themes of concern to club members might prove valuable. In the Suggested Readings accompanying this essay, I have listed six books that have broadened my own perspective and appreciation for diversity. Once the group is underway, members are more likely to find choosing books a challenge, not because of too few possibilities, but because of too many.

The diversity club allows its members to get some grounding and deeper understanding about established cultural communities as well as those new to our society. Ideally, between monthly meetings, members would exchange visits and encourage socializing across the cultural lines imposed by separate or even segregated housing and other factors. How distant we are from each other can be graphically illustrated by the segregation apparent in our society during our times of worship. The diversity club can help us bridge such distances.

Lastly, the club can promote coalitions of interest instead of the coalitions of color or gender or sexual orientation we are so familiar with now. Diversity is much more than intellectualizing about the topic. Through the reading clubs, a group of people, on a voluntary basis, can "walk the walk" by creating voluntary structures to help make our House of Democracy healthier, stronger, and freer than we found it.

REFERENCES

Angelou, M. (1993). *Wouldn't take nothing for my journey now.* New York: Random House.

Cummins, J. (1989). *Empowering minority students.* California Association for Bilingual Education.

Morrison, A. M. (1992). *The new leaders: Guidelines on leadership diversity in America.* San Francisco: Jossey-Bass Publishers.

Takaki, R. (1989). *Strangers from a different shore: A history of Asian Americans.* Boston: Little, Brown.

Woods, J. D., with Lucas, J. H. (1993). *The corporate closet.* New York: The Free Press.

Whyte, M. (1987). *The Japanese educational challenge: A commitment to children.* New York: The Free Press.

Section II: Implementing Multicultural Perspectives in the Classroom

SELF-REGULATED LEARNING AND TEACHING:
AN INTRODUCTION AND OVERVIEW

by
Reinhard W. Lindner

The construct of self-regulated learning has varied origins and flies under the banner of several theoretical frameworks. The basic issue addressed, however, is focused on the notions of volition and (internal) control. While not entirely ignored, these represent relatively neglected topics within the discipline of psychology, particularly learning related psychology. Nevertheless, a growing body of literature suggests that optimal academic performance is strongly tied to the degree of self-regulation the learner is capable of exercising (Borkowski, Carr, Rellinger & Pressley, 1990; Jones & Idol, 1990; Lindner & Harris, 1992b; Zimmerman & Martinez-Pons 1986; Zimmerman, 1990). Although the self-regulated learning perspective is not, at present, a theoretically unified one, according to Zimmerman (1990, p. 4), "a common conceptualization of these students has emerged as metacognitively, motivationally, and behaviorally active participants in their own learning." In other words, whether one espouses a social-cognitive, information processing, or sociocultural orientation, there nevertheless appears to be general agreement that self-regulated learners are purposive and goal oriented (proactive rather than simply reactive), incorporating and applying a variety of strategic behaviors designed to optimize their academic performance.

While many students, barring those who are totally tuned out, are, to some degree and on some occasions, active in the manner Zimmerman describes, self-regulated learners have been found to be both more keenly aware of the relation between specific behaviors and academic success and more likely to systematically and appropriately employ such behaviors (Zimmerman & Martinez-Pons, 1986). In short, they evidence far higher executive or metacognitive processing than their fellow students. Self-regulated learners control learning outcomes, that is, primarily from within; they are intrinsically motivated, self-directing, self-monitoring, and self-evaluating. They also appear, however, to be more finely tuned than their less successful counterparts to situational demands, hence exhibiting greater flexibility in adapting to the variable and sometimes uncertain challenges that exist in the classroom, particularly at the high school and college levels. The question, of course, is: how did they get to be this way?

My own approach to this issue has been to first seek to define, on the basis of the literature surrounding this topic as well as my own investigations, the components of self-regulated learning and then to attempt to capture the dynamics of the learning process from a self-regulated perspective. The model that has resulted from this effort reflects an information processing orientation. With regard to the question of origin, or developmental dynamics, however, I favor a sociocultural approach (Rogoff, 1990).

Components of Self-Regulated Learning: An Information Processing Model

In terms of the self-regulation of cognition the basic mechanism involves: 1) analysis of the task, 2) construction of a plan or strategy, 3) implementation, 4) monitoring by periodically comparing execution to an internal standard, and 5) modification of the plan, when necessary. The entire process should be thought of as recursive rather than as simply linearly executed. The working information processing model of self-regulated learning which I have developed consists of six dimensions: A) epistemological beliefs, B) motivation, C) metacognition, D) learning strategies, E) contextual sensitivity, and F) environmental utilization/control (see Appendix A). In short, in seeking to understand the dynamics of self-regulated learning I argue that it is best to view each individual as bringing to a learning situation a) a largely unconscious frame of reference (informal epistemology) comprised of beliefs about the nature of knowledge and the process of knowing (Kuhn, 1991; Perry, 1988; Schommer, 1990), b) a particular motivational orientation and set of values (Dweck, 1989), c) the capacity (present in all, but more or less developed in a given individual) for monitoring, evaluating, and, generally, reflecting over one's cognitive activity (Flavell, 1979; Brown, 1987), (d) a specific (to the individual) body of strategic knowledge about how to effectively and efficiently process information (Derry 1990; Pressley, et.al., 1990), e) a characteristic degree of sensitivity to contextual cues that facilitate, or afford, learning or problem solving, and f) a specific level of understanding of how to effectively utilize and/ or control environmental conditions such that learning goals are most likely to be achieved (Nelson-Le Gall, 1985; Newman, 1990; Zimmerman & Martinez-Pons, 1986). Most of the various self-regulated learning strategies reported in the literature (see, for example, Pintrich, Smith & McKeachie, 1989; Weinstein, Zimmerman & Palmer, 1988; Zimmerman & Martinez-Pons, 1986) fall into one or another of the categories I have constructed.

Contextual sensitivity, I should note, although implicit in much of the published literature, is not an area typically identified explicitly as an independent aspect of self-regulated learning. However, the theme that cognitive processes are contextually bound, or "situated" (Rogoff & Lave, 1984; Rogoff, 1990) is becoming increasingly general in the contemporary literature on learning and cognition, particularly as it occurs in educational settings. I therefore decided to define it as a separate dimension of self-regulated learning. Also unique to this model of selfregulated learning is the inclusion of epistemological beliefs as a moderating factor. The particular epistemological orientation (absolutist, relativist, evaluative) or set of beliefs that characterize a given individual imposes powerful constraints on the nature and degree of self-regulation a learner is likely to exhibit (Perry, 1988; Schommer, 1990).

In developing this model, I reasoned that the self-regulated learner must be able to both internally regulate, monitor, evaluate, and modify, when necessary, the learning process and be alert to and utilize or manage contextual (external) factors such as course and instructor demands, where and when to study, who, when, and where to go to for assistance. It is also evident that motivational factors mediate the utilization of both cognitive and environmental resources (Borkowski, Carr, Rellinger & Pressley, 1990). Individuals high in self-efficacy, for example, are more likely to use cognitive and metacognitive strategies and to seek appropriate (instrumental) forms of assistance when needed (Karabenick & Knapp, 1991; Schunk, 1991). At the same time, there is a positive relationship between a sense of personal control over learning outcomes and subsequent motivation (Dweck, 1989; Schunk, 1991) to undertake learning related challenges. Furthermore, self-regulated learners must not only be motivated, they must know how to *sustain* motivation over time and in the face of competing alternatives or demands (Kuhl & Beckman, 1985). Despite the many elements that enter into it, there is sound reason to believe that self-regulated learning is a unified process which involves the integration and utilization of cognitive, metacognitive, motivational, perceptual, and environmental components in the successful resolution of academic tasks (Lindner & Harris, 1992a; Zimmerman & Martinez-Pons, 1986).

Perhaps the interworkings of the model in action can best be grasped by way of an example. Using figure 1 as a guide, consider a student faced with the typical task of preparing for a quiz. For purposes of discussion let us assume it will be a written (rather than multiple choice) quiz. Let us also assume the quiz has been announced one week in advance and the subject is world politics. A number of decisions face the learner even in this simple situation.

Figure 1: Conceptual model of the self-regulated learning process

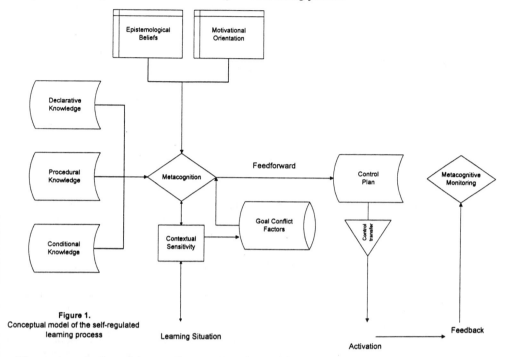

Figure 1.
Conceptual model of the self-regulated
learning process

The strategy the learner eventually pursues depends both on factors internal to the learner and external factors present in the larger situation in which the learning task is set. First of all, the learner brings at least three kinds of knowledge to any task: declarative (knowing that or what), procedural (knowing how), and conditional (knowing when and where to do what). As the learner encounters a particular task, the eventual strategy developed will depend both on the knowledge she possesses and how well she reads the nature and demands of the task (contextual sensitivity). If background knowledge is strong (the task is familiar), the solution path may appear simple and straightforward. If specific knowledge is lacking (regarding the subject matter or the situation or because the teacher is new to the student), a general strategy or plan must be developed. For such a plan to be effective, metacognitive or executive processing will be required. However, the nature of the decisions made at this point will also be driven internally by the largely unconscious epistemological beliefs and motivational orientation the learner brings to the task. If, for example, the learner's epistemological orientation is absolutist in nature, she will interpret the task as primarily a matter of acquiring the "facts," memorizing them and regurgitating them exactly. A relativist, on the other hand, is likely to interpret the task as asking for her opinion on the facts or issue in question.

Motivational orientation too will affect the course of action selected by the learner. If, for example, the learner is *performance* oriented (Dweck, 1989), and the task is challenging (the risk of failure is relatively high), she may choose to minimize effort in order to have a ready-made explanation in the case of failure (I didn't try). Both one's epistemological and motivational orientation exert a tacit but powerful influence on the learner's executive decision-making process. These factors are particularly crucial to investigate if the learning process in a specific individual's case is or becomes maladaptive.

Let us assume, for the purposes of discussion, that our hypothetical learner's epistemological and motivational orientations are relatively salutary. The executive component must effectively define and analyze the learning situation and devise an appropriate action strategy. The efficacy of the strategy devised will be dependent upon the depth of the learner's repertoire of learning tactics and conditional knowledge. Performance will also vary as a function of the number and attractiveness of goal conflict factors (social and other extracurricular activities) present in a situation relative to the effort and actions necessary if the goal of passing the quiz is to be achieved. The stronger the drive to succeed, and the fewer the number and attractiveness of goal conflict factors present, the greater the likelihood that the learner will persist in carrying out the strategy in pursuit of goal attainment. In any case, metacognitive reflection and processing subsequently generates feedforward in terms of a learning plan and goal selection. The plan will next be transformed into action. Action, of course, produces feedback which, if carefully monitored, allows adjustments to the plan over the course of action. Feedback of a different kind also comes upon task completion. Such feedback not only informs the learner if she succeeded but provides a source of conditional knowledge allowing for future construction of more appropriate and adaptive strategy building. Teaching can play a crucial facilitating and informative role at this point in insuring that proper connections between behavior and outcome are made on the part of the student.

The Development of Self-Regulated Learning

In approaching the question of development, as previously noted, I favor a sociocultural approach in the spirit of Vygotsky (1978). That is, I assume that cognition is first other-regulated within the context of the individual's social and cultural relationships. Through social interaction over time, cognitive structures and processes peculiar to each individual arise which come to characterize her conceptual and procedural interaction with the events and individual actors of her world. Ideally, the individual, moving through the *zone of proximal development* (Vygotsky, 1978), gradually becomes increasingly self-conscious and self-regulating. In Vygotsky's terms: "Any function in the child's cultural development appears twice, or on two planes. First it appears on the social plane, and then on the psychological plane. First it appears between people as an interpsychological category, and then within the child as an intrapsychological category" (1981). It is important to note that, from this perspective, the degree to which one self-regulates behavior and thought is primarily a function of the nature and quality of one's interpersonal relationships. I want to also emphasize, however, that self-regulation of *academic* cognition, in the sense that I have been depicting it, is neither a necessary or natural outcome of development. This is not meant to suggest, however, that the contents of one's mind and the nature of one's interactions are strictly determined by sociocultural experience. Individuals clearly play a role in determining their developmental routes and outcomes. Nevertheless, sociocultural experience imposes powerful constraints (for good or ill) on individual development.

The issue of the development of *academic* self-regulation raises not only the question of origin but of individual and group differences. That is, are some individuals and/or groups (for example, socioeconomic, ethnic) more or less likely to develop the skills and attitudes of a self-regulated learner than others, and why?

Self-Regulated Learning and Multicultural Education

I have thus far provided a description and evidence for the general characteristics and development of self-regulated learners. The question many readers will want addressed, however, is: are some learners more or less likely to be self-regulating due to differential cultural or subcultural experiences? The answer (although too complicated to address fully here) would seem to be, yes. This appears particularly true with groups who have traditionally not performed well in our schools and whose status is "castelike or involuntary" (Ogbu, 1992, p. 8). This involuntary status as a minority leads many members of such groups to identify the adoption of certain behaviors (for example, those associated with success in school) as requiring a rejection of their own unique cultural identity and sense of community. The result is an inability or unwillingness to accommodate their behavior to the demands of classroom culture which would facilitate success in that setting. In fact, such individuals are likely to enter the classroom setting with a cultural identity that has been formed in significant ways in opposition to that of the dominant culture (Ogbu, 1992). The problem is further exacerbated by peer pressure and the lack of clear incentives within the context of a social reality that is less than encouraging in terms of future social and/or economic success. Ogbu (1992) has done much to clarify the nature of the different cultural frame of reference such groups bring to the classroom context. I suspect that this issue plays out, in terms of the issue of self-regulation of learning, in several ways.

In the first place, I suspect that some minority groups not only operate from a different *cultural* frame but (perhaps, partly as a consequence) a different *epistemological* frame of reference. In terms of my own research (Lindner, 1994), the evidence suggests that certain epistemological beliefs antithetical to academic success are dominant among, for example, African Americans who have been incarcerated. I hesitate to generalize from such data. However, I do think it indicates that this question demands further investigation. Certainly differences in epistemological criteria on a variety of issues is implicit in the many debates between minority and dominant group members that appear to talk past one another.

Secondly, an individual possessed of an oppositional orientation to behaviors and attitudes that promote success in the classroom seems unlikely to develop either the motivational orientation or processing strategies likely to facilitate academic success. In short, I strongly suspect that members of minority groups of an involuntary status are less likely to demonstrate the kinds of attitudes and behaviors I have defined as underlying academic self-regulation. I have no doubt, however, that if convinced that a strategy of "accommodation without assimilation" (Gibson, 1988) was in their best interest, such individuals could be taught to develop and utilize such skills. Indeed, the (admittedly limited) data we have on *successful* minority students at the college level (Harris & Lindner, 1993) indicates that they utilize self-regulated learning skills to a higher degree than less successful students, irregardless of status.

Applications of Self-Regulated Learning Theory to Instruction

Since experience, and in particular social experience, plays such a powerful role in the development of self-regulation, it should not be surprising that school experiences are crucial in the development of the cognitive tools available to individuals. The school setting is at once a cultural artifact and a living social and experiential context in which the primary focus is literacy-based learning. Some forms of teacher-learner (as well as peer) interaction, however, are clearly more facilitative of self-regulation of the learning process than others. Teaching can be primarily presentative and corrective (focused on what Howard Gardner, 1991, has termed the "correct answer compromise"), wherein the teacher regulates the learning; or dialogic and facilitative, wherein the teacher actively seeks to foster student regulation of the learning process.

The particular instructional model I have been developing (see Figure 2) incorporates the basic assumptions of the *cognitive apprenticeship* approach (Rogoff 1990) and tailors them such that they specifically foster the emergence and development of self-regulated learning.

The self-regulated learning/teaching cycle

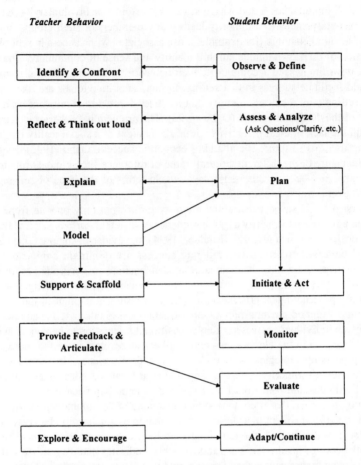

Teacher Behavior

Student Behavior

Identify & Confront

Observe & Define

Reflect & Think out loud

Assess & Analyze
(Ask Questions/Clarify. etc.)

Explain

Plan

Model

Support & Scaffold

Initiate & Act

Provide Feedback &
Articulate

Monitor

Evaluate

Explore & Encourage

Adapt/Continue

As Rogoff (1990, p. 39) notes, cognitive apprenticeship occurs when "active novices advance their skills and understanding through participation with more skilled partners in culturally organized activities." Cognitive apprenticeship is, in other words, a form of socially mediated instruction wherein 1) to-be-learned skills are modeled by a more experienced [adult or peer] "expert," 2) made explicit by the "expert" through think-aloud demonstrations in the application and regulation of the component skills, and 3) over the course of learning the "novice" is induced to accept increasing responsibility for his/her performance of the target skill (Englert & Raphael 1989). Also crucial to the cognitive apprenticeship model is the notion that socially mediated learning is most effective when occurring within the zone of proximal development (Vygotsky, 1978; Rogoff 1990). That is, such instruction attempts to enter a student's optimal region of sensitivity to social guidance in order to facilitate cognitive growth. While space does not permit a complete explication of a self-regulated teaching model, let me attempt to describe its basic skeleton and, on the student side of the process, what it seeks to promote.

Before I begin, allow me to state some preliminary conditions and concerns. It is important to realize that if self-regulated learning is the desired outcome of instruction, then the conditions of learning and instruction must be designed to insure its development. That is, self-regulated learning must be the explicit goal of instruction. Furthermore, instructional policy and the institutional support system that regulates its day-to-day affairs must be such as to facilitate this educational goal. This point may appear obvious. However, it is crucial to emphasize at the outset that traditional schooling in this country, though well intended, has inclined toward fostering learning that is teacher and policy (other) regulated rather than seeking to foster student self-regulation of the learning process. Unfortunately, programs that have set out explicitly to promote self-regulated learning, at this juncture, remain largely experimental in nature (see, for example, Paris, Cross & Lipson, 1984). Having said this, the question of how, in practical terms, to go about the business of nurturing self-regulated learners remains to be addressed.

First of all, it is recommended that teaching for self-regulated learning take place in conjunction with the teaching of content rather than as a separate set of skills. Emphasizing self-regulated learning in the context of content and skill acquisition ensures the greater likelihood of transfer. Secondly, it is crucial that instruction begin at the level of the student. Simply informing students about powerful learning tools will only produce, at best, confusion and discouragement. Thirdly, it is crucial that the collaborative and reciprocal nature of the teaching/learning process inform the entire cycle. Teaching and learning are not two separate activities with entirely independent aims and responsibilities. Rather, they are highly complementary activities with a single aim: the promotion of informed, independent and skillful information processing and decision making. In order to accomplish this overarching goal, it is critical for the teacher to take the mystery out of the learning process by making his thinking visible (by thinking out loud) and through modeling the learning cycle for the student. The ultimate aim, it must be kept in mind, is to transfer control of the performance sought from the teacher to the student. This deceptively simple point is a difficult one for many teachers, particularly those who feel they must always be in control of all that occurs in their classroom. In sum, the teacher's task is to move the student from other-regulation, through the zone of proximal development, to self-regulation.

One begins the cycle by *identifying* for and *confronting* the learner with the problem to be solved, or skill to be taught. In so doing, one should pause and *reflect,* considering (out loud) the reason(s) behind the identification of the problem or the skill to be learned. For example, a highly effective strategy for learning from text involves generating and answering crucial questions such as what, when, who, where, how, and why with regard to text content. Teaching the effective use of this strategy would include explicit identification of the learning goal and the reasoning behind its use. In an effort to clarify and promote comprehension, the teacher may wish, at this point, to have students generate, discuss, and compare possible alternative strategies. The next step involves *explaining* how to effect the strategy followed by explicit and detailed *modeling* of the strategy on the part of the teacher. In the process, the teacher should *articulate* what is being done and why. Once these five steps have been carried through, time should be taken to *encourage and explore* questions or consider strategies generated by students and to consider explicitly other situations in which the strategy or skill being taught could effectively be employed.

At this point, students should be allowed to attempt to apply the strategy or skill on their own under the careful *scaffolded guidance* of the teacher. The basic idea is to provide as much, and only as much, guidance as the student requires. A crucial element in the successful internalization of the learning process is provision of explicit and detailed *feedback* from teacher to student. Finally, the learner's independent action and taking control of the learning process must be carefully nourished and *encouraged.* That the entire cycle I have described is in the form of a dialectic (dialogue) between teacher and learner (designed to regulate learning and cognition) is hopefully transparent. Its aim is to promote an approach and attitude toward learning and behavior that is self-reflective, self-evaluative, and, ultimately, self-regulative. If attained, transfer, in the sense of the regulation of cognition, will, I think follow rather naturally. In fact, such transfer can be viewed as the hidden goal of the self-regulated teaching/learning sequence. The learning/teaching cycle, however, does not end at this point. In fact, there is no real end point to the sequence, just as there is no true end point in learning. At the closing of a particular teaching/learning event, time should, once again, be taken to *encourage and explore* questions or consider alternative strategies generated by students, now that they have applied the strategy or skill on their own. It would be wise, I think, as a particular portion of the cycle is brought to closure, to also consider the possible limitations of a specific skill, concept, or strategy.

I believe it worth noting at this point that what I have been describing as a teaching model for promoting self-regulated learning falls within a family of approaches to instruction called *constructivist* models. A persistent criticism of constructivist approaches to instruction is they place too much of a burden on the learner without sufficient consideration of the kinds and complexity of entry level skills they presuppose (Dick, 1991; Perkins, 1991). Such criticisms have a grain of truth in them. That is, the cognitive demands of complex tasks can be overwhelming and frustrating for a novice learner. As Perkins (1991, p. 18) puts it: "Constructivist pedagogy often imposes sharp demands on learners." It is tempting, therefore, for both teacher and learner to succumb to the allure of a more direct approach to instruction. The answer to this dilemma, however, is not to abandon the constructivist approach. Rather, the answer lies in a pedagogical approach that stresses the crucial role of the *scaffolding* (a pedagogocal technique that seeks to temporarily reduce the cognitive load imposed on the learner when confronted with new and complex tasks or concepts) of the learning process by a sensitive and flexible teacher.

The model I have described above is, admittedly, abstract and sketchy in nature. The main point, again, involves an emphasis on taking the mystery out of learning and the fostering of volitional control on the part of the learner. Since gaining such control is a complex process, such instruction needs to occur early and often in the learning career of students. A specific technique, primarily a form of scaffolding, which I use with my students (many of whom are the products of schooling that fostered other-regulation of learning!), is represented in Appendix B. Basically, prior to entering a new content area in my classes, I pass out this sheet and ask students to begin filling it in. I begin by asking them to clearly define and differentiate (as far as they can, at this point) the topic we will be examining, and to set some specific goal(s) with regard to learning it. Next, I attempt to lead them to draw out whatever knowledge (accurate or inaccurate) they already possess concerning the topic at issue. In this manner, active learning is initiated. Once they have read their text and the topic has been covered in class, I ask students to consider: 1) what questions they have, 2) how confident they would be about taking a test, and 3) what specifically they could do to improve their understanding. That this form of instruction is designed to promote taking charge of the learning process on the part of the student is, hopefully, transparent. It represents a type of *dialogue* between teacher and learner that, if all goes well, will be internalized by the student and become a normal aspect of her learning *modus operandi*. The technique allows for flexibility and for working through the various steps (as needed) of the teaching process previously articulated. This is, of course, only one way to actualize teaching for self-regulated learning. The specific technique employed is, I believe, not nearly as important as the fact that a deliberate, conscious effort is made on the part of teachers to foster self-regulated learning in the classroom.

REFERENCES

Borkowski, J. G., Carr, M., Rellinger, E., & Pressley, M. (1990). Self-regulated cognition: Interdependence of metacognition, attributions, and self-esteem. In B. F. Jones & L. Idol (Eds.), *Dimensions of thinking and cognitive instruction.* Hillsdale, NJ: Erlbaum.

Brown, A. (1987). Metacognition, executive control, self-regulation and other more mysterious mechanisms. In F. E. Weinert & R. H. Kluwe (Eds.), *Metacognition, motivation, and understanding.* Hillsdale, NJ: Erlbaum.

Derry, S. J. (1990). Learning strategies for acquiring useful knowledge. In B. F. Jones & L. Idol (Eds.), *Dimensions of thinking and cognitive instruction.* Hillsdale, NJ: Erlbaum.

Dick, W. (1991, May). An instructional designer's view of constructivism. *Educational Technology, 31*, 31-44.

Dweck, C. S. (1989). Motivation. In A. Lesgold & R. Glaser (Eds.), *Foundations for a psychology of education.* Hillsdale, NJ: Erlbaum.

Englert, C. S., & Raphael, T. E. (1989). Developing successful writers through cognitive strategy instruction. In J. Brophy (Ed.), *Advances in research on teaching, Vol. 1.* Greenwich, CT: JAI Press.

Flavell, J. H. (1979). Metacognition and cognitive monitoring: A new area of cognitive-developmental inquiry. *American Psychologist, 34*, 906-911.

Gardner, H. (1991). *The unschooled mind.* New York: Basic Books.

Gibson, M. A. (1988). *Accommodation without assimilation: Sikh immigrants in an American high school.* Ithaca, NY: Cornell University Press.

Harris, B. R., & Lindner, R. W. (1993). *Cultural influences on self-regulated learning.* Unpublished manuscript.

Jones, B. F., & Idol, L. (Eds.). (1990). *Dimensions of thinking and cognitive instruction.* Hillsdale, NJ: Erlbaum.

Karabenick, S. A., & Knapp, J. R. (1991). Relationship of academic help seeking to the use of learning strategies and other instrumental achievement behavior in college students. *Journal of Educational Psychology, 83*(2), 221-230.

Kuhl, J., & Beckman, J. (Eds.). (1985). *Action control: From cognition to behavior.* Berlin: Springer-Verlag.

Kuhn, D. (1991). *The skills of argument.* New York: Cambridge University Press.

Lindner, R. W. (1994). Self-regulated learning in correctional education students and its implications for instruction. *The Journal of Correctional Education, 45*(3), 122-126.

Lindner, R. W. & Harris, B. (1992a). *Self-regulated learning and academic achievement in college students.* Paper presented at the April, 1992, American Educational Research Association annual convention, San Francisco.

Lindner, R. W., & Harris, B. (1992b). Self-regulated learning: Its assessment and instructional implications. *Educational Research Quarterly, 16, 2.*

Nelson-Le Gall, S. (1985). Help-seeking behavior in learning. *Review of Research in Education, 12,* 55-90.

Ogbu, J. U. (1992). Understanding cultural diversity and learning. *Educational Researcher, 21*(8), 5-14.

Paris, S. G., Cross, D. R., & Lipson, M. Y. (1984). Informed strategies for learning: A program to improve children's reading awareness and comprehension. *Journal of Educational Psychology, 76,* 1239-1252.

Perkins, D. N. (1991, Sept.). What constructivism demands of the learner. *Educational Technology, 31,* 19-21.

Perry, W. G. (1988). Different worlds in the same classroom. In P. Ramsden (Ed.). *Improving learning: New perspectives.* London: Kogan Page.

Pintrich, P. R., Smith, D. A., & McKeachie, W. J. (1989). *Motivated strategies for learning questionnaire.* Ann Arbor: University of Michigan.

Pressley, M., Woloshyn, V., Lysynchuck, L. M., Martin, V., Wood, E., & Willoughby, T. (1990). A primer of research on cognitive strategy instruction: The important issues and how to address them. *Educational Psychology Review, 2,* 1-58.

Rogoff, B. (1990). *Apprenticeship in thinking: Cognitive development in cultural context.* New York: Oxford University Press.

Rogoff, B., & Lave, J. (Eds). (1984). *Everyday cognition: Its development in social context.* Cambridge, MA: Harvard University Press.

Schommer, M. (1990). Effects of beliefs about the nature of knowledge on comprehension. *Journal of Educational Psychology, 82*(3), 498-504.

Schunk, D. H. (1991). *Learning theories: An educational perspective.* New York: Merrill.

Vygotsky, L. S. (1978). (M. Cole, V. John-Steiner, S. Scribner, & E. Souberman, Eds.) *Mind in society: The development of higher psychological processes.* Cambridge, MA: Harvard University Press.

Vygotsky, L. S. (1981). The genesis of higher mental functions. In J. V. Wertsch (Ed.), *The concept of activity in Soviet psychology.* Armonk, NY: M. E. Sharpe.

Weinstein, C. E., Zimmerman, S. A., & Palmer, D. R. (1988). Assessing learning strategies:

The design and development of the LASSI. In C. E. Weinstein, E. T. Goetz, & P. A. Alexander (Eds). *Learning and study strategies: Issues in assessment, instruction, and evaluation.* New York: Academic Press.

Zimmerman, B. J. (1990). Self-regulated learning and academic achievement: An overview. *Educational Psychologist, 25,* 3-17.

Zimmerman, B. J. (1989). A social cognitive view of self-regulated academic learning. *Journal of Educational Psychology, 81,* 329-339.

Zimmerman, B. J. & Martinez-Pons, M. (1988). Construct validation of a strategy model of student self-regulated learning. *Journal of Educational Psychology, 80,* 284-290.

Zimmerman, B. J., & Martinez-Pons, M. (1986). Development of a structured interview for assessing student use of self-regulated learning strategies. *American Educational Research Journal, 23,* 614-628.

Zimmerman, B. J., & Schunk, D. H. (Eds.). (1989). *Self-regulated learning and academic achievement: Theory, research and practice.* New York: Springer-Verlag.

Appendix A

Self-regulated Learning
(Lindner & Harris, 1992)

General definition: A) The ability to monitor, regulate, evaluate, sustain, and strategically modify, when necessary, the learning process and B) sensitivity to, and ability to exercise control over, contextual factors that affect learning outcomes. The basic components of self-regulated learning include 1) epistemological beliefs, 2) motivational processes, 3) metacognitive processes, 4) learning strategies, 5) contextual sensitivity and 6) environmental control and/or utilization. Self-regulated learners are possessed of a belief system that views knowledge as complex and evolving, rather than simple and fixed, and the knower as capable of self-modification. An individual is a self-regulated learner to the degree that she/he is able to effectively monitor and regulate (control) and sustain the learning process, apply a variety of appropriate and efficient strategies to learning problems encountered, maintain a sense of competence, (intrinsic) motivation, and personal agency, accurately diagnose the character and demands of particular learning challenges, and effectively utilize and control environmental factors that have a bearing on learning outcomes.

Six Dimensions of Self-Regulated Learning

A. Epistemologial Beliefs: Defined as relatively enduring and unconscious beliefs about the nature of knowledge and the process of knowing (i.e., the source, certainty, speed of acquisition, etc., of knowledge).

B. Motivation: Refers to goal oriented effort that is a complex function of goal value, goal accessibility, learning orientation, perceived likelihood of success, one's sense of self-efficacy and the factor(s) to which one habitually attributes success and/or failure.

C. Metacognition: Defined generally as 1) knowledge about cognition and 2) awareness and conscious regulation of one's thinking and learning. The executive engine of cognition.

D. Learning Strategies: Refers to both operative knowledge of specific learning tactics (highlighting, summarizing, etc.) and the ability to combine various tactics into an effective learning plan.

E. Contextual Sensitivity: Refers to the ability to "read" the learning context for what it specifies regarding the demands of a particular problem setting and what it affords in the way of problem resolution.

F. Environmental Utilization/Control: Refers to the utilization and management of circumstances and resources external to the self in the pursuit of learning related goals.

Appendix B

What I Know Metacognitive Worksheet

TOPIC/SECTION: _____

_____

LEARNING GOAL(S): _____

_____

Before you begin, consider:

What do I know about this topic already (activate prior knowledge):

    First: Ask yourself, have I read/heard about this topic before?
    Then: Briefly review mentally your prior understanding of the topic.

    NEXT, begin studying. After each major section of text, STOP and ASK:

What do I know about this topic after studying/learning:

    First: Outline or map out the main concepts as presented in your text.
    Then: Summarize the main concepts presented in your own words.

What do I still not know or understand (questions I have):

    First: Return to your text and list concepts which you missed or are still unclear.
    Then: Try to specify what is confusing you about the concepts you identified as unclear.

If I had to take a test on this topic right now, what grade would I expect?

    Circle one: A   B   C   D   F

FINALLY, ask yourself:

What could I do to improve my knowledge and understanding?

    First: Review and evaluate your previous strategy.
    Next: Revise your strategy to enhance your progress toward your goal(s).

ENDING THE SILENCE:
ENCOURAGING DISSENSUS IN THE CONTACT ZONE

by
Hallie S. Lemon

Silence is the weapon of hostility and has a way of breeding violence, first of the body and then the soul.

Jerry Hazen

This quote cannot be found in a textbook on pedagogy but is remembered from a Sunday sermon; the minister added that we can best end prejudice not by realizing that the objects of prejudice are just as good as we are but by realizing that they can be as human as we are, too, and have their dark moments. In our collaborative classrooms, silence among classmates has been replaced by dialogue. Linda Dittmar (1993) recognized this silence as a barrier which students either struggle to break through or keep in place. Breaking silence without conflict in a multicultural classroom appears impossible and, as I hope to show, may even be undesirable. In a classroom of students from diverse cultures, which Mary Louise Pratt (1991) describes as a contact zone, fostering honest dialogue requires structured teaching strategies as well as an understanding of four terms: *dissensus, consensus, confrontation/problem solving,* and *groupthink.*

Kenneth Bruffee (1993) concentrates on redefining higher education as helping students "reacculturate themselves and one another into the community that the teacher represents" (225). He defines reacculturation as switching membership from one culture to another and involves:

...giving up, modifying, or renegotiating the language, values, knowledge, mores, and so on that are constructed, established, and maintained by the community one is coming from, and becoming fluent instead in the language and so on of another community. (225)

College teachers should recognize the learning process as a reacculturation and acknowledge that students will be negotiating from many primary cultures brought with them into the classroom.

Definition of *Dissensus*

Bruffee's definition of learning as reacculturation provides a theoretical foundation for John Trimbur's (1989) description of dissensus, Pratt's (1991) contact zone, and the conversation that occurs at the boundaries of knowledge communities. Boundary discourse is the most positive term for the language of negotiation; it has also been referred to as abnormal discourse and non-standard discourse. However, it is more correctly seen as a complete and acceptable language of one culture negotiating with the language of another culture. In our college classrooms, because no single voice can speak for all the students, the multicultural heritage of the students affects the negotiations.

Trimbur discusses two main criticisms of collaborative learning: first, that consensus stifles the individual voice, and second, that it focuses on the conversation of knowledge communities but fails to realize they are embedded in an "unequal, exclusionary social order" with "hierarchical relations of power" (603). We are teaching our students to participate in the more knowledgeable conversations of our disciplines, to recognize that we all belong to many communities each with its own vernacular language. But "the term vernacular cannot be understood apart from the relation of domination and subordination that it implies" (609).

Given these criticisms, Trimbur wants us to consider the collaborative learning occurring in our college classrooms from a new perspective:

We will need, that is, to look at collaborative learning not merely as a process of consensus-making but more important as *a process of identifying differences and locating these differences in relation to each other* [Italics added]. The consensus that we ask students to reach in a collaborative classroom will be based not so much on collective agreements as on collective explanations of how people differ, where their differences come from, and whether they can live and work together with these differences. (610)

Trimbur suggests that we remind our students that consensus does not often happen in daily situations involving conflicting points of view; often, nobody takes the time to hear all sides of an issue to try to reach a solution that all parties can accept. Therefore, our students should be encouraged to interrupt the conversation "in order to investigate the forces that determine who may speak and what may be said, what inhibits conversation and what makes it possible" (612). Which people are being excluded from the conversation and how are they being excluded? These discussions can serve as "a critical measure to understand the distortions of communication and plays of power in normal discourse" (615).

The second term in my title, **contact zone,** is closely related to Trimbur's ideas and was illustrated by Pratt (1991). Pratt urges us to think of our classrooms as contact zones where "cultures meet, clash, and grapple with each other, often in contexts of highly asymmetrical relations of power" (34). Pratt wants us to establish "safe houses" in our curriculum where dissensus is tolerated and valued: "intellectual spaces where groups can constitute themselves…with high degrees of trust, shared understandings, temporary protection from legacies of oppression" (40). When cultures are discussed and objectified in a multicultural course, "all students [will see] their roots traced back to legacies of both glory and shame; all the students [will experience] face-to-face the ignorance and incomprehension, and occasionally the hostility, of others" (39).

Richard Miller (1994) notes, "Required self-reflexivity does not, of course, guarantee that repugnant positions will be abandoned…. [It] does not mean that this approach wields sufficient power to transform the matrix of beliefs, values, and prejudices that students (and teachers) bring to the classroom" (407). We still need strategies for dealing with resistant students, but Miller believes that close attention to what our students say and write in the contact zone may provide "the most promising pedagogical response" (408). Pratt also notes "moments of wonder and revelation, mutual understanding and new wisdom—the joys of the contact zone" (39). How does the notion of dissensus, which exists within the contact zones of our multicultural classrooms, affect our understanding of collaborative learning itself?

Dangers of Consensus

Teachers have viewed consensus as the ultimate outcome of collaborative work and feared conflict in group discussions, perhaps intervening to stop any heated verbal disagreement. Weiner (1986) uses Trimbur's earlier definition of consensus to show how important it has been thought to be to the nature of collaborative work: "intellectual negotiation which leads to an outcome (consensus) through a process of taking responsibility and investing collective judgment with authority" (55). In fact, Weiner asserts that this attempt to reach consensus is the main element that "distinguishes collaborative learning from mere work in groups" (54). Consensus or "…collective judgments in groups" (55) is necessary for the groups to accomplish the goal of the activity; Weiner describes a successful task description as one that contains instructions to "require a member of the group to record this consensus in writing" (56).

72

In the same article, however, Weiner quotes a letter from Trimbur warning new practitioners of collaborative learning to understand "the process of social negotiation that underwrites consensus" (54). In this letter, Trimbur already seems to be working toward the concept of dissensus defined in his 1989 article. Noting that most successful collaborative activities allow students to understand the underlying causes of differing views, he would have us teach students that they can "agree to disagree" (54).

Dittmar (1993) is another who warns a harmonious exchange might indicate a "bland melding of cultures" (36). Allan Cox (1991) in "Consensus as a Killer of Creativity" argues we don't want consensus, which he defines as an "attempt to secure virtual unanimity among a group of people," because it wastes time, leads to "mediocre options," and discourages commitment to the decision. "Something that is everybody's task becomes nobody's task" (15). He defines effective teamwork as "managing diversity" in today's corporations: they now have access to new viewpoints and ways of meeting problems because of the past experiences and traditions of their multicultural workforce. The team members realize sometimes their ideas are implemented, sometimes not, but they are always solicited and considered. Cox encourages confrontation between these often conflicting ideas; the leader needs to be one who "chooses between the competing options he has spurred through vital exchanges among his [or her] team members" (15).

Confrontation/ Problem Solving

Learning how to value and manage conflict successfully is another skill we should be teaching our students in a multicultural classroom. Wilson and Hanna (1986) acknowledge conflict can be dysfunctional or functional and can at times provide benefits. When used effectively, the advantages of conflict may include: 1) increased involvement of members, 2) an outlet for hostility, 3) greater cohesiveness of the group, and 4) a greater chance for commitment to the decision (268). They explain both poor and effective conflict-management strategies labeling confrontation/problem solving as a win-win strategy while compromise is considered a lose-lose method. What do these labels tell us about forcing compromise on our students to achieve consensus?

Wilson and Hanna's key is to focus on long-term goals rather than solutions to individual problems. Blaming the other person involved will not help; energies need to be directed toward defeating the problem. An example of this comes from management efforts to keep health insurance costs down. Workers had full coverage with no deductible, but the company was concerned about yearly increases averaging 15%; workers, forced to pay the same percentage increase each month to cover their dependents, wanted the company to pay part of this. A compromise would have split the difference and given employees half of what they were asking. However, an integrated solution, like those favored by Wilson and Hanna, resulted when the overall insurance picture was studied. In this instance, the employees accepted a $100 deductible that brought the total cost down for both the company and employees and allowed the company to pay a portion of dependent coverage while the employees' $100 deductible was made up through reduced dependent payments.

One way to arrive at an integrated solution such as this one is to employ good listening skills (something that can be taught) as well as to confirm understandings and conclusions being discussed; participants should be encouraged to come to the group with tentative solutions and answers, even researching them beforehand. Obviously in my example, both sides had to understand the effects of a deductible in reducing insurance costs before discussing it.

Current studies are being done to learn more about the ways learning groups function and about conflict in groups. Some of the findings may be surprising to many teachers. Thia Wolf

(1990) has noted that the litany of complaint heard when the students begin to work is actually part of the process; it unites the group as they begin to relate to the assignment. Some of the comments a circulating teacher may hear as off the task may be part of the necessary socialization process that goes on, or they may be used deliberately to break the tension that occurs when the groups are on track, either negotiating ideas or evaluating each other's work. A membrane is established, and neither the teacher nor a student should break it.

Theodore F. Sheckels (1992) outlines the types of talk in collaborative groups into Task Talk, Role Talk, Consciousness-Raising Talk, Encounter Talk, and Non-Verbal Dimensions. The teacher's attitude toward encounter talk is often hostile, but Sheckels suggests it shouldn't be because conflict often indicates boundary-seeking and is positive. He identifies only three behaviors as negative: dominating (not allowing other people to speak), clowning (undermining the seriousness of the lesson), or blocking (preventing discussion of the issues). Robert Brooke (1987) defines the activities students "engage in to show that their identities are different from or more complex than the identities assigned them by organizational roles" as the students' *underlife* (142). He suggests that what appears to the teacher to be disruptive behavior is actually students "...actively connecting ideas in the classroom to their own lives outside the classroom" (145).

Geoffrey A. Cross (1993) in a book-length ethnography of a collaborative writing group suggests teachers train students to understand and manage conflict. He defines confrontation as "the meeting of mutual needs" (135). Students should be encouraged to elicit information from the dissenters and keep a **conflict-process log** to identify group conflicts and ways of managing them. Discussion of these process logs may be one way to deal with resistant students. He warns that groups, knowing a compromise will always be reached, will begin discussion with expanded demands; some compromise solutions "may be so weakened as to be ineffective" (135). Although a decision must eventually be reached, Wolf notes that controversy is very much a part of euphoria in groups; teachers should be more wary of groupthink.

Groupthink

In my own classrooms, I am worried about groups that reach conclusions too soon, so I often deliberately try to complicate matters for them. If, for example, a group reaches a complete interpretation of a complex essay in a few minutes, I will ask questions about aspects that they have not considered. Usually, one student has noted at least some of the complexity but has been silenced by fear of a confrontation. These groups who find the easy consensus may exhibit characteristics of groupthink, a term outlined by Irving Janis in 1972 and charted in a subsequent book by Janis and Leon Mann (1977). They have outlined the antecedent conditions for groups guilty of groupthink and subsequent poor decision making, among them: 1) high cohesiveness, 2) insulation from others, 3) lack of good procedures for finding information, and 4) directive leadership.

Janis and Mann claim these conditions lead a group to believe itself to be invulnerable. Such a group tends to rationalize its decisions, to stereotype other groups, and to believe it is in the right. It censors itself, not allowing in ideas that would alter its views. The results often show an incomplete survey of choices and objectives, a biased processing of information, and a failure to work out alternative plans or scenarios. Janis (1972) offers suggestions to prevent groupthink, including regularly appointing someone from the group to challenge all ideas that are proposed; this role could be added to that of discussion leader and/or recorder.

When our groups are too homogeneous and reach conclusions too quickly, we should look for the signs of groupthink. Dittmar (1993) cites the diversity of views in a successful class in direct contrast to a second class that was less successful: "about half the class consisted of young high school graduates, all European American graduates of parochial schools, and mostly of one ethnicity" (30). However, heterogeneous grouping may not always be possible in our classrooms, so what other strategies can we employ to encourage dissensus in our classrooms?

Strategies to Encourage *Dissensus*

Reither and Vipond (1989) provide successful ways to use collaborative strategies that might encourage the type of discussion Trimbur is calling for in his article. They focus on the knowledge-making aspects of collaboration. "We make our meanings not alone, but in relation to others' meanings, which we come to know through reading, talk, and writing" (862). They suggest structuring entire courses so "students collaboratively investigate a more or less original scholarly question or field" (863). "The teacher is responsible for orchestrating and acting as an expert co-researcher, modeling the process" (863). Reither's senior Shakespeare class investigated what Shakespeare had to know to write his plays; Vipond's introductory psychology class investigated the psychology of humor.

My example in NCTE's *Talking to Learn* (1990) was developed for a sophomore composition class; for their final project, each group of students teaches the other groups; they choose an art form illustrating the topics we have been discussing all semester. By allowing them to choose material from their culture (underlife) that they will teach, we can discuss the forms that are accepted, those that are considered unacceptable, and the forces that determine acceptance, thus acknowledging the dissensus of our classroom community.

A demonstration of Trimbur's own use of collaborative learning to encourage dissensus comes from his 1993 workshop at the University of Chicago's Critical Thinking Seminars. First, he asked us to view a short clip from Spike Lee's film *Do the Right Thing*: a yuppie character had ridden his bicycle over the new shoes of one of the neighborhood youths causing a loud confrontation. The workshop participants watched the clip three times and responded in writing each time: 1) what did we see; 2) how did it make us feel; and 3) what did the scene mean. Trimbur encouraged us to interpret the scene in terms of our own experience. Then he arranged the participants into groups of five with a discussion leader and recorder. The three writings we had done (five minutes each) were our admission ticket to the discussion; we couldn't participate in the groups unless we were prepared. After each person had read aloud the last writing he or she had done, we tried to reach a consensus in responding to three questions. We were asked to 1) explain how the responses were alike and different and describe the similarities and differences; 2) explain the similarities and differences and identify the assumptions members of the group seemed to be making in their responses; and 3) finally, if we had time, decide whether we could agree on the meaning of the sequence. These directions were asking us to look for ways our responses varied and to find explanations for the differences.

Since I was the recorder for our group at this workshop, I still have my notes and can describe how the five of us differed in our reactions to the same film clip. One felt anger at the failure of the characters to get along; another identified with the "Mouthy One" who had to back down; a third felt racism is a disease and is getting worse; a fourth didn't like noisy confrontations; and the fifth feared the verbal conflict because verbal conflict was threatening to him. We discussed why we reacted differently: some of us assumed ways of disagreement that don't involve so much noise and some reacted the ways we are accustomed to in our disciplines. The English teacher started a thesis/proof response based on the characters while the economist saw the economic theories involved in the effects of racism. We did not have time in the seminar session to answer Trimbur's third question; however, in planning this activity for a semester's course, teachers can schedule in sufficient time.

Although gender did not come up in our particular discussion, it is often the first difference groups discover in the way they react to material. Cross (1993) encourages members of groups to be conscious of gender and job-role influences on the way decisions are made. Instead of ignoring a female point of view as being too emotional, for example, groups should listen to this voice. He notes that intended audiences are likely to be both male and female; therefore, writers must "identify and analyze previously tacit gender perspectives...[so] androgenous prose will result" (137).

We can incorporate dissensus into our classrooms in many ways. Besides those indicated above, Bruffee (1993) suggests assigning questions to which there are no clear or correct answers (Task A) or assigning questions to which there are answers accepted by the prevailing knowledge community and asking the group to explain how these answers were reached (Task B). A third possibility is to allow the groups to find an answer, present the prevalent answers of the academic community, and then negotiate between the two.

Collaborative pedagogy is an effective teaching strategy; in Volume 2 of *Multicultural Education,* Teri Faulkner and I reviewed the studies showing how collaborative strategies have been proven to be especially valuable in diverse classrooms. Designing curriculum based on the theories of collaborative learning requires us to help students recognize they are already members of many communities of knowledgeable peers (Bruffee 1993). David Jaques (1984) reminds us that many of the goals of a college education such as developing a critical and informed mind, developing an awareness of others' interests and needs, and developing a social conscience are all "processes which are experienced mostly if not totally within well-organized study groups" (64). The process itself is what is important: "The end is the means" (63). We should not try to short-circuit this means by eliminating all conflict or dissensus from our classrooms.

REFERENCES

Brooke, R. (1987). Underlife and writing instruction. *College Composition and Communication 38,* 141-153.

Bruffee, K. (1993). *Collaborative learning: Higher education, interdependence, and the authority of knowledge.* Baltimore: Johns Hopkins.

Cox, A. (1991, July 2). Consensus as a killer of creativity. *Chicago Tribune, p.* 15.

Cross, G. (1993). *Collaboration and conflict: A contextual exploration of group writing and positive emphasis.* Cresskill, NJ: Hampton Press.

Dittmar, L. (1993). Conflict and resistance in the multicultural classroom. In J. Q. Adams & J. R. Welsch (Eds.), *Multicultural education: Strategies for implementation in colleges and universities, Vol 3.* (pp. 29-37.) Macomb, IL: Illinois Staff and Curriculum Developers Association.

Faulkner, T. M., & Lemon, H. S. (1992). Collaborative learning: Building community in a culturally diverse classroom. In J. Q. Adams & J. R. Welsch (Eds.), *Multicultural education: Strategies for implementation in colleges and universities, Vol 2* (pp. 3-11) Macomb, IL: Illinois Staff and Curriculum Developers Association.

Jaques, D. (1984). *Learning in groups.* Beckenham, Kent: Croom Helm.

Janis, I. L. (1972). *Victims of groupthink.* Boston: Houghton-Mifflin.

Janis, I. L., & Mann, L. (1977). *Decision making.* New York: Free Press.

Lemon, H. S. (1990). A speaking project about the arts that acknowledges the students' underlife. In *Talking to learn: Classroom practices in teaching English, Vol. 24.* Urbana, IL: National Council of Teachers of English.

Miller, R. E. (1994). Fault lines in the contact zone. *College English 56,* 389-408.

Pratt, M. L. (1991). Arts of the contact zone. *Profession 91,* 33-40.

Reither, J. A., & Vipond, D. (1989). Writing as collaboration. *College English 51,* 855-867.

Sheckels, T. F. (1992). Research in small-group communications: Implications for peer response. Paper presented at the Conference on College Composition and Communication, Cincinnati, OH.

Trimbur, J. (1989). Consensus and difference in collaborative learning. *College English, 51,* 602-616.

Trimbur, J. (1993). Workshop presented at the University of Chicago Bringing the World into the Classroom Conference, Chicago.

Weiner, H. S. (1986). Collaborative learning in the classroom: A guide to evaluation. *College English, 48,* 52-61.

Wilson, G. L., & Hanna, M. (1986). *Groups in context.* NY: Random House.

Wolf, T. (1990). The teacher as eavesdropper: Listening in on the language of collaboration. In D. A. Daiker & M. Morenberg (Eds.), *The writing teacher as researcher,* (pp. 277-289). Portsmouth, NH: Boynton.

COURSE ORGANIZATION AND THE CHALLENGES OF STUDENTS' MULTIPLE INTELLIGENCES

by

Savario Mungo

Educators in higher education, much like educators at all levels, are concerned about being able to reach an increasingly diverse student population. Traditional tried and true methods do not seem to work anymore. Motivation to learn and to participate seems harder to instill in more and more of our students. Is this because diversity means a lowering of ability among the student population? Of course not. What we are facing in higher education is a challenge to relate our teaching styles and approaches more closely to the needs and characteristics of our students. This shift to a new paradigm, one in which we accept the idea that if students don't learn the way we teach, we should teach the way they learn, is difficult; it can also be challenging and exciting.

The movement to infuse multicultural concepts into our courses and to respond to diversity throughout our curriculum has provided us with an opportunity to use new approaches and strategies. If we use this opportunity, we will be able to relate more closely to a diverse student population and make the paradigm shift a reality. Faced with this challenge, many teachers, myself included, have looked to research on learning styles for direction. I have found the approach holding the greatest promise is based on Howard Gardner's multiple intelligence theory.

Multiple Intelligence Theory

The following quote from Gardner about his multiple intelligence theory indicates its usefulness:

It is of the utmost importance that we recognize and nurture all of the varied human intelligences, and all of the combinations of intelligences. We are different largely because we all have different combinations of intelligences. If we recognize this, I think we will have at least a better chance of dealing appropriately with the many problems that we face in the world. (1987, p. 193)

Thus Gardner offers an underlying principle that allows us to clearly address student differences as we develop our strategies.

Gardner, in *Frames of Mind* (1983), provides a means of mapping the broad range of abilities humans possess by grouping these capabilities into seven comprehensive categories of intelligences:

1. Linguistic - the capacity to use words effectively, whether in speech or in writing;
2. Logical/Mathematical - the capacity to use numbers effectively and to reason well;
3. Spatial - the ability to perceive the visual-spatial world accurately and to perform transformations upon those perceptions;
4. Bodily/Kinesthetic - expertise in using one's whole body to express ideas and feelings and the facility to use one's hands to produce or transform things;
5. Musical - the capacity to perceive, transform, and express musical forms;
6. Interpersonal - the ability to perceive and make distinctions in the moods, intentions, motivations, and feelings of other people; and
7. Intrapersonal - self-knowledge and the ability to act adaptively on the basis of that knowledge.

According to Gardner, all people possess all seven intelligences, with some of them highly developed in a person, some of them less developed. Since most people can develop each intelligence to an adequate level of competency, we should not type individuals according to one or the other. The goal is to allow everyone to develop more fully all of their intelligences (Armstrong, 1994).

Assuming our students are probably highly developed in at least one of the seven intelligences and moderately developed in others does not, of course, mean we necessarily know which intelligences are stronger for which students. Our choice, therefore, is clear. In order to implement this theory, we need to develop strategies and approaches that address all of the seven intelligences, offering a variety of approaches to insure that every student, no matter what his or her strongest intelligence is, will be able to relate that intelligence to a class activity. Hopefully, each student, depending on the intelligence that is his or her strength, will be turned on by the activity addressing that strength and thus will be encouraged to use other intelligences in other activities and assignments. Though this theory cannot come to fruition overnight and demands ongoing development, it is possible to integrate strategies that address most of the seven intelligences for the major concepts or topics taught. If all seven cannot be addressed in a particular instance, they can all be addressed periodically throughout the course.

Although this may seem a difficult task, I know from experience that it can be done, having developed activities, assignments, and strategies for my classes over the past several years to address the diversity in my classrooms and having chosen Gardner's theory of multiple intelligences as a guide. I use activities that address most, if not all, of the seven intelligences for every major concept or topic I teach. The approach is twofold. First, I organize each course so requirements, assignments, and assessment measures address the seven intelligences. In this way, all students have an opportunity to use their strength of intelligence, as well as to develop more fully their other intelligences. Second, I develop many specific activities and strategies within a course's major concepts and topics to relate to the seven intelligences.

Course Requirements, Assignments, and Activities

One of my major concerns is that course requirements reflect my attempt to understand and build on students' diversity. These requirements are developed around a variety of the seven intelligences so each student has the opportunity to experience initial success in at least one aspect of the course and thus be motivated to pursue success in others. The initial success can be in activities or assignments related to their strength of intelligence. Then, as they address other activities and assignments, they will be encouraged to participate more fully and to develop further additional intelligences with the result being a more positive and comprehensive learning experience.

The following examples of course requirements, activities, and strategies illustrate how this might work. Though individually they reflect what many educators already do, the combination of activities shows how the multiple intelligences approach to classroom diversity can be most effective.

Text Assignments

All students must be able to read and understand the texts used for a course. However, additional activities can not only enhance an understanding of the text, but also allow for the diversity of intelligences.

Chapter summaries. Ask students to complete and hand in a summary of each chapter, giving them a number of ways to do so, from summarizing the highlights to elaborating on the parts of the chapter they felt they learned most from. Require them to turn in the chapter summaries the day of the test on a particular chapter. This enables them to review their notes and the chapter in preparing for the test.

Chapter discussion groups. Divide the class into chapter discussion groups, with four or five students per group. The groups will stay together throughout the course. For each chapter, prior to the test on that chapter, have students hand in their summaries and then meet in their discussion groups to discuss the chapter. In each group have a recorder and a leader, roles that rotate each time the group meets. The recorder keeps track of the important issues discussed, and the leader keeps the discussion focused. At the end of the session each member of the group signs the recorder's notes, which are handed in to the instructor. The whole class then briefly discusses the issues raised in the small groups. Students who do not hand in a chapter summary can participate in the group discussion, but cannot sign the recorder's notes. Each person signing the recorder's notes receives points in addition to their chapter summary point total.

The discussions can be handled in a number of ways to add variety and interest to a class. For example, students can discuss what each found to be the most important aspects of the chapter or the instructor can offer questions for them to focus on. Cooperative learning strategies, such as JigSaw, can also be used. In this approach the instructor assigns a specific section of the chapter to each member of the discussion group. If, for example, there are four members in the discussion groups, the chapter is divided into four parts, with each student assigned a part. The students read their assigned section, write a summary of it, and make copies of it for each person in their group. Thus in each group, the students will get a summary of each part of the chapter. When the class arrives for the discussion, students from each group who read the first section will meet for about ten minutes to share what they have in their summaries. In these "expert" groups, students can add information to their own summaries if they missed an important point or concept. After these discussions, students return to their original chapter discussion groups and pass out their summary copies, verbally explaining anything gained from the expert group. At the end of the discussion, students hand in their chapter summaries.

Written tests on text readings. Although most tests follow a similar format, short answers and essays, variation can enhance student understanding and encourage them to study harder. In my own classes, the first chapter test is always open book. This allows students to understand the type of tests required on text assignments and encourages them to read the subsequent chapters with greater care and a better understanding of the expectations of the instructor.

If JigSaw is used to discuss a chapter, the test on that chapter can be done as a group assignment. Since members of the group were responsible for specific sections of the chapter, they should be responsible for the questions for their own section. Taking the test as a group allows each member to contribute answers to the section he or she reads and summarizes. The sharing and interaction experienced during this type of test enhances student collaboration and support for each other. It also forces students to face up to their responsibilities since they will be accountable for part of each group member's grade on the test.

Adherence to Diversity and Multiple Intelligence

Students who have difficulty reading the text and taking tests on those readings are allowed the opportunity to gain an understanding of the text not only through reading, but also through discussing the chapters with peers in groups, summarizing their ideas, listening to others explain what they learned from the text, and adding to their own summaries of important aspects of the readings. Taking the test on the first chapter with an open book approach removes the initial fear students have when faced with the unknown. Too often, a text reading assignment and the follow-up test on the readings primarily reward those with a strong linguistic intelligence strength. The above text activities address student diversity by allowing students to use, and be evaluated on, the results of engaging several different intelligences. The activities address interpersonal, intrapersonal, spatial, and mathematical/logical intelligences in addition to linguistic intelligence. This enables many students to gain an understanding of a chapter in the text while encouraging them to continue reading subsequent chapters and improve their linguistic intelligence.

Group Reports

All students are assigned a group presentation. The following structured approach has proven to be most successful. All students are given the opportunity to select from a series of topics to be covered in class and then are assigned to groups based on their choices. Groups of four or five are most effective when the following format and rules apply.

1. Reports are to be in a semi-debate format, with students determining one or more current controversial aspects of the topic and researching the issues. Sides are chosen and students present their debate to the class in a very structured format. Not a debate in the sense that one side wins or loses, the success of the exercise is determined by how well the overall debate brings forth all the important aspects of the controversy. Thus each side helps and supports each other in finding material for arguments and rebuttals so a balanced presentation is possible. Students have the option of using any media, simulation, or other devices to make their points.
2. Students are to use a minimum of four sources for their data and develop a bibliography for all class members.
3. Students are to develop an outline of their topic and arguments for each member of the class, thus enabling the class to follow the report and to take notes as needed.
4. The debate is to be followed by a question and answer (Q & A) period in which the class questions the presenters. Each presenter is to stay in character and on his or her particular side of the debate throughout the Q & A. The instructor can initiate the Q & A by raising particularly interesting questions for each side.
5. Each student in the group is to submit an individual position paper on the topic as a whole.

In evaluating these group reports, I give group points in the following categories: opening and closing statements, bibliography, outline, and research. I give individual points for arguments, rebuttals, students' position papers, and the Q & A. Each student who is not part of a particular group report is required to complete a minimum of two article reviews related to the group topic and is able to participate in the Q & A period of the reports.

Adherence to Diversity/Multiple Intelligences

Too often group reports turn students off because they fear they will be stuck with a lower grade because only a group grade is given. In the format proposed, opportunities for both individual and group evaluations exist. In addition, students often have the concern that some members of the group will not pull their weight and thus will let the group down. Because multiple intelligences are addressed in this format, the potential for each student to be turned on by some aspect of the process will enable each student to contribute more fully. In the above structure, each of the multiple intelligences is addressed. The intrapersonal intelligence and linguistic intelligence is addressed throughout the report but particularly in the research, individual presentation, position paper assignment, and verbal report. Mathematical/logical and spatial intelligences are addressed in organizing and sequencing the report and in preparing the outlines. The kinesthetic and musical intelligences can be addressed as students use their creativity in developing their presentation to the class, and finally, the interpersonal intelligence is addressed during the group meetings leading up to the final preparation of the report. It is hoped some aspect of this assignment, from preparation to article reviews to Q & A, will address each student's strength of intelligence, and that each in collaboration with other group members, will have the opportunity to enhance and further develop his or her other intelligences.

Films/Videos

Since class presentations of short videos or excerpts from films to support a point or enhance a topic or concept are often extremely useful, I try to find at least one film or video related to as many class topics as possible. In addition to showing films and videos in class, I assign students films/videos to view at a media center outside of class. For each film viewed as part of the course students are asked to write a film review. Periodically, they use their chapter discussion groups as film discussion groups to discuss the films they have seen. The groups can either discuss what each found most useful in the films, or they can respond to questions posed by the instructor. Either way, students have an opportunity to share what they learned as well as to learn from those who saw the film differently.

Simulation/Games

As often as possible, I use simulations and games to make points important to the class topics. These are usually whole class activities, and many are either commercial games or simulations developed by the instructor.

Class Activities Exercises

Shorter than games and simulations, (usually 5-15 min.) numerous activities related to such topics as listening, verbalizing one's needs, and cross-cultural communication, as well as other topics related to specific class concepts, are available. I use these in conjunction with class topics or overall course development as often as possible. Most involve physical as well as verbal activity and require group interaction.

Assessment

If an instructor decides to use a variety of assignments and to initiate requirements such as those outlined above, each of the assignments must become part of the overall course evaluation. I assign points to each required assignment in the course, including quizzes, chapter summaries, article reviews, film reviews, discussion groups, oral reports, position papers, and attendance and participation. A student who does not do well in the quizzes has the opportunity to do well on the film reviews and in the discussion groups. Since each are worth points that are part of the overall course evaluation, students can gain points most easily in assignments related to their strength of intelligence and work on improving their performance on assignments related to their less developed intelligences. What should be avoided is basing the total evaluation of students primarily on the results of their performance on written tests that favor those with strong linguistic intelligence. If we teach to multiple intelligences, we must assess with those multiple intelligences in mind.

Adherence to Diversity/Multiple Intelligences

Using films and videos on a regular basis addresses the spatial intelligence of many students. In addition, by requiring film reviews and film discussion groups similar to those related to chapter texts, other intelligences such as linguistic, intrapersonal, interpersonal, and mathematical/logical are addressed. The use of simulations, games, and class exercises on a regular basis will allow students with strong spatial, bodily kinesthetic, and interpersonal intelligences to succeed. Instructors can effectively respond to student diversity if they combine media, activities, and discussions with readings and lectures. By combining activities that address multiple intelligences with assessments that reward success in a variety of intelligences, the potential for student involvement and learning will be greatly enhanced.

Classroom Climate

The above series of course structures, assignments, activities, and tests can be best implemented if a very open and positive classroom climate is created. To establish an environment in which students feel comfortable and safe in offering their opinions and debating issues with other class members and the instructor is a challenge for educators. No magic answer to attain this environment exists, but certain strategies that enable students to experience a level of comfort and trust do. The following are two ongoing activities I have used successfully to get students to risk participating and communicating. Whether these or similar activities are used, the point remains: in order to build on students' diversity and have them actively participate in class, a major effort must be made to create a comfortable and safe class climate.

Reaction Logs

An additional channel of communication between the class and the instructor, reaction logs are handed in by each class member at *every* class period beginning with the second meeting. These contain a student's reactions to either the previous class session, report, or activity or a reaction to any topic related to class content. They also provide an opportunity for students to comment on the discussion if they were unable to contribute in class, to ask questions they want the instructor to answer, or to critique the class structure, assignments, or their own progress. To be effective the instructor must read each one, answer every question, and comment on every log. They must be confidential, being read only by the student and the instructor, and must be returned promptly, that is, the next class day. Logs can be long or short, but they must be written. They are not graded, but are required.

This activity, since it is ongoing throughout the course, involves a commitment on the part of the instructor to read all of the logs before returning them to the students. After the first few logs are returned, students understand the purpose and, after reading the instructor's comments, are not intimidated by the assignment. What occurs is a very positive, ongoing discussion between the instructor and the majority of the students. Of course, some students will object to keeping a log and may not use it in the spirit intended. However, many students, not very verbal in class sessions, are grateful for a chance to communicate their ideas in this format. The practice establishes a good rapport and a level of trust, contributes to a positive class climate, and addresses student diversity. The reaction logs also provide an ongoing critique of various aspects of the course that the instructor can use in revising and upgrading the course.

Discussion Wheel

At the start of a course, either the first or second class period, divide the class into groups of six to eight students and distribute a discussion wheel to each group. Each discussion wheel consists of three paper discs of diminishing sizes, placed one on top of the other with the smallest on top, and attached through the center with a brad. Thus the three circles or discs are layered, with the smallest in front, the next largest in the middle, and the largest in the back. The inner disc is divided into eight sections, the middle disc is divided into four to six sections, and the outer disc is divided into six or eight sections. The inner disc sections are numbered one through eight. The names of individuals such as parents, friends, and relatives are written in the sections of the middle circle while words identifying general concepts, like anger, happiness, bias, prejudice, and wealth are written on the outer disc. An unlimited variety of options can be used.

When using the wheel, students are asked to pick a number from one to eight for themselves. A student in each group is given the discussion wheel upside down. He or she rotates the inner and middle discs without looking at them, then turns the disc over. Finding his or her number, the student matches the number with the closest section in the middle disc, for example, "friend," and with the closest section on the outer disc, for example, "anger." The student then shares with the group something in his or her life that is related to "friend" and "anger." These are brief sharings, only one or two minutes each. The disc is passed around the group, with each student again rotating the discs and proceeding as the first student.

After using an instructor disc a few times, the groups are given materials and asked to develop their own discs using any topic they wish. The instructor can develop additional discs based on these ideas or ask students to construct the discs for a subsequent discussion. This activity is done periodically throughout the course to provide the opportunity for student discussion of difficult topics in a nonintimidating, controlled environment. The discussion discs can, of course, include topics related to course content as well as interpersonal concerns.

In summary, I have found that establishing a positive class climate, developing activities to address student diversity, and incorporating a combination of assignments and approaches such as those I have described, allow students to strengthen their multiple intelligences. The result is more active, successful, and exciting classes for both students and instructor.

REFERENCES

Armstrong, T. (1994). *Multiple intelligences in the classroom.* Alexandria, VA: Association for Supervision & Curriculum Development.

Armstrong, T. (1993). *Seven kinds of smart.* New York: Penguin Books.

Ballanca, J., Chapman, C., & Swartz, E. (1994). *Multiple assessment for multiple intelligences.* Palatine, IL: IRI/Skylight Publishers.

Campbell, L., Campbell, B., & Dickinson, D. (1992). *Teaching and learning through multiple intelligences.* Seattle: New Horizons for Learning.

Campbell, C. (1993). *If the shoe fits...How to develop multiple intelligences in the classroom.*

Palatine, IL: IRI Skylight Publishing.

Gardner, H. (1983). *Frames of the mind: The theory of multiple intelligences.* New York: Basic Books.

Gardner, H. (1987). Beyond I.Q.: Education and human development. *Harvard Educational Review, 57*(2), 187-193.

Gardner, H. (1993). Creating minds. New York: Basic Books.

Gardner, H. (1993). *Multiple intelligences: The theory in practice.* New York: Basic Books.

Lazear, D. (1994). *Multiple intelligence approaches to assessment.* Tucson: Zephyr Press.

Lazear, D. (1991). *Seven ways of teaching.* Palatine, IL: IRI/Skylight Publishing.

Lazear, D. (1994). *Seven pathways of learning.* Palatine, IL: IRI/Skylight Publishing.

MEDIA LITERACY:
AN EDUCATIONAL BASIC FOR THE INFORMATION AGE

by
Carlos E. Cortés

Where is the wisdom we have lost in knowledge? Where is the knowledge we have lost in information?

T. S. Eliot ("Four Quartets")

The mass media teach. Yet classroom teachers and others involved in schools continue to refer to themselves as the educational system. Nonsense! Students learn through schools, but people, including students, also learn outside of schools through the societal curriculum—that massive, ongoing, informal curriculum of families, peer groups, neighborhoods, churches, organizations, institutions, mass media, and other socializing forces that educate all of us throughout our lives (Cortés, 1981). The interplay of these informal educational forces has become particularly critical for learning and living in increasingly complex settings.

Moreover, the temporal range of nonschool teaching and learning far exceeds that of schools. Young people begin learning through the societal curriculum before they enter school, and they continue to learn in society as they go to school. For most of us school days end, but societal learning will continue as long as we live. A central element of that lifelong societal teaching-learning process is the media curriculum, the omnipresent bombardment of information and ideas emanating from the mass media (Boorstin, 1961; Czitrom, 1982; Greenfield & Cortés, 1991; Monaco, 1978; Postman, 1985; Stanley & Steinberg, 1976). To help empower young people to process and evaluate information and ideas, to construct knowledge drawing upon the critical evaluation of that information and those ideas, and to develop wisdom using that knowledge, schools should help students learn to analyze media content and messages. For students, this educational process should include helping them learn to grapple with the way media deal with local issues and social themes.

Unfortunately, many school educators have reacted to the media curriculum by ignoring it, except for complaining about media content or the amount of time that students spend with the media, especially television. As Wilma Longstreet (1989) of the University of New Orleans appropriately warned in her article, "Education for Citizenship: New Dimensions,"

We spend years teaching reading and remedial reading while we hardly glance at these newer, more powerful media. Our young are literally at the mercy of television, besieged by far greater amounts of information on each screen than was ever possible on the pages of a book, and we give them no help in sorting and analyzing that barrage of data or in defending themselves from the high level of stimuli that accompany the barrage. (p. 44)

And the media barrage comes from more than television. It emanates from all media—television and motion pictures, radio and recorded music, newspapers and magazines. Moreover, the barrage consists of more than data. The media send fictional as well as nonfictional images and messages, disseminated through programs, films, and publications presumably made just to entertain (and make money), as well as through those intended to provide information and analysis. Some members of the so-called entertainment media proclaim that they merely offer diversion, but in fact they simultaneously teach, whether intentionally or incidentally. Let's reverse the equation. Whatever the stated or unstated goals of the media, people learn from both fictional and nonfictional media sources, although they may not realize that such media-based learning is occurring (Jowett, 1976; Kubey & Csikszentmihalyi, 1990; Schramm, Lyle, & Parker, 1961; Sklar, 1975).

But what can educators do about this? We can help students develop media literacy, the ability to examine, understand, and evaluate media messages. To help students become better informed and more analytical media consumers, we need to address the mass media within the school system as a core element of the teaching-learning process.

The Development of Media Literacy

For many teachers, the development of such media-based pedagogical skills may be a personal challenge, as most have never been exposed to media literacy training or classroom strategies. Both teachers and students can begin by increasing their own media awareness through such techniques as keeping a media curriculum journal. Teachers can document what they observe that the media, including the local media, are teaching, intentional or not, whether by fictional or nonfictional means. Particular attention should be paid to themes of special importance in contemporary society, such as race, ethnicity, gender, religion, intergroup relations, demographic change, government operations, and the environment. This helps teachers and students increase their awareness of the extent, content, and pervasiveness of the media curriculum, including its teaching about their own environments, as well as their propensity to think analytically about the media.

Beyond general awareness comes the development and implementation of media-based pedagogical strategies. This issue can be engaged by addressing the various ways in which the media teach. Based on my more than two decades of media research and teaching, as well as my efforts to integrate, expand, and strengthen media analysis as an element of K-12 and college education, I have concluded (Cortés, 1991) that the media, both fictional and nonfictional, teach in at least five basic ways.

1. They provide information.
2. They help organize information and ideas.
3. They help create, reinforce, and modify values and attitudes.
4. They help shape expectations.
5. They provide models for action.

Let us look briefly at how teachers can enhance their own pedagogy, improve their students' learning, and sharpen students' critical thinking by addressing these five media teaching processes.

1. *Media provide information.* All presentations of information involve interpretation (DuBois, 1991; Gans, 1979). While providing information, media also inevitably interpret— by including and excluding information, structuring presentations of that information, selecting words and images, and commenting on that information. As part of developing media literacy, students need to become aware of the "interpretive inevitability" of information presentations and need to learn to identify and analyze those interpretive techniques and dimensions.

One pedagogical strategy involves having students compare various media treatments of the same subject, such as news coverage of a major event or controversy. Students can compare the ways that different local media cover an election, a government action, a court case, an environmental issue, a conflict involving different elements of a community, or efforts within a community to build intercultural bridges or create cohesion among disparate social groupings. Students can be assigned to examine various newspaper, radio, or television reports or analyses concerning a single event or issue. In doing so, they can engage in such literacy-building exercises as separating fact from interpretation, identifying adjectives and verbs that tilt the presentation of information, examining how different stories exclude information that is included in other stories about the same subject, assessing the impact of such inclusion/exclusion on the messages being delivered by each story, and developing hypotheses about the reasons for this differential treatment. Through this comparative approach, students can improve their capacity for analyzing and assessing interpretive aspects involved when media purportedly just present facts and information.

2. *Media help organize information and ideas.* Through the repetitive presentation of certain themes, the reiteration of similar interpretations of those themes, and the repetition of certain words when identifying or describing a particular subject, media influence how readers and viewers organize information and ideas (Bagdikian, 1983; Dennis, 1978; Wilson & Gutiérrez, 1985). They help create and reinforce reader and viewer mental schema, which in turn influence individual reception, interpretation, and integration of future information and ideas (Keen, 1986). To develop media literacy, students need to become aware of how media influence their own ways of thinking about different subjects and help shape their ways of receiving new media input on those subjects. Here both nonfictional and fictional media can be used as teaching materials.

Students can be asked to read or view a news story on a provocative subject or a fictional media presentation about a certain theme. They can then be asked to interpret, orally or in writing, what they have read or seen. As students express different, possibly conflicting interpretations, they can be asked to consider why they had such differing responses and to hypothesize about what previous media exposure may have influenced these interpretations.

Take, for example, the opening credits portion of the 1987 motion picture, *China Girl,* which rapidly and poignantly dramatizes the dilemma of changing urban neighborhoods. As the credits are shown, the visual sequence focuses on an Italian American neighborhood of New York City. It shows a proud Chinese American family remodeling an old Italian American bakery into a Chinese restaurant while local residents watch with emotions ranging from the nostalgic sorrow of the elderly to the barely restrained bitterness and hostility of the younger generation. This brief sequence can be used to provoke consideration of the multiethnic implications, opportunities, and challenges of immigration and demographic change, a continuous process in contemporary society. Moreover, as part of that discussion or as a written assignment, students can reflect on why they responded differently to that sequence and can consider what previous media exposure may have contributed to their ways of responding to and personally organizing the information and ideas in that sequence.

3. *Media help create values and attitudes.* All news stories implicitly support certain values (for example, the democratic process or the free-market economy) or condemn others (for example, certain kinds of perceived antisocial behavior). Movies and television have always taught values, although those value lessons have changed over time (Matabane, 1988; Peterson & Thurstone, 1933). Hollywood's 1930 Motion Picture Production Code, which governed the content of U. S. motion pictures between 1934 and 1968, provides fascinating reading as well as revealing insights into the values that American filmmakers of that era agreed to teach to the viewing public.

Television, too, teaches values. Likening television to schools and television programs to school courses, sociologist Herbert J. Gans (1967) argued,

Almost all TV programs and magazine fiction teach something about American society. For example, *Batman* is, from this vantage point, a course in criminology that describes how a superhuman aristocrat does a better job eradicating crime than do public officials. Similarly, *The Beverly Hillbillies* offers a course in social stratification and applied economics, teaching that with money, uneducated and uncultured people can do pretty well in American society, and can easily outwit more sophisticated and more powerful middle-class types.... And even the innocuous family situation comedies such as *Ozzie and Harriet* deal occasionally with ethical problems encountered on a neighborhood level.... Although the schools argue that they are the major transmitter of society's moral values, the mass media offer a great deal more content on this topic. (pp. 21-22)

Students can be asked to examine fictional and nonfictional media sources to determine the value lessons that they explicitly or implicitly teach. Advertising can serve as a stimulating source for developing student critical literacy about media value teaching, because advertising seeks to shape values and attitudes and ultimately to promote value-impelled action, from voting for a candidate to purchasing a certain product to joining the military (Culley & Bennett, 1976; Poe, 1976). Drawing upon local media, students can consider the special values being taught or built on by local advertisers. By applying analytical thinking to the examination of media advertising—identifying underlying values being disseminated about both the product and the society at large as well as assessing the techniques used to maximize the effectiveness of this advertising "values education"—students can sharpen their critical thinking abilities.

4. *Media help shape expectations.* Reporting that there had been more than 2,300 research papers on television and human behavior, social psychologist George Comstock (1977) addressed the relationship of media to the shaping of expectations:

Several writers have argued that television is a powerful reinforcer of the status quo. The ostensible mechanisms are the effects of its portrayals on public expectations and perceptions. Television portrayals and particularly violent drama are said to assign roles of authority, power, success, failure, dependence, and vulnerability in a manner that matches the real-life social hierarchy, thereby strengthening that hierarchy by increasing its acknowledgement among the public and by failing to provide positive images for members of social categories occupying a subservient position. Content analyses of television drama support the contention that portrayals reflect normative status. (pp. 20-21)

A dramatic demonstration of that media influence on expectations, particularly expectations about urban life, occurred on the media itself on September 18, 1986, when the popular American television game show, *The $25,000 Pyramid,* was shown in Los Angeles. The show's competition involves two teams, each pairing a celebrity with a contestant. For each team, a series of words appears on the screen in front of one player, who gives clues to guide the partner into identifying the maximum number of words within the time limit.

Suddenly the word *gangs* popped onto one contestant's screen. Without hesitation, he shouted, "They have lots of these in East L.A." (a heavily Mexican American section of Los Angeles). Responding immediately, his partner answered, "Gangs." Under competitive pressure, two strangers had instantly achieved mental communion through their coinciding visions of a Chicano community as synonymous with gangs. Moreover, they had transmitted this ethnic stereotype to a national television audience.

Unfortunately, East Los Angeles does have Chicano gangs. But it also has a multitude of far more prevalent elements—families, schools, businesses, churches, and socially contributing organizations. Yet gangs, not any other element of East Los Angeles life, had rapidly and reflexively linked these total strangers. Why? The answer lies with the media, whose continuous fascination with Latino gangs—from news reports and documentaries to TV series and feature films—has elevated and reinforced them as the popular vision of East L.A. (and many other Latino communities).

One strategy for helping students examine both their own expectations and the media's role in shaping those expectations involves adapting *The $25,000 Pyramid* approach. In order to stretch the thinking of their students, teachers can give them a series of terms about things with which they have had no or little personal contact—a foreign nation, a major political figure, or an ethnic group not present in their own community—and have them react with the first thing that pops into their mind. Then ask them to try to recall or hypothesize where they obtained the ideas and expectations that prompted these reactions and later to test their hypotheses by keeping a journal in which they record and analyze the fictional and nonfictional media treatment of these topics for an extended period of time. (In using such a strategy to introduce a unit on Gypsies to a fourth-grade class, a teacher in one of my in-service courses discovered that her students' "knowledge" and "expectations" concerning Gypsies had been influenced by viewing old Frankenstein and Wolfman movies on television!)

5. *Media provide models for action.* Media have sometimes intentionally, sometimes unintentionally, provided models for action (Rosen, 1973; Singer & Kazdon, 1976; Tuchman, Daniels, & Benet, 1978; Woll & Miller, 1987). Personal research on the history of the U. S. motion picture treatment of race and ethnicity has revealed numerous examples of that media role modeling.

During World War II, the American media used both fictional and nonfictional presentations to appeal to Americans of all backgrounds to sacrifice for their country. For example, by flooding theaters with feature films that included explicitly multiethnic military units, Hollywood spread the message that Americans of all racial and ethnic backgrounds should be willing to fight for their country (regardless of what racial and ethnic discrimination they had encountered in American society). And they did fight, with honor (Koppes & Black, 1987). Similarly, many post-World War II movies role modeled opposition to antiethnic bigotry and discrimination. In these films, villains were often driven by racial, ethnic, and religious prejudice, whereas heroes took direct action to confront such bigotry. In such a manner, movies encouraged people to take individual action to oppose bigotry and acts of discrimination .

Students can be asked to examine different media to determine what role models they provide, including role models presented in the local media. In what respects do media use such models to call explicitly for action (for example, as through advertisements)? In what respects do media laud or condemn other types of action, thereby encouraging or discouraging such behavior? Or in what respects do the media send mixed messages, sometimes condemning, sometimes approving, sometimes even glorifying similar actions? Finally, students can suggest what elements of this media role modeling seem to be most effective or ineffective and discuss what media techniques render them so.

Conclusion

By continuously involving students in the analysis of these five types of media message systems, schools can play a major role in preparing young people for a future in which the analytical use of information will become increasingly vital. By continuously involving students in the analysis of media message systems about life in general and about their own cultural milieus in particular, schools can help prepare students for effective and sensitive living in their communities. This involves helping them to develop critical thinking, including media literacy, in order to increase their ability to deal more effectively as thoughtful consumers of that omnipresent lifelong educator, the mass media.

School-based media analysis can help students take a major step toward developing such media literacy. In a world in which they are enveloped by the media, in which they are bombarded with information, ideas, and messages in both informational and entertainment form, the ability to engage the media consciously and effectively is necessary for developing greater control over their own destinies (Wurman, 1989). As one avenue to the wisdom necessary for the information age, students must learn to use, not be used by, the media.

REFERENCES

Bagdikian, B. (1983). *The media monopoly.* Boston: Beacon.

Boorstin, D. J. (1961). *The image or whatever happened to the American dream.* New York: Atheneum.

Comstock, G. (1977). *The impact of television on American institutions and the American public.* Honolulu: East-West Communication Institute, East-West Center.

Cortés, C. E. (1981). The societal curriculum: Implications for multiethnic education. In J. A. Banks (Ed.), *Education in the 80's: Multiethnic education* (pp. 24-32). Washington, D.C.: National Education Association.

Cortés, C. E. (1991). Pride, prejudice, and power: The mass media as societal educator on diversity. In J. Lynch, C. Mogdil, & S. Mogdil (Eds.), *Prejudice, polemic or progress?* (pp. 367-381). London: Falmer.

Culley, J. D., & Bennett, R. (1976). Selling women, selling Blacks. *Journal of Communication, 26,* 160- 174.

Czitrom, D. J. (1982). *Media and the American mind from Morse to McLuhan.* Chapel Hill: University of North Carolina Press.

Dennis, E. E. (1978). *The media society: Evidence about mass communication in America.* Dubuque, IA: William C. Brown.

DuBois, E. C. (1991). The Civil War. *American Historical Review, 96,* 1140-1142.

Gans, H. J. (1967). The mass media as an educational institution. *Television Quarterly, 6,* 20-37.

Gans, H. J. (1979). *Deciding what's news: A study of CBS Evening News, NBC Nightly News, Newsweek, and Time.* New York: Random House.

Greenfield, G. M., & Cortés, C. E. (1991). Harmony and conflict of intercultural images: The treatment of Mexico in U. S. feature films and K-12 textbooks. *Mexican Studies/Estudios Mexicanos, 7,* 283-301.

Jowett, G. (1976). *Film: The democratic art.* Boston: Little, Brown.

Keen, S. (1986). *Faces of the enemy: Reflections of the hostile imagination.* New York: Harper & Row.

Koppes, C. R., & Black, G. D. (1987). *Hollywood goes to war: How politics, profits, and propaganda shaped World War II movies.* New York: Free Press.

Kubey, R., & Csikszentmihalyi, M. (1990). *Television and the quality of life: How viewing shapes everyday experience.* Hillsdale, NJ: Lawrence Erlbaum.

Longstreet, W. S. (1989). Education for citizenship: New dimensions. *Social Education, 53,* 41-45.

Matabane, P. (1988). Television and the Black audience: Cultivating moderate perspectives on racial integration. *Journal of Communication, 38,* 21-31.

Monaco, J. (Ed.) (1978). *Media culture.* NewYork: Dell.

Peterson, R. C., & Thurstone, L. L. (1933). *Motion pictures and the social attitudes of children.* New York: Macmillan.

Poe, A. (1976). Active women in ads. *Journal of Communication, 26,* 179-200.

Postman, N. (1985). *Amusing ourselves to death: Public discourse in the age of show business.* NewYork: Viking.

Rosen, M. (1973). *Popcorn Venus.* New York: Coward, McCann, & Geoghegan.

Schramm, W., Lyle, J., & Parker, E. B. (1961). *Television in the lives of our children.* Stanford, CA: Stanford University Press.

Singer, R., & Kazdon, R. (Eds.). (1976). Television and social behavior. *Journal of Social Issues, 32.*

Sklar, R. (1975). *Movie-made America: A cultural history of American movies.* New York: Random House.

Stanley, R. H., & Steinberg, C. S. (1976). *The media environment.* New York: Hastings House.

Tuchman, G., Daniels, A. K., & Benét, J. (Eds.). (1978). *Hearth and home: Images of women in the mass media.* New York: Oxford University Press.

Wilson, C. C., & Gutiérrez, F. (1985). *Minorities and media: Diversity and the end of mass communication.* Beverly Hills, CA: Sage.

Woll, A. L., & Miller, R. M. (1987). *Ethnic and racial images in American film and television: Historical essays and bibliography.* New York: Garland.

Wurman, R. S. (1989). *Information anxiety.* New York: Doubleday.

BUILDING CULTURAL BRIDGES:
A BOLD PROPOSAL FOR TEACHER EDUCATION

by
Geneva Gay

One of the most compelling features of current school demographics is the growing socio-cultural gap between teachers and students. Although the percentage of citizens and students who are Hispanic, Asian, Indian, African American, poor, and limited English speaking is increasing significantly, the number of teachers from similar backgrounds is declining. This distribution has some major implications for the professional preparation of teachers and for how classroom instruction is conducted. The discussion that follows describes some of the specific demographic characteristics of students and teachers, explains some of the implications of these for teacher education, and offers some suggestions for how teacher preparation programs should be designed to respond to these demographic realities.

Student and Teacher Demographics

The percentage of students of color in U. S. schools has increased steadily since the 1960s. They now compose 30% of the total population of elementary and secondary schools. During the 1980s Hispanics and Asians/Pacific Islanders accounted for the greatest increases, by 44.7% and 116.4%, respectively (*The Condition of Education,* 1992). Although their percentages are not evenly distributed throughout the United States, the trend of increasing numbers of children of color in all school districts across the country is. Already, in at least 18 states and Washington, DC, between 30% and 96% of the public school students in grades K-12 are children of color (*Digest of Education Statistics,* 1992; *Education That Works,* 1990).

The increasing number of ethnically and culturally diverse students is attributable to two major factors—the relative youth of groups of color and their higher birthrates; and increased immigration from non-White, non-Western European countries in Asia, the Caribbean, Central and South America, Africa, and the Middle East. By the beginning of the 1990s, more than one third of Hispanics (39%) and African Americans (33%) were 18 years old or younger, compared to 25% of Anglos. Also, a greater proportion of the population of these groups fell within the prime childbearing years and produced a larger average number of children per family unit. The median ages of Hispanics, African Americans, and Anglos were 25.5, 27.3, and 33.1 years, respectively (*The Condition of Education,* 1992; *Statistical Abstract of the United States,* 1991).

During the 1980s, the pattern of immigration to the United States shifted radically from previous generations. People coming from Western European nations declined to a mere trickle, whereas those from other parts of the world, such as Southeast Asia, Central and South America, and the Caribbean, increased (*Statistical Abstract of the United States,* 1991). The reunification of Germany, the fall of the USSR, the democratization of Eastern European nations formerly under communist control, and political shifts in Arabic nations also are having a major impact on immigration patterns. As more people from these parts of the world arrive in the United States, even more strands of ethnic, religious, cultural, and language diversity are being added to the American mosaic. The overall impact of these demographic changes on U. S. society led *Time* magazine, in its April 9, 1990 cover story, to describe it as the "browning of America" (Henry, 1990).

Increasing levels of poverty are another salient characteristic of today's students.

According to the latest statistics from the Bureau of the Census *(Statistical Abstract of the United States,* 1991), 38.4% of Hispanic and 44% of African American children under the age of 18 live in poverty. Rather than stabilizing or declining in the near future, these rates are expected to continue to increase.

The statistics on ethnic identity, immigration, and poverty among public school students have major ramifications for teacher education because there are direct correlations between these social descriptors and the educational opportunities and outcomes of different groups of students. Also, they are significant because the ethnic, racial, and cultural diversity among school teachers and administrators does not reflect similar trends.

Ethnic minorities now compose less than 15% of the teaching force, and less than 12% of school administrators. About 8.0% of all K-12 public school teachers are African Americans, 3.0% are Hispanics, 1.4% are Asians/Pacific Islanders, and 0.9% are American Indians/Native Alaskans *(Status of the American School Teacher,* 1992). Among public school principals and central office administrators there are 8.6% African Americans; 3.2% Hispanics; 1.1% American Indians, Eskimos, and Aleuts; and 0.6% Asians/Pacific Islanders *(The Condition of Education,* 1992; De La Rosa & Maw, 1990; *The Hispanic Population in the U. S.,* 1991)

Demographic Implications Greater than Numbers

A closer scrutiny of the demographics summarized above suggests that the problem is greater than the numbers and that the solution is more complex than merely recruiting teachers of color. There is a growing cultural and social distance between students and teachers that is creating an alarming schism in the instructional process. In addition to racial disparities, other key factors accounting for these widening gaps are residence, generation, gender, social class, experiential background, and education levels.

Many teachers simply do not have frames of reference and points of view similar to their ethnically and culturally different students because they live in different existential worlds. Whereas a growing percentage of students are poor and live in large urban areas, increasing numbers of teachers are middle class and reside in small- to medium-size suburban communities *(Statistical Abstract of the United States,* 1991; *Status of the American School Teacher,* 1992). Furthermore, there is not much mobility in the profession, which means that the teaching population is aging, and relatively few opportunities are available for significant numbers of new and younger individuals to enter the profession. The most recent summary of U. S. teachers compiled by the National Education Association *(Status of the American School Teacher,* 1992) indicates that their mean age is 42 years. Although 60% live within the boundaries of the school district where they are employed, only 37% live in the attendance area of the school where they teach. This percentage drops to 17.3 for schools in large systems, where the greater number of ethnically diverse and poor children are enrolled. The overwhelming majority of teachers continue to be Anglo (86.8%). More than 72% are female. By comparison, the student population in public schools is increasingly children of color.

Disparities in educational levels also contribute to the growing social distance between students and teachers. More and more teachers are achieving higher levels of education, whereas students of color and poverty are becoming less educated. Teachers with five years of college education and a master's degree, or its equivalent, are common throughout the country.

Another distancing phenomenon in who teaches and who is taught is that students are far more technologically adept than most teachers. Thus they are accustomed to high levels of multiple sensory stimulation and mediated information processing. These conditions are rather alien in most conventional classrooms, which tend to emphasize single sensory stimulation, similarity, passivity, and mental activities (Goodlad, 1984). These orientations and dispositions challenge the basic foundations of how teaching and learning are customarily organized and practiced. This challenge is apparent in the frustrations frequently voiced by teachers throughout the United States that they can no longer teach; they have to entertain. From the vantage point of students, many of them find it difficult to become personally invested in classroom learning because too often it lacks the "special effects" that characterize the dissemination of information they are accustomed to from constant exposure to technological media. Consequently, many of the assumptions, premises, programs, and strategies that have been used previously to teach students do not work any more. Therefore, radical changes must be made in how teacher preparation programs are conceived, designed, and implemented to meet these new challenges.

In classroom interactions, these sociocultural factors can become impenetrable obstacles to effective teaching and learning. The conduits or carriers of personal meaning in teaching and learning are examples, illustrations, vignettes, and scenarios. Understandably, teachers tend to select these from their own personal experiences and frames of reference. These examples, which are supposed to make subject matter and intellectual abstractions meaningful to culturally different students, often are irrelevant, too. The experiences, values, orientations, and perspectives of middle-class, highly educated, middle-aged Anglo teachers who live in small to mid-size suburban communities are very different from those of students who are poor, undereducated, racial and ethnic minorities, living in large urban areas. Yet establishing effective communication between students and teachers is imperative for academic success. Preparing teachers to connect meaningfully is the ultimate challenge of teacher education in an ethnically and culturally pluralistic and technologically complex world. Meeting this challenge requires reform in both the conceptual frameworks and substantive components of the preparation programs.

New Conceptual Frameworks Needed

In addition to the idea of *social distance,* there are several other behavioral science and multicultural education paradigms that offer some new and challenging directions for preparing teachers to work effectively with culturally diverse students and issues. Five are discussed here: cultural discontinuities, stress and anxiety, learned helplessness, situational competence, and cultural context teaching.

A growing body of behavioral science research and scholarship suggests that the burden of school failure does not rest on individual students and teachers but is nested in the lack of "fit" or syncretization between the cultural systems of schools and diverse groups. Spindler (1987), and other contributing authors to *Education and Cultural Process,* refer to this phenomenon variously as *cultural incompatibilities, cultural discontinuities,* and *cultural mismatches.* They and others (Gibbs, Huang, & Associates, 1989; Kochman, 1981; Shade, 1989; Trueba, Guthrie, & Au, 1981) agree that many of these mismatches occur at the level of procedures rather than substance. That is, culturally diverse students often have difficulties succeeding in school because *how* they go about learning is incompatible with school expectations and norms, not because they lack desire, motivation, aspiration, or academic potential. Opportunities to participate in the substantive components of teaching and learning frequently are a condition of the extent to which students conform to the "correct procedures and social protocols" (Holliday, 1985) of teaching. Failure to master these virtually ensures academic failure as well.

Some of the most crucial cultural discontinuities in classrooms occur in the areas of cultural values, patterns of communication and cognitive processing, task performance or work habits, self-presentation styles, and approaches to problem solving. That many of these incompatibilities happen without deliberate and conscious intent does not distract from their importance. If anything, this increases their significance as obstacles to successful teaching and learning in culturally pluralistic classrooms and as variables to be targeted for inclusion in multicultural teacher preparation programs.

Living and functioning effectively in culturally pluralistic classrooms can be highly stress provoking for both students and teachers. Trying to negotiate two or more different cultural systems can take psychoemotional priority over attending to academic tasks. *Stress and anxiety* correlate inversely with task performance. As psychoemotional stress levels increase in culturally pluralistic classrooms, teaching and learning task performance declines, thereby reducing the overall quality of academic efforts and achievement outcomes (Beeman, 1978; Gaudry & Spielberger, 1971). Teachers spend inordinate amounts of time on classroom control and maintaining the Anglocentric cultural hegemonic status quo. Culturally different students spend much of their psychoemotional and mental resources defending themselves from attacks on their psychic sense of well-being. Many find themselves in what Boykin (1986) calls a "triple quandary," having to negotiate simultaneously in three often disparate realms of experience: the mainstream school culture, their natal ethnic cultures, and their status as members of oppressed, powerless, and unvalued minority groups.

These conditions do not create "safe and supportive" environments for learning, one of the commonly accepted requirements for effective schooling. Instead, the result is classroom climates charged with adversarial opposition, distrust, hostility, and heightened levels of discomfort and tension. Neither students nor teachers can function at their best under these circumstances. Thus being able to identify stress-provoking factors in crosscultural instructional interactions and knowing how to alleviate them can be a vital way to improve the overall quality of teaching in pluralistic classrooms.

An assumption held by many teachers is that children from certain ethnic groups and social classes are "universally disadvantaged or incompetent" because they do not do well on school tasks. These teachers further assume that the normative ways of doing things in school, whether they deal with social adaptation or academic issues, are the only "correct" and acceptable ones. Research conducted by cultural anthropologists, social psychologists, ethnographers, and sociolinguists (Boggs, Watson-Gegeo, & McMillen, 1985; Florio & Schultz, 1979; Greenbaum, 1985; Holliday, 1985; Kochman, 1981) indicate that ethnically and socially diverse students are very capable in their own cultural communities and social contexts. But these skills do not necessarily transfer to schools. A case in point is African American youths who are verbally adept, creative, imaginative, and fluent among other African Americans but appear inarticulate and unthinking in the classroom. The Kamahameha Early Education Program (KEEP) demonstrates the positive benefits of modifying the schooling process to incorporate the social competencies native Hawaiian children exhibit in their homes and cultural communities (Au & Jordan, 1981; Boggs, WatsonGegeo, & McMillen, 1985).

Furthermore, all individuals are not equally capable in all intellectual areas. Some are artistic; others are more scientific, mechanical, literary, or musical. Gardner (1983) reaffirms this point in his work on multiple intelligences, and Barbe and Swassing (1979) explain the merits of teaching to different students' modality strengths. But teachers frequently do not extend this principle to functioning in different cultural systems. They assume that deficiency in one area extends to all others. Thus children who are poor and from racial minority groups become "culturally deprived," "at risk," "learning disabled," and "socially maladaptive," and *all* of their educational experiences are so affected. Children with limited English proficiencies are too often assumed also to have limited intellectual potential in mathematics, science, computers, and critical thinking. These orientations need to be replaced with ones that emphasize *situational competence* and the understanding that all students are competent in some things within certain environments. The challenge is for teachers to determine what individual strengths and cultural competencies different students bring to the classroom and to design learning experiences to capitalize on them.

Irrespective of their ethnic identity, socioeconomic status, gender, or cultural background, most children begin school eager to demonstrate their abilities and excited about engaging in new learnings, experiences, and interactions. However small the rest of the world might think their achievements are, these youngsters see them as major accomplishments. They do not focus their energies on what they do not have and cannot do; they naturally take great pride in showing off what they do have and can do. They have the dispositions and perspectives on their own experiences that Giovanni (1970) praised in the poem, "Nikka Rosa," while she also lamented these strengths being ignored or abused by those who do not understand them. Giovanni explains that what she remembers most about her childhood is selfpride, a strong sense of accomplishment, love, and happiness, not the constraints of poverty that others outside her social network feel define her essence.

These positive perceptions of personal competence begin to erode for many culturally different students shortly after they start their formal schooling. A persistent message is sent to them, in innumerable ways, of all the things they do not have and cannot do. The longer they stay in school, the more persuasive this message becomes. They become helpless, insecure, and incompetent. This concept of *learned helplessness* is crucial to understanding the plight of these students in schools and developing teacher attitudes and behaviors to avoid its perpetuation.

Basic principles of learning (Gagne, 1985) suggest that students are more likely to master new learnings when they build on previous learnings. These principles apply to the content to be learned, as well as to the structures, conditions, and environments under which learning occurs. Ecological psychologists have found that setting, environment, and climate are important factors in fostering desired behavior (Shade, 1989). Thus students who are accustomed to work being framed in informal social relations and group structures outside school will perform better if this tradition is continued in the classroom, rather than in formal, highly competitive, and individualistic situations.

This continuity can be achieved by doing cultural context teaching. That is, placing the mechanics and technical components of teaching and learning into the cultural frameworks of various ethnic, racial, and social groups. Stated somewhat differently, cultural context teaching is synchronizing various cultural styles of teaching and learning and creating culturally compatible classrooms that provide genuine invitations and opportunities for all students to engage maximally in academic pursuits without any one group being unduly advantaged or penalized (Barbe & Swassing, 1989; Shade, 1989).

Cultural context teaching is somewhat analogous to *segmented marketing* in business and industry. As the United States evolved from a factory-driven to consumer-driven economy, corporations moved rapidly from total reliance on mass media advertising to marketing strategies designed for specifically targeted segments of the population. The shift involves identifying the values, institutions, connections, concerns, experiences, and motivations of key consumer segments; affiliating with esteemed individuals, organizations, and activities that embody these features to enter into the "circles of trust" of different consumer groups; and packaging products and services to match the lifestyles of the various groups (Swenson, 1990). The merits of these strategies are readily apparent—"increased consideration translates into increased sales" (Swenson, 1990, p. 12).

Educational institutions are very susceptible to the opinions of business and industry. They have a long tradition of borrowing models from the corporate world and using economic reasoning to justify program priorities. Education, like other consumer goods and services, must be marketed effectively if it is to "sell" and succeed. Just as mass, homogeneous advertising is obsolete in the economic marketplace, so is it in the educational marketplace.

The questions now are: a) What knowledge and skills do teachers need to acquire to respond to the practical implications of *consumer-segmented teaching* and other paradigms for understanding cultural pluralism in the classroom? and b) How should teacher preparation programs be redesigned to address these needs?

Teachers as Cultural Brokers

No one should be allowed to graduate from a teacher certification program or be licensed to teach without being well grounded in how the dynamic of cultural conditioning operates in teaching and learning. To achieve this goal, the preparation programs should be designed to teach teachers how to be *cultural brokers* (Gentemann & Whitehead, 1983) in pluralistic classrooms and to be competent in *cultural context teaching* (e.g., *segmented marketing of pedagogy*).

A cultural broker is one who thoroughly understands different cultural systems, is able to interpret cultural symbols from one frame of reference to another, can mediate cultural incompatibilities, and knows how to build bridges or establish linkages across cultures that facilitate the instructional process. Cultural brokers translate expressive cultural behaviors into pedagogical implications and actions. They model maneuvers within and negotiations among multiple cultural systems without compromising the integrity of any. They provide mechanisms for establishing continuity between ethnically and socially diverse cultures and mainstream school culture. Cultural brokers are *bicultural actors* who are able to straddle or syncretize different cultural systems and integrate elements of ethnic cultures into classroom procedures, programs, and practices (Gentemann & Whitehead, 1983). How they function epitomizes cultural context teaching at the levels of interpersonal interactions with students, pedagogical strategies employed in the classroom, and the infusion of multiculturalism throughout the entire instructional process.

Several skills are necessary for teachers to become cultural brokers. These can be classified as acquiring cultural knowledge, becoming change agents, and translating cultural knowledge into pedagogical strategies. They should form the substantive core of all teacher preparation programs.

Acquiring Cultural Knowledge

This component of preparing teachers to be cultural brokers should have three aspects: learning factual information about the specific characteristics of different ethnic and cultural groups, understanding the pedagogical implications of these cultural characteristics, and developing a philosophy for cultural context teaching. The students enrolled in the preparation programs should declare a cultural or ethnic group for concentrated study. They also may choose more than one group to concentrate on with the understanding that this choice will extend the time they spend in the preparation program. When they finish the program, the graduates will have a culturally diverse area of specialization (e.g., African Americans, Mexican Americans, children of poverty), as well as a subject matter major and endorsement.

Knowledge about cultural diversity should be acquired through two primary means: studying the accumulated research and scholarship on different ethnic and cultural groups and firsthand experiences gained from participatory observations in various cultural communities. Both of these should be in-depth experiences, guided by the methodologies, orientations, conceptual frameworks, and knowledge funds generated by behavioral scientists, ethnic studies scholars, and expressive artists (such as cultural anthropologists, social psychologists, sociolinguists, ethnomusicologists, ethnographers, cultural artists, and literary authors). College of Education faculties will need to establish previously unexplored instructional partnerships with some university divisions and scholars. These partnerships in search of accurate and authentic knowledge about cultural patterns and functions are as essential as the more traditional ones between educationists and social scientists designed to increase mastery of the subject matter taught in schools.

Some dimensions of culture are more applicable than others to understanding and mediating cultural conflicts in pluralistic classrooms. These include cultural values, relational patterns, learning styles and work habits, communication styles, rewards and punishments, social etiquette and decorum, cultural ethos, self-presentation styles, and patterns of ethnic identification and affiliation. Students enrolled in teacher education programs should be expected to take relevant behavioral science courses to learn specific content about each of these cultural components for specific ethnic groups. They may take courses in ethnic literature, cultural values, folklore, family, art and aesthetics, celebrations and ceremonies, customs and traditions, and developmental psychology.

The cultural content courses should be complemented with education seminars that have three primary purposes. The first is the extrapolation of pedagogical principles and practices embedded in the cultural content. Seminars should be sequenced so that students' enrollment in the content courses and the seminars coincide with each other or follow closely thereafter. The courses could even be team taught by behavioral scientists and educationists working together. A second component of the seminars is a field-based practicum in which students spend concentrated periods of time in culturally pluralistic school sites. During these experiences, students will function as participant observers to document how the cultural characteristics they are studying are expressed in actual classroom settings and interactions. The third element of the seminars should be the development of students' philosophies for cultural context teaching. The emphasis here is on developing an understanding and appreciation of cultural pluralism in the classroom as a vital, creative, and enriching phenomenon, as well as its potential for transforming the quality of schooling for students from historically disenfranchised groups. The conceptual paradigms discussed earlier should be the foundation of this philosophy.

Becoming Change Agents

To be effective cultural brokers and cultural context teachers, students in teacher education programs must be taught how to be agents. This role requires a commitment to institutional transformation and developing skills for incorporating cultural diversity into the normative operations of schools and classrooms. A four-step process should constitute this aspect of teacher education.

First, teacher education students should be taught skills of critical analysis and self-reflection. These skills will help them learn to analyze systematically the structures and procedures in schools and classrooms and their own habitual ways of behaving in institutional settings from various cultural vantage points; to identify points of conflict between the culture of the school and different ethnic groups; and to determine which of these offer the best and the worst opportunities for negotiation and change to serve the academic needs of culturally different students better.

Second, education students should be taught how to deconstruct mainstream hegemonic assumptions, values, and beliefs embedded in the normative structures and procedures of conventional classroom teaching. This requires a thorough understanding of how cultural values shape classroom policies, procedures, and practices; an awareness of the points in the instructional process that are most susceptible to cultural conflict; and the ability to discern those structural components that are most significant to incorporating cultural pluralism into routine classroom procedures.

Commitments to making teaching more culturally relevant need to be grounded in principles of organizational behavior and change (e.g., Belasco, 1990; Bowditch & Buono, 1985; Meltzer & Nord, 1980; Robbins, 1991). Many teacher education students recognize the need for change and have strong affinities for making their classroom teaching more culturally sensitive. But they do not know how to anchor it in a realistic and reliable operational framework. They seem to believe that desire alone is sufficient to bring about change. In the long run, this naiveté is a serious obstacle to real change. Students must understand the organizational culture, climate, and psychology of schools; why schools are self-perpetuating institutions; obstacles to change; cooperative strategies for planned change; and techniques to initiate and sustain change.

An integral feature of success as cultural brokers is being able to relate well to students from culturally, ethnically, and racially diverse backgrounds. Therefore, a fourth part of becoming effective change agents is developing competencies in cross-cultural communications and multicultural counseling. Both of these fields of research and scholarship have rich data bases from which students can acquire conceptual skills and practical techniques. The emphasis should be on sociolinguistic and paralinguistic communication components (Cazden, John, & Hymes, 1985; Greenbaum, 1985; Hall, 1981; Kochman, 1981; Smitherman, 1977; Trueba, Guthrie, & Au, 1981). In some instances, language studies and principles of bilingual education and second language learning are also appropriate. Techniques of cross-cultural counseling are important because teachers need to know how to help students deal with the stress and strain of living and functioning in culturally pluralistic settings. Some of the specific associated needs are style shifting across cultures, self-declaration for different ethnic group members, dealing with interracial and interethnic group hostilities, editing cultural nuances out of public behaviors, and coping with traumas and anxieties related to functions in cross-cultural settings (Beeman, 1978; Schofield, 1982; Spencer, Brookins, & Allen, 1985).

Translating Knowledge into Practice

Finally, teacher education programs should provide ample opportunities for students to engage in supervised practice doing cultural context teaching and being cultural brokers in actual classroom settings. Through a combination of classroom simulations, sample demonstrations, media protocols, case studies, and field experiences, students should develop skills in diagnosing teaching and learning styles, matching teaching styles with learning styles, creating inviting classroom climates (Purkey, 1978), using culturally sensitive assessment tools and techniques, and integrating culturally diverse content into subject matter curricula. These action strategies will need to be accompanied by corresponding changes in beliefs about what knowledge is of greatest worth for citizenship in a pluralistic world and what are the best ways it can be acquired for students from different ethnic, cultural, racial, and social backgrounds. The overriding principles should be the cultural contextuality of teaching and learning and using alternative pedagogical means to achieve common learning outcomes.

All teacher education students also should be expected to participate in a cultural brokerage internship before completing their preparation program. This internship should take place in actual classroom settings and provide opportunities to practice all of the skills involved in being a cultural broker. It is to be a complement to, not a replacement for, the traditional student teaching experience. The duration of the experience should be long enough for the students to get a sampling of the wide variety of issues and challenges involved in the institutional culture of schools. The internship should be carefully monitored and assessed by experienced classroom teachers or university professors. Successful completion should be a condition of graduating from the teacher preparation program and receiving a license to teach.

Conclusion

The plight of many culturally different students in U. S. public schools is chronic and critical. Because teachers play a central role in resolving it, their preparation must be a prime target of reform. This need is becoming even more imperative, given shifts in school demographics that show rapid increases in the numbers of children who are poor, limited English speakers, immigrants, and members of ethnic groups of color, as well as a decline in teachers from similar backgrounds. The resulting social distance can be an impenetrable obstacle to effective teaching and learning.

Generic teacher education programs that are supposed to prepare teachers to function well in all types of school communities are no longer viable. Instead, preparation must be population based and contextually specific. Nor can participation in multicultural learning experiences be left to choice and chance—it must be mandatory and carefully planned. The best way to translate these ideas into practice is preparation programs that emphasize developing skills in cultural context teaching and how to be cultural brokers in pluralistic classrooms. The essence of these strategies is affirming the cultures of diverse students, establishing continuity and building bridges across different cultural systems, creating supportive classroom climates where diverse students feel welcome and valued, and replacing cultural hegemonic pedagogy with one that models cultural pluralism without hierarchy. Mastering the skills necessary for cultural brokering and cultural context teaching may require longer time in preparation. But it is time well spent, and long-range payoffs are more than worth the relative short-term investments.

Preparing teachers to work better with culturally different students and communities demands action now. Conventional approaches to teacher education must be decentered and transformed at their most fundamental core if teachers are to be maximally prepared to teach students of the 21st century who will be increasingly racially, culturally, ethnically, socially, and linguistically pluralistic.

REFERENCES

Au, K. H. P., & Jordan, C. (1981). Teaching reading to Hawaiian children: Finding a culturally appropriate solution. In H. T. Trueba, G. P. Guthrie, & K. H. P. Au (Eds.). *Culture and the bilingual classroom: Studies in classroom ethnography* (pp. 139-152). Rowley, MA: Newbury House.

Barbe, W. B., & Swassing, R. H. (1979). *Teaching through modality strengths: Concepts and practice.* Columbus, OH: Zaner-Bloser.

Beeman, P. N. (1978). *School stress and anxiety: Theory, research, and intervention.* New York: Human Sciences Press.

Belasco, J. A. (1990). *Teaching the elephant to dance: Empowering change in your organization.* New York: Crown.

Boggs, S. T., Watson-Gegeo, K., & McMillen, G. (1985). *Speaking, relating, and learning: A study of Hawaiian children at home and at school.* Norwood, NJ: Ablex.

Bowditch, J. L., & Buono, A. T. (1985). *A primer on organizational behavior.* New York: Wiley.

Boykin, A. W. (1986). The triple quandary and the schooling of Afro-American children. In U. Neisser (Ed.), *The school achievement of minority children: New perspectives* (pp. 57-92). Hillsdale, NJ: Lawrence Erlbaum.

Cazden, C. B., John, V. P., & Hymes, D. (Eds.). (1985). *Functions of language in the classroom.* Prospect Heights, IL: Waveland.

The condition of education. (1992). Washington, DC: U. S. Department of Education, National Center for Education Statistics, Office of Educational Research and Information.

De La Rosa, D., & Maw, C. E. (1990). *Hispanic education: A statistical portrait.* Washington, DC: National Council of La Raza.

Digest of education statistics, 1991. (1992). Washington, DC: U. S. Department of Education, Office of Education Research and Improvement, Center for Educational Statistics.

Education that works: An action plan for the education of minorities. (1990). Cambridge, MIT, Quality Education for Minorities Project.

Florio, S., & Shultz, J. (1979). Social competence at home and at school. *Theory Into Practice, 18,* 234-243.

Gagne, R. M. (1985). *The conditions of learning and theory of instruction* (4th ed.). New York: Holt, Rinehart & Winston.

Gardner, H. (1983). *Frames of mind: The theory of multiple intelligences .* New York: Basic Books.

Gaudry, E., & Spielberger, C. D. (1971). *Anxiety and educational achievement.* New York: Wiley.

Gentemann, K. M., & Whitehead, T. L. (1983). The cultural broker concept in bicultural education. *Journal of Negro Education, 54,* 118-129.

Gibbs, J. T., Huang, L. N., & Associates (1989). *Children of color: Psychological interventions with minority youth.* San Francisco: Jossey-Bass.

Giovanni, N. (1970). *Black feeling, Black talk and Black judgment.* New York: William Morrow.

Goodlad, J. I. (1984). *A place called school: Prospects for the future.* New York: McGraw-Hill.

Greenbaum, P. E. (1985). Nonverbal differences in communication style between American Indian and Anglo elementary classrooms. *American Educational Research Journal, 22,* 101-115.

Hall, E. T. (1981). *The silent language.* New York: Anchor.

Henry, W. A., III. (1990, April 9). Beyond the melting pot. *Time,* pp. 28-31.

The Hispanic population in the U. S. (1991, March). (Current Population Reports, Series P-20, No. 455). Washington, DC: U. S. Department of the Census.

Holliday, B. G. (1985). Towards a model of teacher-child transactional processes affecting Black children's academic achievement. In M. B. Spencer, G. K. Brookins, & W. R. Allen (Eds.), *Beginnings: The social and affective development of Black children* (pp. 117-130). Hillsdale, NJ: Lawrence Erlbaum.

Kochman, T. (1981). *Black and White styles in conflict.* Chicago: University of Chicago Press.

Meltzer, H., & Nord, W. R. (1980). *Making organizations humane and productive: A handbook for practitioners.* New York: Wiley.

Purkey, W. W. (1978). *Inviting school success: A self-concept approach to teaching and learning.* Belmont, CA: Wadsworth.

Robbins, S. P. (1991). *Organizational change: Concepts, controversies and applications.* Englewood Cliffs, NJ: Prentice-Hall.

Schofield, J. W. (1982). *Black and White in school: Trust, tension, or tolerance.* New York: Praeger.

Shade, B. J. R. (Ed.). (1989). *Culture, style and the educative process.* Springfield, IL: Charles C. Thomas.

Smitherman, G. (1977). *Talkin' and testifyin': The language of Black America.* Boston: Houghton Mifflin.

Spencer, M. B., Brookins, G. K., & Allen, W. R. (Eds.). (1985). *Beginnings: The social and affective development of Black children.* Hillsdale, NJ: Lawrence Erlbaum.

Spindler, G. D. (Ed.). (1987). *Education and cultural process: Anthropological perspectives.* Prospect Heights, IL: Waveland.

Statistical abstract of the United States (111th ed.). (1991). Washington, DC: Department of Commerce, Bureau of the Census.

Status of the American school teacher 1990-1991. (1992). Washington, DC: National Education Association, Research Division.

Swenson, C. A. (1990). *Selling to a segmented market: The lifestyle approach.* New York: Quorum.

Trueba, H. T., Guthrie, G. P., & Au, K. H. P. (1981). *Culture and the bilingual classroom: Studies in classroom ethnography.* Rowley, MA: Newbury House.

INTEGRATING RACE, CLASS, GENDER, AND SEXUAL ORIENTATION INTO THE COLLEGE CURRICULUM

by
BarBara M. Scott

Historically, curriculum change in American higher education has taken place sporadical-ly, occurring more in some areas of higher education than in others. It has never taken place systematically, occurring more by accretion than by design (Levin, 1992). The challenge of "multiculturalism," its inclusion in the curriculum, has likewise developed sporadically and more by accretion than design. Higher education institutions as well as individual faculty have responded variously to this challenge of inclusion. Overall, the result has been a mixed bag of approaches to and implementations of curricular change.

The attention to curricular multiculturalism has manifested itself in a range of college course offerings in gender and ethnic studies such as Women's Studies, African American Studies, Hispanic American, Chicano, or Latino Studies, Native American Studies, Asian American Studies, and Gay and Lesbian Studies. Less often, multicultural changes are incor-porated into the disciplines: adding new course material to existing courses, developing new multicultural courses, and promoting new multicultural scholarship.

Curricular multiculturalism is both a challenge and an opportunity. Probably one of the biggest challenges of multiculturalism is the development of a consensus as to what the term actually means. In broad but simple terms, for most academics, multiculturalism refers vari-ously or collectively to valuing diversity; teaching about difference; facilitating student's recognition and acceptance of human difference; exploring diverse cultures in order to help students view events, concepts, issues and problems from diverse cultural and ethnic perspec-tives and to illuminate students' own world views. This too is what teaching about the inter-section of race, class and gender is all about.

A multicultural curriculum also provides an opportunity, an opportunity for faculty to develop and further a critique of the traditional curricula: to consider how we, according to Elizabeth Higginbotham (1990), relate to a curriculum assumed to be raceless, genderless, and classless, and how that relationship is shaped by our own race, gender, and social class background. For many of us who have long ago attempted to meet the challenge of diversity in our curriculum, the idea of integrating issues of race, class, gender, and sexual orientation into the curriculum seems to be a straightforward way of dealing with diversity and certainly for me, compatible with a "sociological imagination" (in the C. Wright Mills tradition). In the sociological tradition, such an approach enables students to transcend the "safe" but often misleading, inadequate, or stereotypical information about different cultures and groups that lead to invalid (often racist, sexist, elitist, and/or homophobic) generalizations, apathy, or the assumption that "human beings are the same everywhere." It also helps them to both recog-nize and appreciate their own uniqueness while at the same time recognizing historical and sociological differences among individuals and across groups.

As a sociologist, I am interested in facilitating students' ability to think critically and to understand the links between their own personal biographies (cultural experiences) and public issues (larger social structures). Not getting bogged down in the multicultural debate gives me the advantage of getting right to the heart of diversity: that race, class, gender, and sexual ori-entation are interlocking systems of experience that together produce profound differences in individual biographies and, as categories of experience, shape all social institutions and belief systems (Andersen & Collins 1992). Such a focus also enables students to use their own relevant life experiences as the basis of sociological analysis and academic learning.

In recent years, a plethora of information in the form of articles, primary research, workshops, seminars, conferences, roundtable discussions, and faculty development programs about the rationale, goals, assumptions, and trends of multiculturalism has become available to institutions of higher education and individual faculty who are interested in curricular change. While this information explosion includes a variety of discussions about the process of curriculum reform, there are fewer discussions on the practical "how-to" level. Some of the most important exchanges of hands-on data, cross fertilization of ideas, and sharing of resources and information about multiculturalism and curriculum integration have taken place in workshops like those sponsored by the Center for Research on Women at Memphis State University. Those workshops have assisted a variety of faculty over the years in our quest to develop a curriculum that reflects the diversity of human experience.

I personally owe a debt of gratitude to the various workshop faculty and faculty participants over the years at Memphis State University and especially my friend and colleague Kathy Ward at Southern Illinois University for facilitating exchange and sharing resources, information, and experiences about curriculum integration. It has been this kind of practical, hands-on experience that has helped me most as I continue the process of curriculum integration or transformation: to think and rethink who I am, what my teaching objectives are (what I genuinely want to share with my students), and to develop new perspectives on race, class, gender, and sexual orientation. This essay is deeply rooted in these experiences. Perhaps the most important insight I have gained is that curriculum integration is a process not a demonstrated product.

Yet, the questions are ever present: "How do I achieve curriculum integration?" "Where do I start?" Many faculty, particularly women and people of color, are burdened with heavy teaching responsibilities, committee responsibilities, student advising as well as a host of other responsibilities that go along with the professorship and maintenance of that status. So, what can we do to get started that takes these practical realities into consideration? This paper relates some of my ideas and experiences as well as the collective wisdom and experience of many others engaged in the process of curriculum integration. It has grown out of my ongoing struggles to facilitate recognition, understanding, and appreciation of human diversity in my teaching. Rethinking my teaching objectives, seeking new information, developing new perspectives on race, class, gender, and sexual orientation have become the order of the day for me. As I have worked on transforming my own classroom and course content, within the context of the limitations imposed by a heavy teaching load and the expectation to publish, I have developed some strategies that address these questions and have reaped tremendous rewards in terms of the teaching/learning process. As a result, I have increasingly engaged in modelling the process for my peers based on my personal teaching experiences.

This essay is primarily practical in purpose. It is a working paper intended for faculty, already overburdened and overtaxed, who do not receive release time or monetary compensation to develop new courses or to transform old ones. The focus of the discussion is strategies to get started: how to make a course more inclusive of race, class, gender, and sexual orientation.

What Is Curriculum Integration?

Curriculum integration is a dialectical process between course restructuring or transformation and changing classroom environments. You cannot change one without the other. Building on the ideas of Higginbotham (1988), curriculum integration can be viewed as consisting of three central components: 1) Increasing personal knowledge—adding to and deepening one's personal knowledge about race, class, gender, and sexual orientation; 2) Restructuring course syllabi and content—transforming the content and structure of courses to meet the learning needs, learning styles, and life experiences of a diverse student population; and 3) Changing classroom dynamics—changing the classroom interactions so as to provide a safe and more inclusive environment for all students. Some faculty address these issues one at a time while others are engaged in all three simultaneously.

Why Bother with Curriculum Integration?

Why bother? Because issues of diversity are part and parcel of our rich human history. In addition, we are teaching and living in an increasingly diverse society, one in which European American males, for example, will soon be a minority in the work place. Yet people of color and women continue to be ignored, negatively represented, shrouded in myth, stereotype, or misrepresentations in our college curriculum. This situation can have devastating effects for all of us. For example, "two-thirds of African American children in grades K-12 know very little about their identities, and European American children grow up knowing little but stereotypical knowledge about other racial and ethnic groups" (Brewer, Scott & Ward, 1990, p. 2).

We have an academic responsibility and a moral obligation to provide students with an inclusive education that will enable them to deal with the contingencies of living in a diverse world. Research shows that when students are taught from an inclusive curriculum they are eager to learn; they are more engaged in the teaching/learning process. They want more inclusive course content throughout the education process. Faculty who are involved in integrating diversity into their curriculum report that their teaching is revitalized, their student evaluations improved, and their overall job satisfaction increased. Thus the mandate to be inclusive seems apparent.

How Do I Begin?

To begin we will most certainly have to think about what it is we want to share with students. We will have to think about new strategies or adapt old ones as we restructure or develop new syllabi. In general, while there are no easy answers, I have found a few fairly easy and relatively painless steps that can help move faculty, staff, and students toward phase five of curriculum development: a transformed curriculum that includes all people and genuinely represents the diversity in human society, culture, and individual experiences. (See, for example, McIntosh, 1983, 1988).

Personal Assessment

The process of curriculum integration should begin with an overall assessment of where we are in terms of teaching an inclusive curriculum. We can ask ourselves: What do I already know? What don't I know but need to know about race, class, gender, sexual orientation? How can I find out more? Where can I find the information I need? This kind of personal assessment or inventory begins the process of increasing our personal knowledge, our familiarity with the growing body of literature on, by, and about women, ethnic groups, lesbians and gays, persons with disabilities, and the elderly. It is likely we do not have to go beyond our own university library and resource centers to find this literature, to become familiar with feminist periodicals and those covering multicultural issues. We can utilize bibliographies such as those available through the Clearinghouse Search System on Women of Color and

Southern Women at Memphis State University's Center for Research on Women or through data bases for social sciences or humanities.

In this process we need to rethink that which passes as knowledge, to rethink the process that results in "legitimizing" knowledge or knowledge validation, and to consider that "traditional" knowledge, or what passes as legitimate knowledge, has been historically produced, reproduced, and validated by people whose race, class, gender, and sexual orientation were primarily European American, middle class, male, and heterosexual. In seeking to increase our knowledge about race, class, gender, and sexual orientation as well as disability and age, we need to question what constitutes knowledge when people other than European American males are part of the legitimizing process. We cannot simply rely on traditional sources of knowledge when increasing our own personal knowledge or when deciding on materials for class use and student consumption. We must explore the areas/sources of information previously defined as nontraditional. Much of the relevant information/knowledge is here, in the works of women and people of color.

According to McIntosh (1983, 1988) and others (e.g., Ward & Morrison, 1990), there are roughly five phases of curriculum development.

Phase 1: A European American, "womanless discipline," where women, people of color, lesbians, gays, "others," are simply absent from the curriculum.

Phase 2: "Women and/or African Americans in society," where women and African Americans and maybe one or two other ethnic groups are added to the existing course material but usually discussed as exceptional representatives of their gender or ethnicity; lesbians and gays are invisible.

Phase 3: Women and people of color are regarded as a problem or anomaly. They are regarded in this phase as "other" in comparison to European American men.

Phase 4: Women, people of color, lesbians, gays, persons with disabilities, are studied on their own terms. The specific focus in this phase is on women's worlds or the worlds of lesbians, gays, and people of color. Course content focuses on the world we all live in—one in which race, ethnicity, gender, class, and sexuality are experienced simultaneously by all of us.

Phase 5: The curriculum is transformed, revised, and restructured throughout to be genuinely inclusive of all people and representative of the diversity in our classrooms and the world.

Course Restructuring

Having assessed where we are in curriculum development and having begun the process of increasing our knowledge, we can think about a course we want to transform by asking:

1. What is the goal of this course?
2. What basic assumptions seem to frame the organization of material on the syllabus?
3. How successful is this syllabus? What pleases me about my current treatment of diversity in this course?
4. How would I like to improve the way I address diversity in this course?
5. What are some of the problems or obstacles to transforming my course?

We might further evaluate the course based on the following questions, a modification of those posed by sociologist Margaret Andersen (1988):

1. Where do women, people of color, lesbians, gays appear in my syllabus and assigned and/or suggested readings?
2. Does my syllabus teach that all group experience is grounded in race, class, and gender, or is one group generalized while all others are particularized?

3. Are race, class, gender, sexual orientation, age, and disability segregated in one section of the course?
4. Is race discussed only in the context of poverty and other social problems? Are the experiences of lesbians and gays discussed only in the context of sexuality?
5. Are women and people of color conceptualized primarily as victims rather than as active agents of social change and continuity?
6. Are women, people of color, lesbians and gays viewed on their own terms, not just as the dominant group sees them?
7. Are women, people of color, lesbians, gays seen only through taken-for-granted frameworks of disciplined knowledge? Does my course silence their experiences except when they fit existing concepts and theories in my discipline?
8. Does my course, as presently structured, relegate women, people of color, lesbians, gays to the status of "other?"
9. What would the central themes and questions of the course be if women, people of color, lesbians and gays were a primary reference? If any or all of these groups were at the center of the course?

The goal here is to restructure our courses to be not just inclusive but integrative of all groups. The difference is significant. The goal should be to change our focus from one centered on European American males and/or females as the norm to one that genuinely focuses on diversity, diversity as different, not as superior/inferior. Ask, as Margaret Andersen (1988) suggests, "How would my course change if non-whites, non-white women, or women were at its center?" This requires first and foremost that you take the responsibility and the initiative to know about issues of race, class, and gender. It requires new approaches, new materials, and creative use of old materials.

Getting Started

Start small. Curriculum integration can be an overwhelming job. To lessen the task, begin with one course. Curriculum transformation is a process. It does not happen over night. A relatively nonthreatening way to begin is to add a relevant text or anthology to the required list of readings, or to add themes or topics to the syllabus that reflect the experiences of women, the cultures of people of color, and the diversity of a society with different ethnic groups, genders, classes, sexual orientations, and ages. Another possibility is to include a video, film, or current event such as a speaker or happening on campus or in the community as part of a class presentation or activity. Many of today's students are visual learners and respond well to audio-visual materials. Using media, content analyses of mass media, for example, is an excellent way to begin classroom discussions around issues of race, class, gender, and sexual orientation. Biographical films and documentaries as well as popular cinema can provide the impetus for new understandings and knowledge about diversity. Beginning with the addition of just one film, book, or extracurricular event, or perhaps a poem or a short essay, is okay.

Redefining Concepts and Terms

The reconstruction of our thinking, and thus of our syllabus, to become more inclusive requires transformation on many levels. One of the most basic is the language we use to describe and define different individuals and groups. Consider redefining and reconceptualizing terms that are rooted in racist, sexist, homophobic or ageist thought systems. For example, terms like dominant group, subordinate group, lesser cultures, majority, minority, Third World. Even non-white and people of color are problematic in that they marginalize some groups, making them seem inferior and outside the so-called mainstream while others are the implied superiors against whom all others are gauged.

We can let students help in this kind of de(re)construction or transformation of language. Solving all the problems and limitations of the English language will not be easy or even a realistic goal. The goal is simply to point out to ourselves and to our students the significance of language, its problems and limitations when attempting to think and implement inclusive curriculum.

Restructuring Course Topics/Headings

The nine questions listed above can be used as a guide in restructuring course topics and themes as we try to integrate diversity throughout our syllabus. We can ask, for example, where do people of color, women, lesbians, persons with disabilities appear in my syllabus? Do I spend one class or one week on African Americans? When they are included is the focus, the discussion, or the material male-centered? Is it primarily from an African American or European American male perspective, for instance, that I approach historical discussions of American slavery? Do I spend one class or one week on Native Americans, Latinos, or Asian Americans and then return to "normal," where the experiences of European Americans and males are central and function as the norm? Do I discuss race, class, and gender in terms of victimization but not in terms of agency, survival strategies, change, and continuity? Do I discuss African, Asian, Native, and Latino Americans only in stereotypic and negative contexts: for example, African American women only when discussing female heads of household or teenage pregnancy?

Very often we must reconceptualize in order to present the inclusive reality, to present diverse groups on their own terms. We have to move away from forcing them into European American male (or female) constructs. Think about this: Are the voices of diverse groups silenced when they don't fit existing concepts and theories that we use in our courses? For example, in feminist theory courses we are introduced to liberal, radical, Marxist, and socialist feminism. Sometimes the writings of women of color are added, often as an anomaly. We thus relegate these women to the status of "other," implying a distinction between "real" or "valid" feminisms and something called "women of color" writings. We often reinforce this marginality by telling our students that this intellectual scholarship is less developed, that it is not yet theory (as defined, of course, by European Americans). What we are saying or conveying to our students when we use these labels without discussing the implications of such language serves to perpetuate and maintain the First, Second, and Third World mentality of many of us, the idea that western society has achieved a level of modernity and sophistication superior to all other societies.

Choosing Textbooks and Other Course Material

We must pay attention to whether our choice of textbooks is not only diverse in the coverage of various groups, but also accurate in content and free of racist and sexist language. If they are not, we might want to consider putting together a packet of materials and selling it to students at cost. We can also consider using materials from disciplines other than our own to supplement or reinforce our disciplinary information.

In investigating the coverage of diversity in course materials, it is important to recognize early on in the curriculum integration process that African Americans are not the only non-Europeans in the United States or the world. Some students and faculty commonly use African American and people of color synonymously. Including the experiences of one group, however, does not mean we have developed an inclusive curriculum. Many groups must be considered in an inclusive course: Native Americans (e.g., Cherokee, Apache), Asian Americans (e.g., Japanese, Chinese, Filipinos, Vietnamese), Latinos (e.g., Cubans, Puerto Ricans, Chicanos, Central Americans), lesbians, gays, older women, women with disabilities. Actively looking for and integrating scholarship by and about these various groups may not be easy, but the reward, relative to the teaching/ learning process, is well worth the effort.

As I indicated earlier, curriculum transformation requires new approaches and new materials or the creative use of old materials. For example, in discussions of sociological theory, I use the writings of African Americans such as Ida B. Wells, Oliver Cox, and W. E. B. Du Bois; the writings of many diverse women such as those found in anthologies like *This Bridge Called My Back* (Morago & Anzaldúa, 1983) and *Making Face, Making Soul: Haciendo Caras* (Anzaldúa, 1990) or slave narratives, poetry, and fiction. I've found women's fiction generally, and that of African American women specifically, so fertile with sociological insights that I currently teach a sociology course on African American women in which I use only fiction by and about African American women. I begin the course with the reading and discussion of Toni Morrison's *Beloved* (1987), a historical fiction that can be viewed as a modern slave narrative. It can provide the basis for understanding the intersection of race, class, and gender in the lives of African American women with historical specificity. Another example is my use of Marge Piercy's novel, *Woman on the Edge of Time,* as required reading in a social stratification course. The blend of fiction with research data provides an excellent framework for raising questions, provoking discussion, and facilitating students' understanding of the interlocking nature of race, class, and gender in the lives of women like Piercy's Chicana main character.

In addition to textbooks and other course materials we can have speakers address diversity issues. However, caution is necessary here. We cannot make these people spokespersons for their entire group, whatever it is. Students should understand the guests can only present their own viewpoints. This can be discussed when we prepare ourselves and our classes for the visit by exploring the topic the speaker will address. Unless the speaker's remarks have context and meaning, students might interpret this as busy work, a time filler. Making students responsible for information given by the guest speaker through a summary, critique, or test will also increase their awareness of the subject's importance. Similar preparation and follow-up can underscore the importance of presentations by other speakers brought to campus to address issues of diversity.

Just as important is preparing ourselves on the issues to be discussed. How can we do this? Where is the time? We can attend conferences or workshops on diversity and apply for summer teaching fellowships, sabbaticals, or mini-sabbaticals in order to have some time for increasing our knowledge. Some faculty have started research projects on diversity or issues relevant to diversity in order to acquire new knowledge. As we do begin this process we will have to be prepared to change or throw out old lecture notes. Much of the new research on diversity challenges previous theories and assumptions that we have been teaching. For example, theories of mobility that previously explained only European American male upward mobility are being replaced with theories that take into account the experiences and patterns of achievement and mobility found among women, African, Asian, Native Americans, Latinos, and other groups (See, for example, Scott, 1988). Key labels for historical periods are also being challenged; the Renaissance, for instance, is being reconsidered since most women did not experience a renaissance during the period so labeled. Sometimes we will find our students are more aware of the new research and literature than we are and will challenge our presentation in direct ways, such as asking for the source of our information, or in indirect ways by bringing articles that provide alternative viewpoints, for example. We should welcome such involvement and encourage students to participate in this way.

Teaching Diversity

Having begun by rethinking my syllabus, how do I actually teach an inclusive syllabus? We can begin by attempting to engage students in the course material by using an active/interactive teaching style, by calling on students, soliciting their input in discussions, using active learning exercises, assigning multicultural projects. Some students learn best by reading and discussing issues in small groups. For the last year I have used small groups for purposes of class discussion, peer tutoring and support, and class assignments in my "classical" sociological theory class. Professors such as Lynn Weber Cannon at Memphis State University use a method of providing students with an opportunity to work together in preparing for class exams. Others, like Kathy Ward at Southern Illinois University, use a mix of videos and photographic books to involve students. Ward has used photo essays, for example, on South Africa, African American women, and a pre-World War II Jewish village in a course on comparative race and ethnic relations to give her students a pictorial sense of the people they are studying. They are asked to select the three photographs that most affect them, write about them, and discuss them in small groups (Ward & Morrison, 1990).

But how do we teach inclusively if we are still asking, still learning about diversity? Without sounding glib, insensitive, or flip, we just do it. It doesn't matter if, for example, **all** of our students are European American or male or middle class or heterosexual. Race, class, gender, and sexual orientation do not just affect African Americans, Asian Americans, Native Americans, Latinos, women, or lesbians and gays. All students need to know how their life experiences are affected by race, gender, class, heterosexuality, age, disability, and their increasingly diverse world. Some faculty have indicated they do not feel comfortable speaking about women or ethnic groups other than their own. Some have expressed discomfort in discussing lesbian and gay issues and experiences. If this is the situation for us, we need to begin examining our own "isms": Why is it we don't feel comfortable? In our classroom we might want to invite guest speakers who are well versed in the subject area we find discomforting. But, we still need to examine our own "isms," become informed about the topic, and hold our students responsible for greater awareness as well.

Creating Positive Classroom Dynamics

Along with restructuring our courses and syllabi we must simultaneously pay attention to classroom dynamics. The classroom **must** be a safe environment for **all** students, a place where risk-taking is minimal. We can begin with the premise that people are going to have attitudes: heterosexuals when we discuss gay and lesbian experiences in a positive way, European Americans when we discuss African, Asian, Native Americans, or Latinos in a positive way; and men when we discuss women in a positive way. We must move beyond these attitudes. We cannot afford to get stuck in them. One way to move beyond them is to establish ground rules, agreements between ourselves and our students that are based on an agreement to listen and learn, to honor each other's differences and experiences. Rather than focusing on attitudes, we can focus on the social forces and the simultaneity of oppressions that keep these attitudes alive. This generally requires each of us, teacher and student alike, to recognize his or her own cultural components, including sexuality, gender, race, and class, whether she or he is in a dominant or subordinate position in relation to these interlocking systems. Such an approach avoids blaming individuals and helps to diffuse defensiveness and attitudes while highlighting difference as a central focus of discussion. We can encourage stu-

114

dents to deal with these differences openly and to treat any anger that arises as a vital aspect of the learning process.

Conclusion

An increasing, accessible body of literature addresses the classroom environment and its significance in the teaching/learning process. My intent in this essay is simply to lay out some of the steps and strategies that I have found to be practical and productive in the curriculum integration process.

I do not want to underestimate the seriousness and tremendous work and effort involved in the curriculum transformation process. I know well that it is not easy, that it does not happen quickly. I have been engaged in this process, consciously and not-so-consciously, for a little better than twenty years now. Restructuring the curriculum to be inclusive is all the more difficult because it involves personal change of an intellectual and political nature. We can eventually transform parts or all of our courses, but it takes time and patience. I continue to hope for and work for a higher education system with a totally transformed curriculum, where human experiences are based on, understood, and celebrated in terms of difference and diversity and not sameness, myths, and generalizations.

REFERENCES

Andersen, M. (April, 1988). Moving our minds: Studying women of color and restructuring sociology. *Teaching Sociology, 16,* 123-132.

Andersen, M., & Collins, P. H. (Eds.). (1992). *Race, class and gender.* Belmont, CA: Wadsworth Publishing.

Anzaldúa, G. (Ed.). (1990). *Making face, making soul: Haciendo caras, creative and critical perspectives by women of color.* San Francisco: Aunt Lute Foundation.

Brewer, R., Scott, B., & Ward, K. (1990). Curriculum integration workshop, presented at the Meetings of the Midwest Sociological Society, Chicago, IL.

Higginbotham, E. (May 31-June 2, 1990). Welcome, in *Integrating race and gender into the college curriculum: A workshop.* Center for Research on Women, Memphis State University.

Higginbotham, E. (1988). Integrating women of color into the curriculum. *Working Paper.* Center for Research on Women, Memphis State University.

Levine, A. (January/February, 1992). A time to act. *Change, 24* (1), 4-5.

McIntosh, M. (1988). White privilege and male privilege: A personal account of coming to see the correspondences through work in women's studies. *Working Paper Series,* Wellesley College.

McIntosh, M. (1983). Interactive phase of curriculum revision. *Working Paper Series.* Wellesley College.

Morrison, T. (1987). *Beloved.* NewYork: Knopf.

Moraga, C. & Anzaldúa, G. (Eds.). (1983). *This bridge called my back: Writings by radical women of color.* New York: Kitchen Table: Women of Color Press.

Piercy, M. (1976). *Woman on the edge of time.* New York: Ballantine Books.

Scott, B. (1988). *The making of a middle class black woman: A socialization for success.* Unpublished doctoral dissertation. Northwestern University. Evanston, IL.

Ward, K., & Morrison, J. (1990). *Curriculum integration workbook.* Carbondale, IL: Southern Illinois University.

A MULTICULTURAL PERSPECTIVE IN THE WOMEN'S STUDIES CLASSROOM

by
Martha E. Thompson

"I'm sick of hearing about the poor, about the blacks, and about the women. Can't we just talk about regular people?"

Student's response to a new course entitled
Social Inequality

"What does a poor black dyke's misery have to do with me?"

Student's response to a selection from *This Bridge Called My Back*

"These statistics don't apply everywhere. Where I work, black and Hispanic women who don't know anything are getting the best jobs."

Student's response to lecture on work

"How did that Hispanic woman get herself in such a mess?"

Student's response to a woman in the video *Neighborhood Women*

"If those women weren't so fat and could speak good English, they could go somewhere."

Student's response to *The Woman's Film*

Comments like the above have typically come just after I have complimented myself on an excellent choice of a reading, film, or lecture topic. Such comments have stunned me with their bitterness and anger. Such comments have exacerbated existing hostilities and widened the gulf between already divided groups of people. Such comments have made me question whether or not I am cut out for teaching. Such comments represent the risk all of us take when we attempt to integrate a multicultural perspective into our curriculum. Such comments demonstrate the importance of integrating a multicultural perspective throughout the curriculum.

This essay is intended as a contribution to the ongoing discussion about how to integrate a multicultural perspective into women's studies courses. The approach I will discuss grew out of my experience in teaching at Northeastern Illinois University, a state-supported university of 10,500 with an established women's studies program. Northeastern has a female majority and a student population highly diversified by age, ethnicity, literacy skills, race, religion, physical ability, political perspectives, sexual orientation, and social class. Most of the students live and work in highly segregated neighborhoods or communities.

In recent years, the greater availability of books, articles, films, and research centers analyzing the interrelationship of race, class, and gender has made it possible to integrate a multicultural perspective into every aspect of women's studies courses (e.g., Andersen & Collins, 1992; Asch & Fine, 1988; Anzaldúa, 1990, Bookman & Morgen, 1988; Collins, 1990; Rothenberg, 1992; The Research Clearinghouse and Curriculum Project on Women of Color and Southern Women; Wellesley College Center for Research on Women). Materials that integrate race, class, and gender are necessary for multicultural education, of course, but are not sufficient (Dines, 1994; Belkhir, Griffith, Sleeter, & Allsup, 1994).

As the above comments suggest, students are keenly aware that race, class, and gender are interconnected issues. The problem I have faced is how to expand their understanding of the connections without reinforcing their preconceived ideas. I have found that simply exposing students to new ideas about the connections between race, gender, and class is not enough. Their perceptions of these concepts are too deeply entrenched to be challenged by mere exposure. Students need to have opportunities to practice thinking in different ways in a safe environment. The process of creating a multicultural classroom in women's studies must include structuring a supportive environment in which students can experience the benefits of diversity when grappling with women's studies issues. Creating a supportive classroom environment is important because of the prejudices most students bring into the classroom.

The potential for developing an understanding of the intersections of gender, race, and class in a multicultural classroom is enormous. Abstract ideas can be developed, discussed, or tested from different sets of social experiences. Complexities and contradictions, suggesting new directions, can more easily be revealed and explored. Having the opportunity to communicate ideas to a multicultural audience can sharpen students' speaking, writing, and thinking skills. However, to work in such a way, diverse students with varying interests in women's studies and varying skills need a supportive environment and the opportunity to develop relevant knowledge and abilities. In the following pages, I will discuss strategies I have used to create such an environment and to nurture people's abilities to analyze concrete experience, discuss complex ideas, and formulate effective social action.

Structuring a Supportive Classroom

To structure a supportive classroom, I use techniques that encourage students to empathize with each other. To develop empathy, students need an opportunity to encounter the unique experiences of each individual in the classroom, to witness the feelings generated by these experiences, and to discover the influence of social forces on each individual's experience. Almost all of the strategies I use begin with students' writing and then reading or summarizing what they have written to a small or large group. Sometimes students work in pairs reading and commenting on what the other has written. Writing assignments give students an opportunity to practice a particular skill and to receive feedback. Students indicate that routinely writing before speaking gives them an opportunity to formulate their thoughts, makes them more confident in participating in class discussion, and improves their writing.

One strategy I have found consistently successful is to ask students to write about their own experiences with the assigned reading topic and then to read their essay to the rest of the class. For example, if students have done reading concerning race, gender, and class (e.g., Andersen & Collins, 1992, Section II), their assignment might be the following:

Write an essay in which you describe an incident or experience which first made you aware of race, class, or gender. Describe what you were doing, who you were with, what happened, how you felt about the experience, and what you did in the situation. Reflect on how this experience may have influenced you.

I ask for volunteers to share what they have written. When people share their stories, race, class, and gender are no longer abstract concepts but become key words to describe a variety of unique experiences and feelings.

Another strategy for building a sense of common purpose is to create small groups based on some combination of similar knowledge and experience (Thompson, 1993). For example, in creating groups for a discussion of feminism, I asked students to write about their familiarity with feminist literature and their experience with feminist groups. Based on individuals' self-assessments, groups were created by identifying clusters of people along the two dimensions of knowledge and experience. One group consisted of individuals who had read feminist literature prior to the course and had participated in at least one feminist group; another group was comprised of individuals who had not read any feminist writing prior to the course and had never participated in a feminist group; another group consisted of individuals familiar with feminist literature, but who had never participated in a feminist group; an additional group consisted of people who had participated in a feminist group, but had not read any feminist writings. All the groups were mixed by age, ethnicity, gender, and race.

Groups were asked to draw upon their reading (e.g., Andersen, 1993; Collins, 1989) and their own experience to discuss how gender, race, and class might affect people's involvement in feminism. For students to be able to begin to talk with each other, I have found it effective to give small groups a specific task to accomplish. For instance, to initiate a discussion of how gender, race, and class might affect involvement in feminism, I might ask each group to come up with five to ten images or ideas their reading associates with feminism. Once they have a list, they pick one or two images or ideas and then discuss how these images or ideas (e.g., women are discriminated against; patriarchy is the root of women's oppression; women's liberation is central to all struggles for revolutionary change) help explain the experiences of two or more groups that differ by class, gender, or race (e.g., middle-class African American men and middle-class African American women; poor white women and poor Latinas). The idea is to encourage students to discuss feminism in the context of specific groups.

Following small group discussions, a representative selected by the group presents the highlights of the discussion to the rest of the class. This process of reporting reveals that people with different levels of knowledge and experience can contribute to a common effort if able to work at their own level of competence. Feedback from students indicates that the collective description, analysis, or evaluation is always more complex and thought-provoking than that which any individual initially brought to the class or a single group developed.

Creating groups with commonalities takes careful planning before class to arrive at questions that will allow real commonalities and differences to emerge and takes class time to organize. I have found the results well worth the effort. When groups consist of people with similar self-assessments of knowledge and experience, participation is greater, the quality of the work is higher, and students are more likely to feel connected to each other than when groups are randomly created. Students who are knowledgeable, experienced, or skilled have indicated they can freely participate in these small groups without dominating them or getting bored. Students with less knowledge, experience, or skills have indicated they are not embarrassed or lost, but can freely participate in the group discussion at their level of competence. Throughout the course, the membership of groups changes since individual students' competence and experience vary, depending on the particular task the groups are assigned, giving students the opportunity to work with almost all other class members at one time or another.

Nurturing Effective Thinking

To encourage students to think effectively about the intersection of race, class, and gender, they need not only a structured, supportive environment, but also the opportunity to develop their critical skills. I break the process into stages of analysis, theory, and action (Sarachild, 1975; Hartsock, 1979) and work with the students to develop the knowledge and skills required for each stage. I describe each of these stages below.

Analyzing Personal Experience

The first step is to gather and analyze information about women's lives. The knowledge required includes knowing how women's lives have been trivialized and ignored by traditional sources of information and understanding that we must actively seek information about women from different social strata and life circumstances. The skills essential for this step include gathering information systematically, identifying patterns and variations, and developing or identifying concepts that reflect what has been observed. To gather and analyze this information requires an assumption that the lives of ordinary people are an important source of information and insight.

To increase the likelihood students will view ordinary people as important information sources, I select materials in which writers or speakers discuss the complex forces in their lives with intellectual and emotional depth and acknowledge the contradictions they experience in behavior, feeling, and thought. Whenever possible, I use materials describing the experiences of women and men who differ by age, class, disability, ethnicity, race, religion, and/or sexual orientation (e.g., Andersen and Collins, 1992; Rothenberg, 1992; Anzaldúa, 1990; Browne, Connors, & Stern, 1985; Driedger & Gray, 1992).

Thinking Thematically

Regardless of the work used, students need an opportunity to learn how to collect and analyze the information offered. Grounded theory (Glasner & Strauss, 1967) is an inductive strategy of theory building in which information is gathered, grouped into categories, and compared and contrasted with information from different groups or situations until no new information emerges. In adapting this approach to a classroom, I ask students to list key words or phrases from their reading to describe the experiences, emotions, or behaviors of a group of women. For example, when talking about feminism, I might ask students to identify words or phrases people use to describe feminism. Students have come up with words and phrases such as, "woman-centered," "equality," "man-hater," "empowerment of women," "lesbian," "humanism," "moving into action," "women's liberation." After words and phrases are listed, we go through the list item by item to group them. In working with the above list, for instance, students are likely to group "man-hater" in a different category than "woman-centered." Though different groups of students come up with different combinations of words and phrases, most students understand that the idea is to explore the relationship the words have to each other. Any set of words can be grouped into different categories. One possible grouping of the list above is *stereotypes* (e.g., manhater), *focus on women* (e.g., woman-centered, lesbian, women's liberation, empowerment of women), *focus on female-male relations* (e.g., equality, humanism), *action-oriented* (e.g., moving into action). From this grouping, we see that to explore feminism, we will need to focus on women only, as well as on women in relation to men; we will need to consider social action and be prepared to grapple with stereotypes.

I make it clear these labels are concepts, words representing general ideas we can use to guide our discussion of ways feminism applies to different groups of women or situations. At this point, I might give students an assignment to reread earlier selections or new selections to compare and contrast different groups or situations in relationship to the concepts we have just identified. What stereotypes about feminists, women, or other groups, for example, do they find in their reading? Do they find a discussion of *relationships between women and men?* In what ways does a writer *focus on women?* What *actions* does the writer suggest?

Through this process of comparison and contrast, students see the utility of a concept that applies to a diversity of experiences; they can also see variations in the ways different groups of women experience what the concept is attempting to describe. In this instance, students find, of course, that feminists are not the only group stereotyped; they also find feminist writers differ in the extent they focus on women and on the relationships between women and men; and they discover feminists differ in their orientation to action. Once we have discussed these initial concepts, we generate a list of questions we have about the topic or issue we have been addressing. This sets the stage for evaluating others' ideas about the issue. For instance, what stereotypes are associated with different groups we are studying? Is the primary focus of a writer on a group of women only or on relationships between women and men? Does a writer or group propose social actions? What kinds of actions?

<u>Evaluating Ideas</u>

Students generally enjoy analyzing people's experience but have a more difficult time evaluating ideas they read. They need support and guidance to read carefully, systematically, and critically. I assign works that use everyday language, not jargon or unnecessarily complex vocabulary or sentence structure and have many concrete examples and illustrations (e.g., Andersen & Collins, 1992; Anzaldua, 1990; Asch & Fine, 1988; Bookman & Morgen, 1988; Browne, Connors, & Stern, 1985; Cordova, 1986; Rothenberg, 1992). I also work with students to develop an approach to reading. Initial assignments explicitly identify what to look for in the reading:

1. What is the main point of the essay?
2. What are the key concepts and how are they defined? How do they relate to each other?
3. What does the writer say about how her or his writing fits with other writing on this topic? Is it a new area of discussion? Is it an addition to an ongoing discussion? Is it a challenge to another point of view?

I also introduce students to ways of using their earlier analyses of women's lives to evaluate ideas. One approach is to ask students to see how many of the questions raised earlier by the class are answered. For example:

1. Does the writer consider any concepts similar to those we developed from our analysis of women's experience? How does the writer define the concept? How similar is it to the understanding we developed?
2. Does the writer address the intersection of gender, race, and class? How does the writer deal with the intersection?

I usually lead the first evaluation discussion with the whole class. Later evaluation discussions typically occur in small groups followed by reporters sharing the highlights of each group's discussion with the rest of the class. This strategy for evaluating feminist scholarship is generally well received by students. Because their own analysis of women's experience is part of the standard of evaluation, students do not feel manipulated or coerced into accepting a particular viewpoint.

<u>Formulating Social Action</u>

The process of bringing a multicultural perspective into the women's studies classroom involves formulating effective social actions. To develop and evaluate effective feminist actions, students benefit from knowing about historical and contemporary visions, the current state of the issue under discussion, a range of actions feminists have taken, and the consequences of those actions. Key skills for students to learn are translating abstract ideas into concrete realities and implementing a concrete idea.

Using the skills developed earlier, students can draw on the writings of activists to develop familiarity with visions and strategies for change (Bunch 1983a; 1983b). For students, translating abstract ideas into concrete realities and developing attitudes supportive of a range of actions requires special attention. One strategy I have used is to have small groups brainstorm ways an individual, a particular group (e.g., our class), or society can implement an idea and then have each group share its ideas with the rest of the class. The small groups are typically comprised of people with similar knowledge about the topic under discussion and similar experience in taking risks (See earlier discussion of creating a supportive classroom). In a class session on building bridges among diverse groups, for example, the class was divided into groups based on their familiarity with readings about racial prejudice and discrimination and their experience with taking public action against racism. The task was to identify how they could individually and in a group implement the idea of building bridges in their everyday lives. Because groups had a different set of knowledge and experiences to draw upon, the class identified a long list of immediate actions, including options for the least to the most experienced bridge builders in the classroom. Asking students to try one of these strategies for bridge building and then to report on it to the class encourages students to take risks and to develop a deeper understanding of social action.

Another strategy I have used to encourage students to implement their ideas is to ask students to write a letter to a particular audience (e.g., the student paper, a local newspaper, a family member, a friend) about an issue related to one we have discussed. Students can be encouraged to deal in some way with the impact this issue may have on women from diverse backgrounds or experiences. Even if students do not send the letter, writing to an outside audience about a contemporary issue gives class members a concrete focus for discussing how they feel about taking risks and the possible consequences of action or nonaction. Seeing the variety of audiences and strategies students choose when addressing issues also expands students' appreciation of the strengths of a multicultural group for formulating social actions.

Conclusion

Diversity can be an asset in the classroom if women's studies teachers consciously create opportunities for the uniqueness of each student to be revealed while simultaneously building on commonalities and differences to involve students in the process of analyzing women's experience, evaluating ideas, and formulating social actions. For students to develop their skills and confidence they must begin by working at their level of competence with others who have similar levels of knowledge and experience. Encouraging groups to combine their work with others builds solidarity among the diverse groups while simultaneously contributing to a more complex understanding of society.

Involving students in collectively analyzing experience, evaluating ideas, and formulating actions requires that women's studies teachers genuinely view students as rich resources of insight. To assist students in discovering their abilities, we need to create opportunities for students to develop their knowledge and skills. Since I began to work constructively with diversity in the classroom, I have been richly rewarded by the work students have done, supportive and stimulating classes, and improvements in students' reading, writing, and thinking skills. My own enjoyment of and commitment to teaching have been renewed and enhanced.

ACKNOWLEDGEMENTS

122

Thanks to students in women's studies courses for their ideas, feedback, and inspiration. Thanks also to J. Q. Adams and Janice R. Welsch for their helpful comments on an earlier version of this essay and to Shelly Bannister, Diane Haslett, and Susan Stall, members of my writing group for their encouragement, suggestions, and insights.

REFERENCES

Andersen, M. (1993). *Thinking about women: Sociological perspectives in sex and gender.* NewYork: MacMillan.

Andersen, M., & Collins, P. H.(Eds.). (1992). *Race, class, and gender: An anthology.* Belmont, CA: Wadsworth.

Anzaldúa, G. (Ed.). (1990). *Making face, making soul, haciendo caras.* San Francisco: Aunt Lute Foundation.

Asch, A., & Fine, M. (Eds.). (1988). *Women with disabilities: Essays in psychology, culture, and politics.* Philadelphia, PA: Temple University Press.

Belkhir, J., Griffith, S., Sleeter, C., & Allsup, C. (1994). Race, sex, class and multicultural education: Women's angle of vision. *Race, Sex, & Class, 1*(2), 7-22.

Bookman, A., & Morgen, S. (Eds.). (1988). *Women and the politics of empowerment.* Philadelphia, PA: Temple University Press.

Browne, S. E., Connors, D., & Stern, N. (Eds.). (1985). *With the power of each breath: A disabled women's anthology.* Pittsburgh, PA: Cleis Press.

Bunch, C. (1983a). *Going public with our vision.* Denver: Antelope Publications.

Bunch, C. (1983b). Not by degrees: Feminist theory and education. In C. Bunch, & A. Pollack (Eds.), *Learning our way: Essays in feminist education* (pp. 248-260). Trumansburg, NY: The Crossing Press.

Collins, P. H. (1990). *Black feminist theory: Knowledge, consciousness, and the politics of empowerment.* Cambridge, MA: Unwin Hyman.

Collins, P. H. (1989). The social construction of black feminist thought. *Signs: Journal of Women in Culture and Society, 14*(4): 745-773.

Cordova, T. et al. (Eds.). (1986). *Chicana voices: Intersections of class, race, and gender.* Albuquerque, NM: University of New Mexico Press.

Dines, G. (1994). What's left of multiculturalism? *Race, Sex, & Class, 1*(2), 23-34.

Driedger, D., & Gray, S. (Eds.). (1992). *Imprinting our image: An international anthology by women with disabilities.* Canada: Gynergy.

Glaser, B. G., & Strauss, A. L. (1967). *The discovery of grounded theory.* Chicago: Aldine.

Hartsock, N. (1979). Feminist theory and revolutionary strategy. In Z. R. Eisenstein (Ed.), *Capitalist Patriarchy* (pp. 56-77). New York: Monthly Review.

Rothenberg, P. S. (Ed.). (1992). *Race, class, and gender in the United States*. New York (2nd ed.): St. Martin's Press.

Sarachild, K. (1975). Consciousness-raising: A radical weapon. In *Feminist revolution* (pp. 131-137). New Paltz, NY: Redstockings.

Thompson, M. E. (1993). Building groups on students' knowledge and experience. *Teaching Sociology, 21*(1): 95-99.

BEYOND VASCO DA GAMA:
UNLEARNING EUROCENTRIC PHALLACIES
IN THE CLASSROOM

by
Nada Elia

I was attempting to solve a crossword puzzle once when I came across a clue that struck me as unfathomable: "the first man who circled the southern tip of Africa." I left its space blank and moved on to the next line, hoping the empty squares would fill up as I completed the puzzle. But my roommate, who was looking over my shoulder, eagerly volunteered "Vasco da Gama." As an Arab in the United States, I have come to expect a lot of Eurocentric tunnel vision. But this was extreme in its presumption that not one of the millions of Africans, who for thousands of years had lived by the shores of southern Africa, could accomplish such an achievement until a Portuguese sailor showed them how.

As I wondered at how even highly intelligent Americans can accept such blatant false-hoods as facts, I was reminded of yet another incident that had puzzled me upon my arrival in the U. S. It was fall, the beginning of an academic year, and the end of the baseball season. During a class break, some students were discussing the World Series with the professor. I asked the professor, who seemed quite a sports fan, what countries were competing. "Canada and the U. S.," he said. Eager to learn new things—baseball not being a popular sport in the Middle East—I went on with more questions, about which countries had participated in the series and which had made the semi-finals. "Only Canada and the U. S. play in the World Series," the professor responded matter-of-factly. Oddly enough, in a doctoral program in comparative literature at a respectable American university, I was alone in finding it absurd that any competition involving only two countries should claim to be universal. But more so, I was acutely aware of the arrogance behind this claim.

Today, as a teacher fully committed to offering my students a multicultural education and primarily concerned with providing alternatives to Eurocentric views, I begin each of my courses with my crossword anecdote, or the World Series one. For the last four years, I have taught courses in world literature and postcolonial literature in Indiana and Illinois. My students have been primarily European Americans, who took my class because it is required of education majors. In a few years, they will likely be teachers themselves. This article does not address a teacher's need to recognize the diversity of students ever present in all classrooms, even the most seemingly homogeneous—for diversity is not only ethnic, but manifests itself in numerous ways, in, for example, different sexual orientations, religious upbringing or the lack of it, having experienced child neglect and/or abuse, growing up in a traditional family or the much more common "contemporary" one. Rather, I want to provide the teacher with some suggestions as to how to approach students required to take multicultural classes they have little initial interest in or much prejudiced resistance to.

Over the last few years, I have developed a few strategies that counter the resistance of students hostile to diversity, as well as encourage them to view a multicultural education as a plus, as a wealth of information that, far from seeking to replace the traditional canon, attempts instead to revive it, to infuse it with a vitality that spares it the fate of Greek tragedy: classic, epic, but falling short of addressing contemporary issues.

On the first day of class, I ask my students for the name of the first person to have circled the southern tip of Africa. Occasionally, a student will volunteer the infamous piece of infor-mation. If nobody does, I write it on the board: Vasco da Gama. Then I tell my students that he was Portuguese and give them the dates of his birth and death: 1469-1524 A.D. Hungry for information (or eager to secure their A) they write it all down. I go on to ask them if they can suggest any reasons as to why no African had been able to circle Africa's southern tip, though they had navigated those shores for thousands of years before the first Europeans arrived there. Of course, no one can provide a satisfactory answer. There isn't one; that Vasco da Gama should be the first simply doesn't make sense.

My approach may be deemed a little harsh for a first day of class, but it has been my experience that this reality check is extremely effective. If it were a student who provided the name Vasco da Gama—and more often than not that student is a crossword puzzle fan—I make sure that they do not feel foolish by pointing out that, according to numerous reference books, they are correct. Moreover, haven't all the rest of the students copied the data down without any questions? Then I ask my students to please cross out whatever notes they have taken, since my class requires critical thinking, not dictionary knowledge, and, as we have just seen, the two are frequently at odds. Critical thinking, I explain, does not always provide the answers, but it avoids incorrect answers. Thus we will never know who made the first lap around the Cape of Good Hope, but we do know it does not make sense that it should be a Portuguese sailor.

Moreover, I find it important to lay the ground rules in that first session: we are here to unlearn certain misinformation we have received, as much if not more than we hope to learn new material. And during the semester, when students are understandably frustrated at the lack of answers to some of the questions we raise, I can refer to this session and ask them "Do you want convenience? I can give you the 'Da Gama equivalent'...." When I present lack of closure in these terms, they stop pressing for the correct answer. Indeed, da Gama has become one of my favorite historical examples, for he also allows me on that first day of class to introduce my students to the evils of racism (the denial of the humanity of Africans), sexism (Were there no women on Da Gama's ship? Why not?), and classism (Surely he had a whole crew to help him; why aren't they mentioned?). Da Gama also makes a good starting point for a discussion of European cultural hegemony and the numerous factors that contributed to the successful imposition of one paradigm over others.

Again, the importance of our first class must be emphasized, for it clearly establishes that the class allows, indeed favors, alternative modes of thinking. In a recent article, Linda Dittmar (1993) argues against leaving sensitive themes such as homosexual love till the end of a course. I agree with her, for the hegemonic discourse that has silenced these topics fully surrounds us, and the fourteen to sixteen weeks that make up a semester are barely sufficient for their discussion in a mature way. We should treat our students as adults. They are adults: they can drive a car, juggle credit cards, and, with very few exceptions, are of voting age. As I realize that the transition from sheltered home life to college campus is not easy, I help them recognize, or question, prejudices in a friendly environment.

One way I have found very effective in promoting individual thought is requiring students to formulate an opinion about the material they have just read. I require students to turn in, on the day we start discussing a new text, an index card with the following:
- three to five questions raised by the text;
- a page reference to a passage they would like discussed in class; and
- an opinion about the reading. Did they like it? Why or why not?

I emphasize to my students they will receive full credit for the index card, regardless of contents, the quality of their questions, or the positiveness of their response. Moreover, I stress that it is fully up to them to identify themselves, if they want to, when I answer their questions in class or read out their opinion. I identify them only in the case of the passage they would like to have us discuss together, since I then ask them to lead the discussion themselves. Whether it is because they indeed feel distance from the dominant discourse they would publicly express or because they are merely testing out alternatives or challenging assumptions, the students offer a rich array of responses that allow for lively debate.

The index cards are useful in many ways. They allow me to evaluate students' needs from the questions they ask and to prepare the next lesson accordingly. They give insight into the students' readings of texts. Through student-led discussion of the passage they have chosen—and quite frequently, two to three will choose the same passage, spontaneously creating group discussion—the learning experience becomes collaborative. Finally, students whose opinions would otherwise be underrepresented feel empowered when I read out their opinions. Here I do use my prerogative as a teacher in that I privilege original thoughts by sharing these with the rest of the class. In doing so, the traditionalists are not silenced, for they are, of course, entitled to respond, and most speakers of the hegemonic discourse feel safe speaking up.

A teacher communicates knowledge best when s/he successfully avoids alienating even the most resistant students, and humor plays an important role, helping in many instances to release tension. A few weeks into a course, as I feel my students weary of our politicized class, I tell them about the press conference I am calling next week, for I have a major announcement to make: I have discovered penicillin! Well, why not? Columbus discovered America, didn't he? Why can't I discover penicillin? Thus humor is not used to distract students from the seriousness of the matter at hand, but rather to present it to them in more acceptable ways, especially when their long-held beliefs are being shattered.

Despite my efforts to break classroom hierarchy, my students are ever aware that I am the authority, that I have special power in the classroom. When I am willing to show them that I, too, am quite fallible, they feel safer about acknowledging mistakes they have made. I tell them how readily I misjudged someone when I assumed that a man I had just met at a bar was drunk, simply because of his accent. He was an African American from a small town in Arkansas. Had I made a racist assumption? I meant no harm, but did I hurt him? Are we ever blameless?

It is easy to denounce racism. It is more challenging to do so without alienating European American students whose belief in a glorious heritage is shattered as they discover their ancestors, just like everybody else's, have at times murdered, pillaged, raped, stolen, and engaged in racial wars. When a student writes that s/he is ashamed of being white, it is essential to explain that shame and guilt can be paralyzing feelings or incitement to action, to change. Most are happy to know there is a positive way out. Yet I would in no way suggest my method is infallible. Very recently, I had a student who grew more angry at me, or the material I was presenting, with each class period and finally exploded during our discussion of the mistreatment of Native Americans by the Europeans. This student claimed that denouncing racism and sexism only aggravates these issues, and he argued that tolerance of others cannot be promoted through a discussion of past wrongdoings. Clearly, as a white male, he felt he had come under attack one time too many. Rather than turn this episode into a one-on-one confrontation between him and me, I asked the rest of the students if they in any way agreed with him. If that were the case, I would change my approach. Fortunately, the students came to my aid, as they explained to him the necessity of knowing how and why certain acts were wrong. Reassured, I was able to add that, just as with addictions or sexual abuse, one has to acknowledge the problem in order to treat it.

Because students learn in different ways, a combination of strategies is necessary when introducing them to concepts they have been trained to regard with suspicion, whether these concepts be feminism, anti-imperialism, or homosexuality. One simple yet effective way is to punctuate class handouts with empowering proverbs. Among my favorites are:

"Until the lions have their historians, tales of hunting will always glorify the hunter."

"The mind of a bigot is like the pupil of the eye: the more light you shine on it, the more it contracts."

"Freedom is merely privilege extended, unless enjoyed by one and all."

"Columbus didn't discover America, he invaded it."

I have included these on my syllabi or exams. You can ask students to contribute their own. One semester, our class started a racist/sexist/homophobic jokes bulletin board. This project was enlightening to those students for whom the prejudice was not evident, and who by the middle of the semester felt comfortable enough to inquire about how a joke was offensive. A bonus I had not anticipated was the broader audience this display reached, as other classes met in the same classroom and frequently commented on our clippings. Photocopies of the collage of some very prominent U. S. figures accompanied by the line "History has set the record a little too straight" never fails to affect students, as they realize that some of their heroes or role models were homosexual.

Students are also less likely to reject new concepts when they are presented to them not solely as the teacher's opinion, but as material of interest and validity to many of their classmates. Again, the index cards are helpful, since reading a positive student response to an alternative text makes the promoters and/or duplicators of the dominant discourse realize the diversity of opinions among their peers; the teacher's perspective is not singled out as that of a hostile authority to be resisted. This is especially helpful when the instructor is visibly other or when s/he openly acknowledges holding alternative views that are feminist, Marxist, or Afrocentric.

Some texts I have used in my classes have elicited very strong responses in my students. Two stand out at the top of a list of works that have sparked some of our best debates: Nawal al-Saadawi's *Woman at Point Zero* and Mehdi Charef's *Tea in the Harem*. The first is the narrative, defiant and unrepentant, of a prostitute on death row for killing her pimp. It is disturbing, as it confronts us with ugly aspects of life we would rather ignore. *Woman at Point Zero* also allows for a discussion of homosexuality, through hints that the prostitute may be lesbian, as well as for a critique of religion's role in the subjugation of women. The book does not contain a single passage that could be termed obscene even by the prudish. I generally also assign chapters from *Sex Works: Writings from Women in the Sex Industry,* which represents the views of COYOTE (Cast Off Your Old Tired Ethics) and WHISPER (Women Hurt in Systems of Prostitution Engaging in Resistance).

Tea in the Harem is the autobiography of a young immigrant in the Parisian housing projects. He writes of doing drugs, torching neighborhood cars, pimping, harassing a teacher, all before being jailed for taking a joyride in a stolen car. Written in street language, the text is explosive. I am ever surprised at how readily my students say they relate to this criminal. Like the prostitute in *Woman at Point Zero,* he is also a victim, pulling us into the gray zone where absolutes are questioned. One of my students, a senior in law enforcement, wrote me that he feels he will be a different, more understanding police officer now that he has taken my class.

To counter the resistance of students who believe sexism is a thing of the past or only present today in non-Western cultures, no book has proven more helpful than Gerd Brantenberg's *Egalia's Daughters*. Through a humorous role reversal, this novel by a contemporary Norwegian novelist successfully denounces the continuing pervasive male dominance in modern European society. After reading it, my students no longer find it perfectly natural, and fair, that they should be called fresh**men** their first year at college, or that they should earn a **bachelor's** degree, or a **master's** or that, even if they choose to retain their names after marriage, they will still be carrying a man's name, their father's. Men who say they would readily change their baby's diaper at a restaurant have to reconsider when they realize most baby-changing facilities are in women's restrooms. Interestingly, it has been my experience and that of my friend and colleague, Loretta Kensinger (who first suggested the novel to me), that most women thoroughly enjoy the novel, while men find it extremely disturbing.

Another text that produces a divided reaction allowing for valuable classroom discussion is the play, *Trial of Dedan Kimathi,* by Ngugi wa Thiong'o and Micere Githae Mugo. In this case, the divide falls along racial lines, since African American students find it empowering, while European Americans criticize it for any number of reasons, including that it is a racist text, a charge that is definitely incorrect. The polarized responses to both of these selections allow for an enriching exchange of ideas. Another text, Buchi Emecheta's *Second Class Citizen,* tells of a Nigerian woman's successful struggle to overcome sexism at home as well as both sexism and racism in England. The response to this novel is generally unanimous, overwhelmingly positive, facilitating discussion of some of its underlying themes: domestic violence, marital rape, a woman's right to reproductive choice, mental emancipation.

These texts are but a few of a multitude of readily available, easily accessible titles that make the move away from a canon loaded with Eurocentric phallacies not only possible, but fun. Whether in women's studies classes or in general survey of literature courses, sociology courses or multicultural studies, we can and should assign them. We make a difference. We impact our students, who will impact others. Let us realize this potential for positive change by exposing our students to alternative texts, worldviews, and instructional methods.

REFERENCES

Brantenberg, G. (1985). *Egalia's daughters.* (L. Mackay, Trans. In cooperation with Brantenberg). Seattle: Seal.

Charef, M. (1989). *Tea in the harem.* (E. Emery, Trans.). London: Serpent's Tail.

Dittmar, L. (1994). Conflict and resistance in the multicultural classroom. In J. Q. Adams & J. R. Welsch (Eds.), *Multicultural education: Strategies for implementation in colleges and universities, Vol. 3.* Macomb, IL: Illinois Staff and Curriculum Developers Association.

Emecheta, B. (1983). *Second class citizen.* New York: Braziller.

Saadawi, N. (1983). *Woman at point zero.* (S. Hetata, Trans.). London: Zed.

wa Thiong'o N., & Mugo, M. G. (1976). *The trial of Dedan Kimathi.* London: Heinemann.

MULTICULTURAL MATHEMATICS

by

Melfried Olson, Judith K. Olson, and Howard L. Hansen

Introduction

"What does it mean to do mathematics?" Before trying to provide an answer to this question two comments are in order. First, to say that a person learns mathematics by doing mathematics brings several assumptions to the forefront: that learning mathematics is an active pursuit; that mathematics is learned in a contextual framework; and that mathematics is a pattern of communication. Second, each of these assumptions brings us to the role of culture in the teaching and learning of mathematics. In every culture there are ways of knowing mathematics. These ways of knowing may differ from culture to culture and certainly impact the manner in which students engage in, value, and learn mathematics. That is, these differences may influence how mathematics is valued, how learners interact when learning mathematics, or what it means to *know mathematics*. Each of these ideas has implications for interaction with students in the mathematics classroom.

Why is the multicultural question in mathematics important? According to Banks (1994), "Multicultural education, as its major architects have conceived it during the last decade, is not an ethnic- or gender-specific movement. It is a movement designed to empower all students to become knowledgeable, caring, and active citizens in a deeply troubled and ethnically polarized nation and world" (p. 1). The National Council of Teachers of Mathematics (NCTM) addressed this issue for school mathematics. Under the topic of *Opportunity for all*, NCTM (1989) states:

The social injustices of past school practices can no longer be tolerated. Current statistics indicate that those who study advanced mathematics are most often white males. Women and most minorities study less mathematics and are seriously underrepresented in careers using science and technology. Creating a just society in which women and various ethnic groups enjoy equal opportunities and equitable treatment is no longer an issue. Mathematics has become a critical filter for employment and full participation in our society. We cannot afford to have the majority of our population mathematically illiterate. Equity has become an economic necessity. (p. 4)

Similar issues in mathematics education are addressed by the National Center for Research in Mathematical Sciences Education (NCRMSE, 1994):

Mathematics instruction has been more accessible to students who are members of society's dominant racial, cultural, social class, and gender groups than to those who are not. From a perspective of equity and fairness, all student groups need access to mathematics instruction and opportunities to excel in mathematics. The reform of school mathematics provided the educational community with possibilities for addressing the needs of an increasingly diverse student population. As they develop policy, research, and practice, educators will need to combine concerns for both equity and reform. If they fail to do so, students who do not come from dominant groups may, once again, be denied full participation. The options educators have and the choices they can make are in the areas of curriculum pedagogy, assessment, and school contexts that facilitate student learning. (p. 1)

While Lynn (1994), NCRMSE, Federal Cooodinating Council for Science, Engineering, and Technology (1993), and NCTM discuss the equity issue in pre-college mathematics and science, many believe that the issues of equity, especially in mathematics and science, for higher education are just as valid. Olson and Olson (1991) give three principles from which faculty members can try to build success: all students can learn mathematics; all students should be given the opportunity to learn mathematics; and ideas and programs should not be discarded because they are not perfect. No matter what mathematical concepts and skills they possess, students in higher education generally are more academically successful than those who do not access higher education. Faculty in higher education must face the reality that they get the best students who complete high school. They must decide how to deal with these students. If this group is multicultural, the problem may even be more difficult. What can be done? As indicated above, no perfect answer to this challenge exists. However, the following three ideas may be useful: developing meaningful mathematical tasks, establishing high expectations, and providing student mentoring.

Meaningful Mathematical Tasks

Among the dimensions of multicultural education identified by Banks (1994) that can be addressed by mathematics teachers are content integration and the knowledge construction process. Content integration is concerned with how teachers use examples from a variety of cultures to illustrate key concepts and generalizations in their discipline. While mathematics teachers can insert multicultural content into their instruction, this can also reinforce stereotypes if it is the only attempt made to include multiculturalism. An analysis of the knowledge construction process is probably of more importance to mathematics teachers. According to Banks (1994), "A multicultural focus on knowledge construction includes discussion of the ways in which the implicit cultural assumptions, frames of reference, perspectives, and biases within a discipline influence the construction of knowledge" (p. 6). In general, the issues of multicultural mathematics education demand a review of significant concerns in mathematics teaching. A critical area is personal/cultural knowledge: the concepts and interpretations that students derive from personal experiences in their various cultural settings. For example, Slavin (1983) indicates that many African American and Mexican American students are more likely to succeed in a cooperative learning environment.

College instructors of beginning level classes often face a challenge concerning meaningful mathematical tasks. Many textbooks are written from a skills-to-application basis rather than a skills-from-application basis. This often means that students must wait to see the significance of the applicability of the mathematics they are learning. The appropriate choice of a meaningful mathematical task should assist the student in making use of mathematics while simultaneously learning more about the content of mathematics. According to NCTM (1991) these mathematical tasks should

engage students' interest; develop students' mathematical understandings and skills; stimulate students to make connections and develop a coherent framework for mathematical ideas; call for problem formulation, problem solving, and mathematical reasoning; promote communication about mathematics; represent mathematics as an ongoing human activity; display sensitivity to, and draw on students' diverse background experiences and dispositions; [and] promote the development of all students' dispositions to do mathematics. (p. 25)

The tasks chosen by instructors frame students' opportunity to learn, structure thinking about concepts and procedures, convey messages about the role of mathematics, help define what doing mathematics means, and assist in the development of students' problem-solving ability. "In selecting, adapting, or generating mathematical tasks, teachers base their decisions on three areas of concern: the mathematical content, the students, and the ways in which students learn mathematics" (NCTM, 1991, pp. 3-4).

The selection of mathematical tasks to achieve all of the goals described above is not trivial. However, it is significant that the selection of meaningful mathematics tasks clearly includes the concepts described for a multicultural education. The selection of an appropriate mathematical task is just the beginning of the process. Implied in the descriptions of mathematical tasks is the need for pedagogy different from the traditional methods. This, too, meets the criteria for a multicultural education. The instructor must be more of a director of instruction, one who poses questions, asks students to clarify and justify ideas, monitors discussions, and determines when to expand on ideas presented by students. An instructor who chooses to operate in this manner must also begin to analyze teaching and learning. Instructors must observe, listen, and gather information to assess students differently. Instructors must give more meaningful direct feedback to students, which helps to begin the mentoring process described later.

The focus on meaningful mathematical tasks suggests that an alternative to the traditional classroom culture would be developed. It can be argued that, largely as a result of traditional instruction, students have developed beliefs about mathematical classroom culture that are often counterproductive. For example, students often view mathematics as a collection of rules to be memorized and look to the teacher as the authority figure who has the one right answer. Several current practices need to be reexamined to change these cultural beliefs. One must think about such matters as what students already know and what they can work on next, the issue of prerequisite skills, who should do the talking, and how students should work together. One quick classroom culture check for an instructor is to answer the following question upon teaching a class, "What did you do in class today?" If the response begins with "Today, I covered..." much is said about classroom culture. If this is a consistent response, the instructor may be creating a classroom culture that reinforces counterproductive beliefs about the learning of mathematics. Classrooms must become places where *students and instructors* work together.

The following statement by Woodrow (1986) shows the significance the choice of task has in the learning environment. He states:

It is a commonly held belief that mathematics is an essentially acultural subject. It is arguable whether this is a valid statement—the nature of argument and the language of implication are both culturally determined—but it is certainly not true that the teaching of mathematics can be acultural. The attempt to convey the ideas and concepts to the learner must take place using the metaphors and imagery available to the learner, and these are clearly the consequence of the society and culture within which the learner lives. (p. 229)

It is not surprising that those persons who hold the view that mathematics is culture free find it difficult to consider that differing pedagogical methods may be needed to reach a larger number of students. However, if one accepts the notion of socially constructed mathematical knowledge, both individual and broader cultural influences can be recognized. A person with this perspective will go beyond the quasi-trivialized inclusion of multiculturalism through historical remnants to the realization that cultural perspective may affect ways of thinking mathematically.

Usiskin (1994) provides a definite challenge to any mathematics teacher when he states, "Every mathematics course should allow for individual differences in **interest** by including a wide variety of activities and contexts which bring out the brilliance, surprise, applicability, and structure of mathematics, and in which students are given choices" (p. 12). While his comments are aimed at pre-college mathematics courses, the comments apply to college mathematics courses as well. This calls for mathematics instructors to bring out the interesting aspects and applicability of mathematics that drew many faculty members to the study of mathematics in the first place.

A perceived difficulty associated with the use of meaningful mathematical tasks is that to explore topics in depth usually means fewer topics are covered. The predicament—one can only know something about which one has thought, yet can only think about something one knows—is real. An instructor must decide whether to provide students with a large volume of topics less well connected or a small volume of more connected topics.

In summary, those who teach mathematics must wrestle with a new paradigm of teaching. Teachers must recognize that individuals investigate and internalize their world and the role of mathematics in that world in a relationship unique to their cultural setting. Teachers must be prepared to teach mathematics beyond the dualistic approach that continues to be fostered by almost all societies. Almost every teacher of mathematics has heard, or, heaven forbid, stated, "At least in mathematics there is a right answer." Mathematics instructors interact with students who bring a dualistic view of mathematics to the learning situation. If the students are reinforced in that idea by the manner in which the subject is taught, instructors should not be surprised students have questions about the use and value of mathematics.

High Expectations

The selection of meaningful mathematical tasks begins with a focus on sound and significant mathematics. Naturally, this implies high expectations for students and, perhaps more significantly, high expectations that all students can engage in and are capable of learning mathematics. Advocating higher academic expectations is consonant with the expectations of the population in general as well as of traditionally underrepresented groups. When the public was surveyed concerning standards for high school academic work, 61% of Americans agreed standards are too low. Seventy percent of African American parents with children in school share this view (Johnson & Immerwahr, 1994-95). Clark Atlanta University has eliminated remedial mathematics courses in an effort to demonstrate a commitment to higher expectations (Morgan, 1993). Of course, along with these higher expectations, faculty members must commit to diligently working with students and must receive administrative support for their efforts. Higher education must not succumb to the institutionalization of lower expectations through tracking.

At the high school level, Mirel and Angus (1994) report that the effect of increased academic coursework in the public schools between 1973 and 1990 contributed to improved student outcomes, especially among minorities, and did not lead to an increase in the dropout rate. "Unfortunately, the increases in academic coursetaking by minority students have not resulted in subsequent increases in college enrollments, especially on the part of black students" (p. 41).

The connection between questioning and expectations is significant. Teachers enhance the academic integrity of their courses by asking meaningful questions and allowing students opportunities to explore the questions before expecting a response. Questions can frame a situation so that it forms the basis of a meaningful mathematical exploration. Raspberry (1991) reported about a university summer program for engineering students from underrepresented groups that started to show remarkable results, but only after a ten-year period. Project staff made a simple adjustment. They quit treating the students as if they would have academic problems and treated them like the capable students they were.

As students are confronted with meaningful questions, are given enough time to respond, and are allowed alternative methods of explanation, achievement levels improve. Questioning sets an expectation of academic achievement and enhances the personal connection between teacher and student as well as between students. Nelson-Barber and Meier (1990) report that the type of questions asked in classroom settings, and the narrow range of acceptable answers, keep poor and traditionally marginalized students from active engagement and lead to negative perception of student abilities. This is clearly an area in which teachers can have an impact on instruction. Mathematics instructors who focus on teaching concepts find it easy to begin the questioning process. Waiting for students to respond, being nonjudgmental in handling responses, and nurturing all students so they feel free to respond are other matters. Instructors using this approach find it rewarding because of the increased student involvement and higher-order thinking. This journey, once started, is irreversible.

Mentoring

Discussing the success of women in the sciences, Tobias (1990) and Buerk (1986) cite strong mentoring and personal involvement as key factors in that success. Faculty mentoring is frequently seen in its most positive context in graduate studies, especially at the doctoral level. A doctoral student often works closely with one professor. This professor becomes the model from which professionalism as well as content is learned. The importance of professionalism is seen in the connections doctoral students make when seeking funding or responding to postdoctoral opportunities.

Mentoring at this level of intensity for all undergraduate students is likely impossible. However, some aspects of mentoring are possible. As there are not enough African, Asian, Latino, or Native American mathematics faculty members to serve as mentors and role models, all members of the profession must actively engage in this endeavor. Mentoring students in the major, especially in mathematics, is possible due to the relatively small number of mathematics majors at most institutions of higher education. Mentoring all students who take mathematics classes is more difficult. Yet some possibilities exist in addressing this. For example, many majors require students to take a sequence of two mathematics courses. Arrangements can be made for the same instructor to teach a sequence thus creating an opportunity for two-semester involvement with students.

Mentoring can also be connected to the idea of meaningful mathematical tasks and the associated pedagogy. In a broad sense, mentoring includes extended communication opportunities between students and teachers. When appropriate tasks demand students prepare projects, make presentations in class, write about conceptual ideas, and actively engage in problem solving, the opportunity for mentoring is available. In fact, when instructors provide appropriate verbal or written feedback, engage students in problem solving, or ask for reflective action on the part of the student, mentoring exists. Instructional strategies that require students to reflect on the teaching and learning of mathematics, that build upon the experiences of the learner, that involve decision making in context, and from which the student must construct meaning connect well with multicultural education. Banks (1994) states, "Reflective action by citizens is also an integral part of multicultural theory. Multicultural education…links knowledge, values, empowerment, and action. Multicultural education is also postmodern in its assumptions about knowledge and knowledge construction…. Multicultural theorists maintain that knowledge is positional, that it relates to the knower's values and experiences, and that knowledge implies action" (p. 2). These strategies are the foundation upon which students can build mathematical power.

Summary

This article describes three possibilities for meeting the multicultural realities and challenges of the mathematics classroom: developing meaningful mathematical tasks, establishing high expectations, and providing mentoring. These ideas, together with the following three thoughts, are important for mathematics teachers with respect to multicultural education. One, teachers need to restructure their thinking about who is capable of learning mathematics. Habits of mind are hard for teachers to break, especially when teachers can cite examples to support their way of thinking. Being able to cite examples of students from underserved populations who were not successful should not be a reason to conclude that no students from underserved populations can be successful. Similarly, citing examples of students from underserved populations who are successful in mathematics is no reason to conclude the task is complete. Two, all students need to know the part they and their culture have played in the creation and development of mathematical knowledge. We must look to current cultural usage and development as well as to historical examples. Three, instructors should come to know and respect all of their students just as they respect students majoring in their own field of study. Students must be taken as they come and assisted to where they want to go, whether or not they are planning to major in mathematics or a closely related field. Students should not be blamed or have their self-esteem attacked due to lack of knowledge and understanding. The task of the instructor is to move them to knowledge, understanding, application, synthesis. This may be difficult but it is not impossible.

REFERENCES

Banks, J. A. (1994). Multicultural education: Development, dimensions, and challenges. In J. Q. Adams & J. R. Welsch (Eds.) *Multicultural prism: Voices from the field* (pp. 1-14). (Reprinted in Section I of this volume). Macomb, IL: Illinois Staff and Curriculum Developers Association.

Buerk, D. (1986). *Carolyn Werbel's journal: Voicing the struggle to make meaning of mathematics.* Wellesley, MA: Wellesley College, Center for Research on Women.

Federal Coordinating Council for Science, Engineering, and Technology. (1993). *Pathways to excellence: A federal strategy for science, mathematics, engineering, and technology education.* Washington, DC: Author.

Johnson, J., & Immerwahr, J. (1994-1995, Winter). First things first: What Americans expect from the public schools. *American Educator, 18*(4), 4-13, 44-45.

Lynn, E. (1994, Spring). Science and equity: Why it's important. *Dwight D. Eisenhower Mathematics and Science Education Newsletter, 4,* 1, 4-5.

Mirel, J., & Angus, D. (1994, Summer). High standards for all. *American Educator, 18*(2), 4-9, 40-42.

Morgan, J. C. (1993, January 28). Shabazz works math wonders at Clark Atlanta University. *Black Issues in Higher Education Special Report: Recruitment and Retention*, pp. 15, 17.

National Council of Teachers of Mathematics. (1989). *Curriculum and evaluation standards for school mathematics.* Reston,VA: Author.

National Council of Teachers of Mathematics. (1991). *Professional standards for teaching mathematics.* Reston, VA: Author.

National Center for Research in Mathematical Sciences Education. (1994, Fall). Equity and mathematics reform. *NCRMSE Research Review: The Teaching and Learning of Mathematics, 3*(3), 1-5.

Nelson-Barber, S., & Meier, T. (1990, Spring). Multicultural context a key factor in teaching. *Academic Connections*, pp. 1-5, 9-11.

Olson, J. K., & Olson, M. (1991). Including the unincluded in mathematics. In J. Q. Adams, J. Niss, & C. Suarez (Eds.) *Multicultural education: Strategies for implementation in colleges and universities* (pp. 41-45). Macomb, IL: Western Illinois University Foundation.

Raspberry, W. (1994, July 19). Setting the highest goal for the brightest—they will achieve. *Chicago Tribune*, p. 12.

Slavin, R. E. (1993). *Cooperative learning*. New York: Longman.

Tobias, S. (1990). *They're not dumb, they're different: Stalking the second tier*. Tucson, AZ: Research Corp.

Usiskin, Z. (1994, Winter). Individual differences in the teaching and learning of mathematics. *UCSMP Newsletter, 14*, 7-14.

Woodrow, D. (1988). Multicultural and anti-racist mathematics teaching. In A. J. Bishop (Ed.). *Mathematical enculturation: A cultural perspective on mathematics education* (pp. 229-235). Boston: Kluwer Academic.

MOTIVATIONS THAT DRIVE PREJUDICE AND DISCRIMINATION: IS THE SCIENTIFIC COMMUNITY REALLY OBJECTIVE?

by
Duane M. Jackson

We are taught that science, unlike religion and philosophy, is based on empirical evidence, that science is a dynamic process and is self-correcting. Existing theories are constantly being modified or abandoned in the face of new evidence. But what truly sets science apart from other disciplines is **objectivity.** As an African American scientist and a student of history, I do not question the objectivity of science as a discipline, but science is done by individuals, and I question the objectivity of scientists and the scientific community. Prejudice (perceptions) and discrimination (actions based on prejudice) have prevented the scientific community from being objective. I will examine the historical roots of this discrimination in science— scientific racism and the eugenics movement, race, intelligence and the IQ controversy, the misuse of heritability, and the inability of the field of psychology to deal with the issue of race.

When we look for motives behind discrimination and prejudice in science, we see three types of individuals emerge: the don't-know, the don't-want-to-know, and the know-and-will-not-accept. The three types are driven by prejudice but the latter two are also driven by discrimination. Individuals who fall into the don't-know category are simply unaware of the accomplishments and contributions that African Americans have made in science. Don't-want-to-know individuals believe African Americans cannot make contributions in science, in part because such accomplishments undermine the don't-want-to-know type's belief in themselves. Individuals who know-but-will-not-accept are the most dangerous of the three, however, since they will attempt to discredit, block, or conceal the truth about the actual scientific contributions African Americans have made.

Three African American Scientists

When I gave a talk, titled "Carver, Just, and Turner: Scientists Against the Odds," at a predominantly European American institution during Black History Month last year, I began my paper by asking the audience if they knew who George Washington Carver, Ernest Everett Just, and Charles Turner were. The majority of the audience were aware of Carver, but only a few African Americans knew of Just, and no one in the audience had ever heard of Turner. These three men had several things in common. They were all African Americans born in the 19th century who spent part of their careers teaching and doing research in Historically Black Colleges (HBCs).

Just taught at Howard University in Washington D.C., Carver taught at Tuskegee Institute (now Tuskegee University) in Alabama; and Turner taught at Clark University (now Clark-Atlanta University) in Atlanta. Being 19th-century African Americans at HBCs worked against them since HBCs had far fewer resources than their European American counterparts. Further, being educated and intellectual African Americans in the 19th century presented a problem: they were not supposed to exist. That they did challenged the very foundation of the European American belief that African Americans were intellectually and socially inferior.

Just and Turner spent most of their lives in frustration. Both Just and Turner received their doctorates from the University of Chicago. As noted above, Just taught at Howard University;

he spent twenty years during the summer doing research at Woods Hole Marine Biology Laboratory in Woods Hole, Massachusetts. Known worldwide, this laboratory has attracted scientists and students to pursue research in the areas of biology, chemistry, physics, and geology. Just's research on cell membrane activity demonstrated that the cell's cytoplasm and ectoplasm are equally important as the nucleus for heredity. Just was prolific: he wrote two books and over sixty articles. Though he was respected and honored in the scientific capitals of Europe, he received little recognition for his accomplishments in the United States. Because of racial prejudice and discrimination in the scientific community in the United States, he spent the last ten years of his life in voluntary exile in Europe.

Charles Turner, the first African American animal behaviorist, published over fifty papers. His first, *Psychological notes upon the gallery spider* (1892a) published in 1892, appears to be the first published paper in psychology written by an African American. It is believed, but difficult to document, that his paper, *A few characteristics of the avian brain,* published in *Science* (1892b) was the first paper by an African American published in that highly respected scientific journal. Some of his work was published by T. C. Schneirla and E. L. Thorndike, two eminent scientists of the time who initiated detailed laboratory studies in insect (Schneirla) and animal (Thorndike) learning.

Convinced that education was the key to overcoming prejudice, Turner developed an argument drawing from comparative psychology and a comparative study of history.

Among men…, dissimilarity of minds is a more potent factor in causing prejudice than unlikeness of physiognomy…. The new Southerner is prejudiced against the new Negro because the new Negro is very unlike him. He does not know that a similar education and a like environment have made the new Negro and himself alike in everything except color and features. (1902, pp. 163-164)

He goes further to suggest the problem was that "the white trash and the vagrant Negro form a wedge separating the new Southerner from the new Negro so completely that they cannot know each other" (1902, p. 164). He later suggested that the only way to overcome this was to transform the white trash and the vagrant Negro into new Southerners and new Negroes through education. But we shall see that traditional education is not enough to cover some prejudice and discrimination; in fact, in some ways, traditional education has actually perpetuated these problems. This is evident when men of "science" such as Jensen (1969), Herrnstein (1973) Rushton, (1988), and Herrnstein and Murray (1994) in their recently published book, *The Bell Curve,* proposed that genetic differences exist among the races and that these differences create inequalities among the races in regard to behaviors from intelligence to criminality. The educational system has either ignored or, in many cases, been inadequate in educating students about the role genes play in behavior and about the interaction between genes and the environment.

Turner's dream of eventually having a position at a major European American research institution never materialized. He spent his last years as a professor of biology and psychology at Sumner High School and Teacher College in St. Louis where his duties included collecting meal tickets at the school cafeteria.

Carver, Just, and Turner all made major contributions in science. Why then is Carver remembered and Just and Turner forgotten? How was Carver able to gain, to some degree, the respect and recognition of the scientific community for his accomplishments? Several factors could account for this. First, Carver was raised by European Americans. He never knew his father, and his mother disappeared when he was an infant. He was adopted by his former slave master. Additionally Carver, unlike Turner and Just, received the majority of his primary and secondary education from European Americans. Also, Carver taught at an HBC that was an industrial and agricultural school, while Turner and Just taught at HBCs that were liberal arts institutions. Teaching African Americans to be farmers and factory workers was more palatable to the European American community than teaching African Americans to be lawyers, doctors, and scientists.

Carver's research was applied, while Just's and Turner's work was for the most part theoretical. Carver's research on the peanut was far easier to grasp than Just's research on the internal workings of cells and Turner's research on the cognitive abilities of insects. It may have been far easier to accept an African American man doing applied rather than theoretical research.

Finally, however, I propose that the most important factor helping Carver gain some acceptance by the European American scientific community was his political activism. Carver had seen and experienced the brutality of racism, but he had been raised and taught by European Americans. This created a dilemma. He attempted to resolve this conflict by working for racial harmony. He was very active in the Commission on Interracial Cooperation and with the YMCA. Despite all of this, however, even Carver never received full recognition for his accomplishments.

The Eugenics Movement and the Roots of Scientific Racism

The eugenics movement attempted to legitimize racism under the guise of science and served as a foundation for scientific racism. Allen Chase defines scientific racism as "the creation and employment of a body of legitimately scientific, or patently psuedoscientific data as rationales for the preservation of poverty, inequality of opportunity for upward mobility and related regressive social arrangements" (1977, p. 72). According to Chase, during its conception, scientific racism was not concerned much with racial or cultural differences. Although it was anti-Semitic, anti-Catholic, and white supremacist, it was primarily concerned with profit. The founding father of scientific racism, Thomas Malthus, laid out the purpose of scientific racism in 1826: to maximize profits and to minimize taxes on those profits. Malthus also stated in *An Essay on the Principle of Population* (1926) that the state is not obligated to support the poor.

The eugenics movement, founded by Francis Galton, guaranteed a future for scientific racism. Galton (1869) coined the word *eugenics* from the Greek word *eugenes*, meaning well born. The primary purpose of the movement was to improve the races by boosting the birthrate of the "well born" and decreasing the birthrate of the less well born. The eugenics movement has a long history of racism and its doctrines have been used to justify racist ideologies. Galton, in 1869, stated that black people were inferior to the lowest of whites and he went further to state, without empirical evidence, "...that the average intellectual standard of the negro [sic] race is some two grades below our own" (p. 327).

The eugenics movement had an impact on immigration and sterilization laws in the United States during the early part of this century. President Theodore Roosevelt, who was greatly influenced by the eugenics movement, wrote a letter on January 14, 1913 to the Committee to Study and to Report on the Best Practical Means of Cutting Off the Defective Germ-Plasm in the American Population, a committee started by the American Breeders Association's Eugenics Section. Roosevelt stated:

It is obvious that if in the future racial qualities are to be improved, the improving must be wrought mainly by favoring the fecundity of the worthy types.... At present, we do just the reverse. There is no check to the fecundity of those who are subordinate.... (cited in Chase, 1977, p. 15)

The eugenics movement was most fully exploited by Nazi Germany. Its doctrine was perfect for a regime that sought to rule the world by breeding a "master race." The eugenics movement gave scientific justification for breeding programs, the creation of Nazi Eugenics Court, and the extermination of an entire "race." The German Sterilization Act of 1933, which was enforced by the Nazi Eugenics Court, was based on the Model Eugenical Sterilization Law written by Harry L. Laughlin (1922) at the Eugenics Record Office of Cold Spring Harbor in New York.

Dr. Lothrop Stoddard, an American eugenicist, who was widely read by Hitler's closest advisers, went to Germany, met with Hitler, and sat on the Eugenics Court. Stoddard stated "...once the jews [sic] and other inferior stocks were annihilated, the Nazi state would be able to concern itself with the improvements within racial stock that are recognized everywhere as constituting the modern science of eugenics, or racial betterment" (1940, p. 189). Eugenics was interwoven into the very fabric of the Nazi creed. Although the Nazi Third Reich fell almost fifty years ago, we have seen in the nineties in Eastern Europe similar atrocities committed in the name of "ethnic cleansing."

The Search for the Genetic Basis of Intelligence
The Race-Intelligence Controversy

The question as to whether African Americans as a group are genetically inferior to European Americans in regard to intelligence is like a vampire. This question keeps rising out of the grave, and no one seems to have the wooden stake to lay this question to an eternal rest. The notion that different ethnic groups were different in regard to intelligence has its roots in Galton's 1869 book, *Hereditary Genius*. As the title implies, Galton believed that intelligence was inherited, although he had no scientific basis for this conclusion: The test that Galton used to measure intelligence lacked reliability as well as validity, and genetics was not a science until the triple rediscovery of Mendel's work in 1900 (Hirsch, 1982, p. 1).

The first intelligence test to demonstrate reliability and validity (validity in regard to academic performance) was developed by Alfred Binet in 1905. The French government commissioned Binet to construct a test to identify students who had low academic aptitudes. Unfortunately, this test, which was designed to help educators identify students with learning disabilities, has over time become synonymous with intelligence testing. The Americanized version, the Stanford-Binet, was published by Lewis Terman (1916) in a book titled *The Measurement of Intelligence.*

Many of the early pioneers in the American testing movement—Lewis Terman, Henry Goddard, and Robert Yerkes—were members of the eugenics movement. These individuals concluded that the Stanford-Binet test measured an "innate intelligence," and this test could be used to identify genetically inferior individuals (Kamin, 1974, pp. 5-6). Terman in *The Measurement of Intelligence* states:

...[I]n the near future intelligence tests will bring tens of thousands of these high-grade detectives under the surveillance and protection of society. This will ultimately result in curtailing the reproduction of feeble-mindedness and in the elimination of an enormous amount of crime, pauperism, and industrial inefficiency. (pp. 6-7)

...[A]mong spanish-indian [sic] and Mexican families of the Southwest and also among negroes [sic] dullness seems to be racial, or at least inherent in the family stocks from which they come.... Children of this group should be segregated in special classes.... They cannot master abstractions, but they can often be made efficient workers.... There is no possibility at present of convincing society that they should not be allowed to reproduce, although from a eugenic point of view they constitute a grave problem because of their unusually prolific breeding. (pp. 91-92)

However, there was also strong resistance in the field of psychology to the notion that genetics had a role in individual differences in behavior. This resistance was led by the behaviorists who felt that all individual differences could be explained by environmental factors. Watson, in his 1930 book, *Behaviorism,* stated:

Our conclusion, then, is that we have no real evidence of the inheritance of traits. I would feel perfectly confident in the ultimately favorable outcome of careful upbringing of a *healthy, well formed baby* born of a long line of crooks, muderers and thieves, and prostitutes. Who has evidence to the contrary? (p. 103)

He goes on to say:

I should like to go one step further now and say, "Give me a dozen healthy infants, well-formed, and my own specified world to bring them up in and I'll guarantee to take any one at random and train him to become any type of specialist I might select—doctor, lawyer, artist, merchant-chief and, yes, even beggar-man and thief, regardless of his talents, penchants, tendencies, abilities, vocations, and race of his ancestors." I am going beyond my facts and I admit it but so have the advocates of the contrary and they have been doing it for thousands of years. (p. 104)

When we look at the race-intelligence controversy, we see that what Watson said over sixty years ago is still correct. Individuals on both sides have gone beyond their facts.

Problems to Resolve Before the Search Begins

I do not question the legitimacy nor the ethics in the search for the genetic basis of intelligence. But I do strongly believe certain problems must be resolved before this can become a worthwhile scientific endeavor. These problems are: 1) the lack of clear definitions of race and intelligence; 2) the limitations of the investigators in the field; and 3) the misconception that the underlying genetic basis for intelligence consists of a few genes or genetic systems.

What does it mean to be intelligent? Some view the use of language and abstract reasoning as the hallmark of intelligence. Others think intelligence is uniquely associated with the mind and thinking, while still others see intelligence as the ability to learn or to adopt to changes in the environment. Unfortunately, no universally accepted operational definition of intelligence exists. One might think it would be far easier to define race, but this has also been a problem.

Yee, Fairchild, Weizmann, and Wyatt (1993), in a paper titled "Addressing Psychology's Problem with Race," deal with the difficulties science has had in clearly defining race. Yee and his co-writers state that not having a scientific definition for race results in investigators conceptualizing and using race in a variety of ways, causing confusion and controversy. Having no clear definition of intelligence or race limits research design and theory building. It also calls into question "race difference" research: How does one claim a race difference if the researchers have not agreed upon a definition of race that allows them to say the races they are referring to are different races?

The second problem I see is that many investigators involved in searching for the genetic basis of intelligence have limited training. Many psychologists have limited training in genetics, so they go outside their field to geneticists for advice. Most geneticists, however, have little training in psychology.

Finally, there exists an oversimplification of the genetic basis for intelligence and a misuse of the concept of heritability. Heritability is a dynamic population measure that must be recalculated each generation and holds only for the single population investigated at the time it was investigated. Yet we see some investigators using it as a static individual measure.

Evidence tends to support strongly the notion that the genetic basis of intelligence is far from simple. For example, Tryon (1940) demonstrated genetic variation in maze learning in rats when he created a strain of "bright" rats and "dull" rats to run a maze. But in 1949 Searle ran these selectively bred strains through a variety of mazes and found that on some tasks the bright strain was superior to the dull strain and on some tasks the reverse was true. He concluded

The finding...indicates that a "general intelligence" factor, if it exists at all, may be regarded as of little or no importance.... [F]rom this together with the intercorrelational evidence that brights and dulls are differently organized it may be assumed that the differences in the maze-learning ability represent differences in patterns of behavior traits rather than in degree of any single psychological capacity. (p. 320)

The importance of this work is that it demonstrates that "intelligence" even in the rat is complex and not governed by one gene. If there are different genetic systems for maze learning in rats, the number of genes and genetic systems involved in human intelligence, which has still not been clearly defined, must be very large. Yet we see genetic models and misuse of heritability reducing the genetic basis of intelligence to a simple system.

After we have a clear, concise definition of race and intelligence and individuals that have thorough training in genetics and psychology, then we may be able to deal with the complex search for the genetic correlates of behavior and to tackle the far more complex problem of the genetic x- environment interaction. It is also hoped that line of research will be motivated to look for differences among groups rather than the superiority of some groups.

Prejudice and discrimination in science exist because science is done by scientists who are no different from other members of society. However, there is hope in science, for in science, old theories and concepts are modified or abandoned when new evidence is presented. Science can abandon old ideas based on prejudice and discrimination in the face of existing data.

REFERENCES

Chase, A. (1977). *The legacy of Malthus: The social costs of the new scientific racism.* New York: Alfred A. Knopf.

Galton, F. (1869). *Hereditary genius.* London: Macmillan.

Herrnstein, R. J. (1973). *IQ in the meritocracy.* Boston: Atlantic-Little Brown.

Herrnstein, R. J., & Murray, C. A. (1994). *The bell curve.* New York: The Free Press.

Hirsch, J. (1982). Introduction. In Hirsch, J., & McGuire, T. (Eds.). *Behavior-genetic analysis.* Stroudsburg, PA: Hutchinson Ross.

Jensen, A. (1969). How much can we boost IQ and scholastic achievement? *Harvard Educational Review, 39,* 1-123.

Kamin, L. (1974). *The science and politics of I.Q.* New York: John Wiley & Sons.

Laughlin, H. L. (1922). *Eugenical sterilization in the United States, Chicago: Psychopathic laboratory of the municipal court of Chicago* (rev. ed., 1926). New Haven, CT: American Eugenics Society.

Malthus, T. (1826). *An essay on the principle of population, it affects the future improvement of society* (6th ed.). London: Norton.

Rushton, J. P. (1988). Race differences in behaviour: A review and evolutionary analysis. *Personality and Individual Differences, 9,* 1009-1024.

Searle, L. V. (1949). The organization of hereditary maze-brightness and maze-dullness. *Psychology Monographs, 39,* 283-325.

Stoddard, L. (1940). *Into the darkness: Nazi Germany today.* New York: Duell, Sloan, & Pearce.

Terman, L. M. (1916). *The measurement of intelligence.* Boston: Houghton Mifflin.

Tryon, R. C. (1940). *Genetic differences in maze-learning ability in rats.* Thirty-ninth Yearbook of the National Society for the Study of Education. Bloomington, IL: Public School Publishing.

Turner, C. H. (1892a). Psychological notes upon the gallery spider. Illustration of intelligent variations in the construction of the web. *Journal of Comparative Neurology, 2,* 95-110.

Turner, C. H. (1892b). A few characteristics of the avian brain. *Science, 19,* 16-17.

Turner, C. H. (1902). Will the education of the Negro solve the race problem? In D. W. Culp (Ed.). *Twentieth century Negro literature or cyclopedia of thought on the topics relating to the American Negro* (pp. 162-166). Naperville, IL: J. L. Nichols.

Watson, J. B. (1930). Behaviorism. Chicago: University of Chicago Press.

Yee, A., Fairchild, H. F., Weizmann, F., & Wyatt, G. (1993). Addressing psychology's problem with race. *American Psychologist, 48,* 1132-1140.

Section III: Creating and Maintaining a Supportive Campus Climate

DIVERSITY AND MULTICULTURALISM
ON THE CAMPUS:
HOW ARE STUDENTS AFFECTED?

by
Alexander W. Astin

Amidst debates over multiculturalism, diversity, and political correctness by academics and the news media, claims and counterclaims about the dangers and benefits of multiculturalism have abounded, but so far little hard evidence has been produced to support any of these claims. Most of the "evidence" injected into the debate thus far is of a purely anecdotal nature, with the veracity of the ancedotes cited by critics on one side of the argument usually disputed by critics on the other side.

As a political animal, I might have certain strong views about multiculturalism—whether it is a good or a bad idea—but as an educator and a researcher, my most important question about multiculturalism and diversity is how students are affected by campus policies and practices. I recently had the opportunity to examine this question empirically in a major national study of undergraduates attending 217 four-year colleges and universities. Published this year, the study involved 82 outcome measures on 25,000 students who entered college as freshmen in the fall of 1985 and were followed up four years later in 1989. It also included data that enabled us to determine how much each institution emphasized diversity and multiculturalism, and measures of each individual student's direct experience with diversity and multiculturalism.

The following analysis of this study addresses several pertinent questions: How are students' values and beliefs about other races and cultures affected by their institutions' policies on diversity and multiculturalism? What difference does it make in students' attitudes and behavior when their professors emphasize diversity issues in the classroom or in their research? How are students' academic progress and values affected by direct involvement in "diversity" experiences?

Method

The basic purpose of this research project was to determine how various student outcomes are affected by environments. The larger study of student development, which provides the data for the findings reported here, included 82 different student outcome measures covering a wide range of cognitive and affective development: attitudes, values, beliefs, aspirations, and career plans, as well as measures of undergraduate achievement and degree completion and scores on nationally standardized tests such as the GRE, MCAT, and LSAT. Since many of these outcomes were pre-tested when the students entered college as freshmen and post-tested four years later, we can determine how students actually changed during the four years. The study also incorporated more than 190 measures of the students' environmental experiences, including characteristics of the curriculum, faculty, and student peer group (for details, see Astin, 1993). Of particular relevance to this article are seven environmental measures reflecting a) the institution's and its faculty's policies on diversity issues and b) the student's direct experience with diversity and multiculturalism at the institution. Given the centrality of these seven environmental measures to the issue of diversity on campus, more detailed discussion of each is in order.

149

Measures of Diversity/Multiculturalism

The study incorporated three types of environmental measures relating to issues of diversity or multiculturalism: Institutional Diversity Emphasis, Faculty Diversity Emphasis, and Student Diversity Experiences (five measures).

The first two measures are based on the responses of the faculty at each of the 217 institutions to an extensive questionnaire administered during the 1989-90 academic year. The mean faculty responses to a large number of questionnaire items were computed and then factor analyzed in order to identify clusters of items that "go together" as determined by the patterns of faculty responses. Environmental measures for any institution were then obtained by averaging the responses of its faculty separately for each cluster of questions. Institutional Diversity Emphasis, for example, reflects the extent to which faculty believe that their institution is committed to each of the following five goals:

1. to increase the number of minority faculty;
2. to increase the number of minority students;
3. to create a diverse multicultural environment;
4. to increase the number of women faculty;
5. to develop an appreciation for multiculturalism.

By looking at the faculty's perception of the degree of institutional emphasis on diversity and multiculturalism, as one might guess, a considerable variation emerges among the 217 institutions in their degree of emphasis on diversity.

Faculty Diversity Emphasis is defined in terms of four other questionnaire items, which also were shown by the factor analyses to produce similar response patterns:

1. instructional technique that incorporates readings on women and gender issues;
2. instructional technique that incorporates readings on racial and ethnic issues;
3. research or writing focused on women or gender;
4. research or writing focused on racial or ethnic minorities.

Note that Faculty Diversity Emphasis is based on the faculty's own scholarly and pedagogical practices, while Institutional Diversity Emphasis reflects the faculty's perceptions of the overall institutional climate. The latter measure presumably reflects not only faculty values and behavior, but also the policies of the administration and possibly even the trustees. As would be expected, these two environmental measures are substantially correlated ($r = .55$), which means simply that faculty who emphasize diversity issues in their teaching and research are likely to be found in institutions that also emphasize diversity and multiculturalism in their admissions and hiring policies. However, the fact that the correlation is far from perfect indicates that there are some institutions where the institutional emphasis on diversity is strong but where the faculty do not emphasize diversity issues in their teaching or research and, conversely, some institutions where the reverse pattern occurs. The two measures, in other words, are not completely interchangeable.

Student Diversity Experiences were measured in terms of five items from the follow-up questionnaire completed by the 25,000 students during the 1989-90 academic year. Each of these items is treated separately in the analysis:

1. took ethnic studies courses;
2. took women's studies courses;
3. attended racial/cultural awareness workshops;
4. discussed racial or ethnic issues;
5. socialized with someone from another racial/ethnic group.

Analysis of Environmental Effects

The method used for analyzing the effects of these seven environmental variables on the 82 student outcomes has been described in detail in earlier works (Astin, 1991, 1993). Pretests and other entering student characteristics assessed in 1985 are controlled first by means of stepwise regression analyses, after which the possible effects of environmental variables are examined. Basically, the analyses are designed to "match" students statistically in terms of their entering characteristics before evaluating the effects of environmental variables on the outcome measures obtained four years later. In effect, this method attempts to determine whether students change differently under differing environmental circumstances.

Before discussing the specific findings from these analyses, it should be mentioned that 26 of the 82 outcome measures were specifically identified as directly relevant to the goals of general education as spelled out in the considerable literature on this subject (Astin, 1992). These 26 goals include a variety of cognitive and academic outcomes, as well as completion of the baccalaureate degree, interest in and enrollment in graduate study, and several value and attitudinal measures. In reporting the findings, I pay special attention to these 26 measures because one of the critical policy questions is whether or not the overall goals of general education are facilitated by emphasizing diversity and multiculturalism.

Institutional Diversity Emphasis

The effects of Institutional Diversity Emphasis are of some practical as well as theoretical interest, since the factors that make up this environment measure are presumably under the direct control of the institution. Its strongest positive effects are on two outcomes: cultural awareness and commitment to promoting racial understanding. Cultural awareness is one of the developmental outcomes that was identified as particularly relevant to the goals of most general education programs. It is based on the students' estimate of how much their undergraduate experience has enhanced their understanding and appreciation of other races and cultures. The fact that a strong emphasis on diversity enhances the students' commitment to promoting racial understanding is of special interest, given that some critics have alleged that emphasizing issues of race and multiculturalism tends to exacerbate racial tensions on the campus. Quite the opposite seems to be the case.

Emphasizing diversity also has positive effects on several measures of student satisfaction with the college experience: overall satisfaction, as well as satisfaction with student life, opportunities to take interdisciplinary courses, facilities, and the quality of instruction. Institutional Diversity Emphasis also has positive effects on political liberalism, libertarianism, and participation in student protests.

Consistent with its positive effect on the students' personal commitment to promoting racial understanding, Institutional Diversity Emphasis has a negative effect on the belief that racial discrimination is no longer a problem in America. It also has negative effects on the students' chances of joining a social fraternity or sorority, or getting married while in college, and on the belief that the chief benefit of college is to increase earning power. This last measure is another outcome judged as relevant to the goals of most general education programs, since such programs would hopefully weaken the students' tendency to see liberal learning in strictly instrumental or monetary terms.

What, then, are the consequences for students who are associated with a strong institutional emphasis on issues of diversity and multiculturalism? If one were to attach values to the outcomes just discussed, emphasizing diversity appears to have uniformly positive effects, not only on those outcomes that are relevant to the goals of general education—heightened cultural awareness and satisfaction and reduced materialism—but also on the students' commitment to promoting racial understanding. The positive effect on political liberalism could be judged as either a plus or minus, given one's own political preferences. The same goes for participation in campus protests, which might be considered by some as a negative outcome However, to render such a judgment, it is first necessary to determine what effects protest participation itself has on the students' subsequent development. This issue will be addressed shortly.

Faculty Diversity Emphasis

Faculty Diversity Emphasis produces a pattern of effects that is very similar to the pattern associated with Institutional Diversity Emphasis. The strongest positive effects are on cultural awareness and overall satisfaction with the college experience. Faculty Diversity Emphasis also had a positive effect on the students' chances of voting in the 1988 presidential election. This item was included as a measure of "citizenship," another of the 26 outcomes that were included among the goals of general education.

That Faculty Diversity Emphasis and Institutional Diversity Emphasis produce very similar patterns of effects does not mean that these two measures are entirely redundant. Both measures, for example, produced independent effects on cultural awareness, overall satisfaction, and participation in campus protests. By "independent," we mean that the faculty's focus on diversity issues contributes to these outcomes over and above the contribution of the overall institutional emphasis.

Direct Student Experience with Diversity

Let us now consider the effects of individual Student Diversity Experiences. Even though these "effects" were obtained only after all student input and faculty environmental measures were controlled for, the fact that the student experiences occurred after the student actually enrolled in college requires that we interpret these effects with caution. Even so, the pattern and results are very interesting.

Critics of political correctness have focused much of their attack on efforts to diversify the curriculum. Our data base included two items bearing on this issue: the number of ethnic studies courses and the number of women's studies courses taken by the students during their undergraduate years. These two measures produced almost identical patterns of effects on student outcomes. The strongest positive effects were on cultural awareness and commitment to promoting racial understanding, as well as a commitment to helping clean up the environment. There were also weaker, but still significant, positive effects on participation in campus protests, political liberalism, listening ability, foreign language skills, and attendance at recitals and concerts. Only one outcome was negatively associated with taking ethnic or women's studies courses: the belief that racial discrimination is no longer a problem in America. Once again, taking ethnic studies or women's studies courses is associated with a wide range of generally positive outcomes rather than alienating students of different races from each other.

Another controversial issue concerns whether the campus administration should sponsor "cultural awareness" workshops designed to enhance racial/cultural understanding among students from different backgrounds. A large number of outcomes are significantly associated with attending such workshops: commitment to promoting racial understanding, participating in campus demonstrations, cultural awareness, and social activism. Of particular interest is that participation in such workshops is positively associated with undergraduate retention (completion of the bachelor's degree) as well as with six different measures of satisfaction with various aspects of the undergraduate experience and six different measures of academic development (critical thinking, general knowledge, public speaking ability, listening ability, writing ability, and preparation for graduate school). Participation in racial/cultural awareness workshops has negative effects on materialistic values and on two beliefs: that racial discrimination is no longer a problem and that the individual can do little to change society. This last item was included among our 82 outcomes as a measure of "empowerment," the student's sense that he or she can actually make a difference through individual effort and dedication. In effect, participating in such workshops appears to strengthen a student's sense of personal empowerment to effect societal change.

Another item from the list of individual Student Diversity Experiences was the frequency with which the student socialized with persons from different racial/ethnic groups. While this experience has its strongest positive effects on cultural awareness and commitment to promoting racial understanding, it also has significant positive associations with commitment to helping clean up the environment, attending recitals and concerts, and—most importantly—with practically all measures of the student's academic development and satisfaction with college. It has negative associations with the beliefs that racial discrimination is no longer a problem in America and that the individual can do little to change society. It is of some interest to note that socializing with persons from different racial/ethnic groups, in contrast to most of the other diversity experiences discussed so far, does not have positive effects either on political liberalism or on participation in campus protests.

Interestingly enough, the largest number of positive effects was associated with the frequency with which students discussed racial/ethnic issues during their undergraduate years. As would be expected, the strongest effects are on commitment to promoting racial understanding and cultural awareness. This item showed other positive and negative effects that closely follow the pattern associated with the other diversity variables. However, one of the strongest effects not found for most of these other diversity variables is the positive impact on the student's commitment to developing a meaningful philosophy of life. This value, which was also included among the 26 goals of general or liberal education, is what we call our "existential" value question. It was the most popular value question on surveys that we conducted in the early 1970s, but its importance to students has since dropped precipitously. That frequent discussions of racial/ethnic issues should appear to strengthen students' commitment to developing a philosophy of life is interesting and provocative. Could it be that issues of race, culture, and ethnicity represent promising curricular subject matter for confronting some of the existential dilemmas that many contemporary students seem to be avoiding?

Effects of Campus Activism

Since emphasizing diversity on the campus seems to enhance the likelihood that students will engage in some kind of protest activity during their undergraduate years, it is important to ask how activism itself affects the student's development. The strongest positive associations are with political liberalism, cultural awareness, and commitment to promoting racial understanding. In other words, individual participation in campus protest activities does not, as some critics would have us believe, serve to alienate students from each other. On the contrary, it seems to strengthen students' sense of cultural awareness and appreciation and to reinforce their commitment to promoting greater understanding between the races. Campus protest participation is also associated with strengthened commitment to helping clean up the environment and developing a meaningful philosophy of life, growth in artistic interests and leadership abilities, aspirations for advanced degrees, and increased chances of voting in a presidential election. Participating in campus protests is negatively associated with materialistic values and the beliefs that racial discrimination is no longer a problem and that the individual can do little to change society. About the only outcome associated with protest participation that might be considered negative is a positive effect on the student's degree of hedonism (defined in this study as drinking beer, smoking cigarettes, and staying up all night). Hedonism, it should be stressed, was not affected one way or the other by any of the environmental diversity measures or individual Student Diversity Experiences.

In short, participation in campus protest activities is associated with a pattern of outcomes that is quite similar to the pattern associated with diversity activities, with the exception of its positive effects on hedonism, voting in a presidential election, artistic inclination, leadership, and aspiration for advanced degrees.

Reflections

Through these analyses I have attempted to shed some new light on the heated debate over political correctness and multiculturalism on college campuses by seeking some empirical answers to the following questions: Does emphasizing or not emphasizing diversity issues have any real consequences for students? How are students actually affected by some of the policies and practices that conservative critics find so objectionable? The findings present a clear-cut pattern: emphasizing diversity either as a matter of institutional policy or in faculty research and teaching, as well as providing students with curricular and extracurricular opportunities to confront racial and multicultural issues, are all associated with widespread beneficial effects on a student's cognitive and affective development. In particular, such policies and experiences are associated with greater self-reported gains in cognitive and affective development (especially increased cultural awareness), with increased satisfaction in most areas of the college experience, and with increased commitment to promoting racial understanding. Emphasizing diversity and multiculturalism is also associated with increased commitment to environmental issues and with several other positive outcomes: leadership, participation in cultural activities, citizenship, commitment to developing a meaningful philosophy of life, and reduced materialistic values. If we confine our analyses just to outcomes that are relevant to the goals of most general education programs, the effects of emphasizing multiculturalism and diversity appear to be uniformly positive.

Perhaps the only outcome consistently associated with diversity variables that might be considered "negative" is the positive effect on participation in student protests. While protest activities are often seen by some faculty, and especially by campus administrators, as a nuisance or possibly even as detrimental to campus order and tranquility, engaging in such protests seems to be associated with generally positive outcomes for the individual student participating. It is also true that an emphasis on multiculturalism is associated with increases in the student's political liberalism, but how one chooses to value such an effect would depend on one's political orientation.

While these findings provide strong evidence supporting campus attempts to emphasize issues of diversity and multiculturalism, there are other aspects of the PC debate which we have not directly addressed in this study. One particularly touchy issue is speech codes. Perhaps the most bizarre and ironic aspect of the PC debate is that, when it comes to speech codes, people at the extremes of the political spectrum seem to have switched sides. Those on the left who have supported codes that outlaw racist and other forms of hateful speech and conduct on the campus come from the same political camp that has always championed first amendment rights and supported the dismantling of *in loco parentis*. At the same time, those on the political right who have, with the help of the news media, promoted the PC issue, come from a political perspective that has regularly advocated censorship in speech, writing, and the arts and that has endorsed restrictive codes of student conduct on the campus.

Ironically, the PC debate has once again underscored the critical importance of academic freedom and tenure in academia. Tenure, lest we forget, was established primarily to protect academic freedom. I am a living example of the necessity for tenure, since some of what I have to say in my writing and speechmaking does not fall on receptive ears in my own university. While I like to think of myself as a free thinker, there is a serious question in my mind as to whether I might be much more circumspect in what I say and do if there were no academic freedom and tenure. I might even be in a different line of research.

That emphasizing multiculturalism and diversity reinforces political liberalism on the campus, should come as no surprise. Nor should academics necessarily feel defensive or apologetic about such effects. The very values and traditions of academia naturally attract people of a liberal persuasion. An environment that places a high value on teaching, learning, discovery, artistic expression, independence of thought, critical thinking and freedom of speech and expression naturally tends to attract such people, since these are values that have traditionally been very important to people from the left. In the same way, the corporate and military worlds have tended to attract people from the right because business and the military have traditionally placed a high value on power, control, hierarchy, authority, capitalism, free enterprise, and making money.

Academics should more openly acknowledge that the PC critics are right when they claim that the expression of right-wing viewpoints is not warmly received in a liberal campus climate. What the PC critics themselves fail to do, however, is to make any distinction between the right to express a particular point of view and the right to have others agree with it. There is no such thing as a "right" to expect agreement. As a matter of fact, liberal academics don't even agree with each other on matters like speech codes and curricular reform. If the PC critics want people to agree with them, then they should look, instead, into conservative politics, corporate business, fundamentalist religion, or the military.

Despite the liberal leanings of most faculties, I would submit that in academia there is still far more tolerance shown for the expression of deviant viewpoints than in any other social institution. In other words, an employee in business, government, or the military has much less freedom of expression—especially when it comes to expressing deviant political viewpoints—than does an employee in academia. And this is as it should be. This is our tradition, our strength.

One thing that we tend to forget about academic freedom is that it is not merely an end in itself but that it has a larger purpose: the pursuit of truth. The link between academic freedom and the pursuit of knowledge is often overlooked in the PC debate, but the underlying logic is really very simple: the quickest and surest way to the truth is to encourage the expression of diverse points of view and to promote active discussion and debate of these different views. This is really what academic freedom is all about.

RELATED READINGS

Astin, A. W. (1991). *Assessment for excellence: The philosophy and practice of assessment and evaluation in higher education.* Phoenix: Oryx.

Astin, A. W. (1992, Fall). What matters in general education: Provocative finding from a national study of student outcomes. *Perspectives, 22*(1), 23-46.

Astin, A. W. (1993). *What matters in college? Four critical years revisited.* San Francisco: Jossey-Bass.

SPEECH CODES ON CAMPUS: WHAT CAN I SAY?

by
Gayle Tronvig Carper

Introduction

During the 1980s, over 300 colleges and universities created codes of conduct for students and faculty, codes which punished use of language that humiliated or offended others because of insult to the race, color, or gender of another person. The colleges and university committees who created these codes acted with the best of intentions: they reasoned that hate speech, usually defined as verbal or written words or symbolic actions that convey a grossly negative assessment of particular persons or groups based on their race, gender, ethnicity, religion, sexual orientation, or disability harms the victim, the victimized group, the campus community, and society (Kaplin, 1992). The harm was considered to be psychic rather than physical and lasted long after the actual hate speech was forgotten (Kaplin, 1992). Further harm was caused in the feelings of vulnerability, insecurity, and alienation created by hate speech which could undermine the conditions necessary to constructive dialogue on campus (Kaplin, 1992).

However, in the rush to rid higher education campuses of demeaning language, the code committees overlooked a well-established American tradition applicable to public institutions of learning: the First Amendment guarantee of freedom of speech and expression. During the past 200 years, the United States Supreme Court has created standards that must be followed when rules are made that may infringe upon citizens' rights to speak freely or to express their opinions through actions. In general, speech, symbols, and ideas are protected by the First Amendment, subject to certain exceptions. For example, all speech and expressive conduct may be regulated by reasonable and non-discriminatory time, place, and manner restrictions.

Additionally, the First Amendment prohibits restrictions based on the content of speech. The expression of certain words, symbols, or ideas may not be banned because those words, symbols, or ideas might disturb, embarrass, or offend others. However, speech can be regulated and even banned if it falls into certain categories. Speech that has the effect of inciting imminent lawless action and is likely to incite such action may be lawfully punished (*Brandenburg v. Ohio*, 1969). Obscene speech can be prohibited (*Miller v. California*, 1973), and pornographic materials involving children can be banned (*New York v. Ferber*, 1982). A civil remedy is available for speech that creates a hostile or abusive working environment (*Meritor Savings Bank v. Vinson*, 1986). Fighting words, those which by their very utterance inflict injury or tend to incite an immediate breach of the peace, may also be punished (*Chaplinsky v. New Hampshire*, 1942).

Several related constitutional doctrines apply in cases of speech regulation. The vagueness doctrine states that regulations must be easily understood by the reasonably intelligent person and that enforcement of the regulations may not be left to the discretion of an official (*Papachristou v. City of Jacksonville*, 1972). Overbreadth is another constitutional doctrine used to invalidate legislation prohibiting broad categories of speech, some of which may legally be proscribed but which also include a substantial amount of expression protected by the First Amendment. Finally, regulations that may infringe on fundamental freedoms must be written in the least restrictive way possible.

These rules were apparently set aside by the code creators in their efforts to remove uncomfortable language from colleges and universities. Unfortunately, this led to the demise of many of the codes through court challenges.

The Court Cases

The first case brought challenging a speech code was *Doe v. University of Michigan* in 1989. The University of Michigan at Ann Arbor adopted a "Policy on Discrimination and Discriminatory Harassment of Students in the University Environment." This policy provided discipline for

Any behavior, verbal or physical, that stigmatizes or victimizes an individual on the basis of race, ethnicity, religion, sex, sexual orientation, creed, national origin, ancestry, age, marital status, handicap or Vietnam-era veteran status. Sexual advances, requests for sexual favors, and verbal or physical conduct that stigmatizes or victimizes an individual on the basis of sex or sexual orientation.

In an attempt to accommodate the First Amendment, application of the policy was restricted. The prohibited behavior had to "involve an express or implied threat to" or have "the purpose or reasonably foreseeable effect of interfering with" or had to "create an intimidating, hostile or demeaning environment for" the victim's academic efforts, employment, extra-curricular activities, or personal safety. The policy only applied in academic centers such as classroom buildings and libraries and could not be used to regulate conduct in university housing, university publications, or public areas of campus. The policy was accompanied by an "Interpretive Guide" listing examples of sanctionable conduct. Finally, if a complaint was lodged against an individual, the policy administrator had discretion to determine that the complained-of behavior was protected by the First Amendment and refuse to take action under the policy.

John Doe, the plaintiff, was a psychology graduate student with teaching responsibilities. He described his speciality, biopsychology, as the interdisciplinary study of biological bases of individual differences in personality traits and mental abilities. Doe wanted to discuss sexual differences between male and female mammals, including humans, in his classes. One theory he wished to discuss as partial explanation for why more men than women chose engineering as a profession was that men as a group do better than women in some spatially related mental tasks partly because of a biological difference. Doe believed that some students and faculty regarded his theories as sexist. He alleged that he might be charged with a violation of the policy if he discussed them, especially in light of the interpretive guide, where an example of a sanctionable conduct was

A male student makes remarks in class like "Women just aren't as good in this field as men" thus creating a hostile learning atmosphere for female classmates .

Doe brought a civil suit against the university challenging the policy on constitutional grounds and requesting the Federal Court to prevent the university from enforcing the policy. In a lengthy opinion, the court found that the policy violated both the First and the Fourteenth Amendments to the U. S. Constitution.

The court first described the available remedies for discriminatory actions. The Court stated that the

...most extreme and blatant forms of discriminatory conduct are not protected by the First Amendment, and indeed are punishable by a variety of state and federal criminal laws and subject to civil actions. Discrimination in employment, education, and government benefits on the basis of sex, ethnicity and religion are prohibited by the constitution and both state and federal statutes.... In addition, the state provides criminal penalties and civil remedies for assault and battery...for purposes of ethnic intimidation.... Federal law imposes civil and criminal sanctions against persons depriving or conspiring to deprive others of rights guaranteed by the United States Constitution.... Many forms of sexual abusive and harassing conduct are also sanctionable...[both criminal and] civil remedy...

and civil damages.

The policy, however, could not meet constitutional requirements to be included as a legal remedy. The court decided that the university could not "establish an antidiscrimination policy which had the effect of prohibiting certain speech because it disagreed with ideas or messages sought to be conveyed." The court relied on a well-settled principle of law, first stated in 1943:

> If there is any star fixed in our constitutional constellation, it is that no official, high or petty, can prescribe what shall be orthodox in politics, nationalism, religion, or other matters of opinion or force citizens to confess by word or act their faith therein (*West Virginia State Board of Education v. Barnette*, 1943).

The court went on to say that First Amendment principles have special significance in universities, whose mission to educate is promoted by the free and unrestricted exchange of competing and contradictory views. The court also determined that the policy was overbroad and vague. The policy had been applied often over its one-year life to punish protected speech and could continue to do so as written. The terms "stigmatize" and "victimize" were too general and eluded precise definition. Additionally, the policy was unclear as to what kind of "threat" could be punishable and what conduct would "interfere" with an individual's efforts. In short, the university was unable to articulate any principled way to distinguish sanctionable conduct from protected speech. Students of common understanding were necessarily forced to guess at whether a comment about a controversial issue would subject them to punishment. These characteristics of the policy results made the court decide that the policy was unconstitutional.

Doe was followed by several other similar court opinions. The case of *UMW Post v. Board of Regents of U. of Wisconsin* was based on a plan called "Design for Diversity," intended to increase minority representation, multicultural understanding, and greater diversity throughout the University of Wisconsin's 26 campuses, apparently in response to escalating discriminatory harassment incidents, including caricatures and slave auctions, from fraternities. A rule in the student conduct handbook imposed punishment for a student's comment, epithet, or other expressive behavior which 1) was racist or discriminatory, 2) directed at an individual, 3) demeaning to the race, sex, religion, color, creed, disability, sexual orientation, national origin, ancestry, or age of the individual, and 4) created an intimidating, hostile, or demeaning environment for education, university-related work, or other university-authorized activity.

At least nine students had been disciplined for such offenses as name calling based on sex or national origin and for pretending to be immigration officials and intimidating international students. Punishment was usually probation, alcohol assessment, apologies, and some form of sensitivity training. The rule was challenged on the basis of the First Amendment violations, vagueness, and overbreadth.

The university argued that the rule was allowed under the fighting words doctrine since it regulated speech that had minimal social value and harmful effects. According to the university, the kind of expression banned did not serve as a step to the truth, was not intended to inform or convince the listener, was not likely to form any part of a dialogue or exchange of views, did not provide an opportunity for reply, constituted a verbal assault, and was likely to incite violent reaction. The university argued that the compelling reasons of increasing minority representation, assuring equal educational opportunity, preventing interruption of educational activities, and preserving an orderly and safe campus should outweigh any First Amendment rights.

In response, the Court stated that the fighting words doctrine allowed restrictions only on those words, directed at the person of the hearer, that tend to incite an immediate breach of the peace and naturally tend to provoke violent resentment. Breach of the peace was to be narrowly defined as not merely a breach of decorum but must also tend to bring the addressee to fisticuffs.

The Court decided that the rule did not fit the fighting words definition because it did not state that sanctionable speech must cause a breach of the peace. Additionally, the rule could easily apply to many situations where breach of the peace was unlikely to occur. The rule was too broad since it included more conduct than inciting to an imminent breach of the peace and covered non-violent as well as violent situations. The court defined an "intimidating or demeaning environment" as one that makes others timid, discouraged, or inhibited, a state unlikely to incite immediate breach of the peace. The court applauded the university's goals, but held firm to the idea that content-based restrictions limit diversity of opinion and prevent the robust exchange of ideas.

The case *Iota Xi Chapter of Sigma Chi Fraternity v. George Mason University* was a fraternity's suit alleging First Amendment violations for sanctions imposed as a result of an "ugly woman contest" with racist and sexist overtones. The fraternity had for two years held Derby Day events for entertainment and as a source of funds for charity. Fraternity members were assigned to sorority teams to be dressed as ugly women. One contestant appeared painted black, with stringy black hair and clothing stuffed with pillows to exaggerate breasts and buttocks. The contestant also spoke in slang to parody African Americans. A petition signed by 247 students and presented to the university condemned the performance as racist and sexist. The Dean of Student Services held meetings with all sides and concluded that the contest created a hostile learning environment incompatible with the university mission. The university sanctioned the fraternity with suspension from current activities and a two-year probation on all social activities except pre-approved pledging events and "philanthropic events with an educational purpose directly related to gender discrimination and cultural diversity." The fraternity also was required to plan and implement an educational program addressing cultural differences, diversity, and the concerns of women.

In defense of its actions, the university said its mission was to promote a culturally and racially diverse student body, that education was not limited to the classroom, and that it was committed to teaching the values of equal opportunity, treatment, and respect for diversity and individual integrity. The university said the fraternity behavior was antithetical to the mission to create a nonthreatening environment for students, and it could not keep attracting and retaining minority students if behavior like this had to be allowed.

The court decided that the behavior was protected under the First Amendment and relied on a 1992 United States Supreme Court case, *R.A.V. v. City of Saint Paul*. The city of St. Paul, Minnesota, enacted an ordinance that made it a crime

> to place on public or private property a symbol, object, appellation, characterization or graffiti, including, but not limited to, a burning cross or Nazi swastika, which one has reasonable grounds to know arouses anger, alarm or resentment in others on the basis of race, color, creed, religion or gender.

In *R.A.V.*, a teenager charged with violating the statute for burning a cross in the fenced-in yard of an African American family asked for a dismissal of the charge because the statute violated his First Amendment rights. The case ultimately reached the United States Supreme Court which held that the statute violated the First Amendment because it imposed "viewpoint discrimination." In other words, the statute only criminalized fighting words based on race, color, creed, religion, or gender and not any other topics such as "...political affiliation, union membership or homosexuality...." The Court specifically stated that "the point of the First Amendment is that majority preferences must be expressed in some fashion other than silencing speech on the basis of its content" (*R.A.V. v. City of Saint Paul*, 1992).

The court in the George Mason University case decided that the R.A.V. holding applied with equal force to universities. George Mason's rule was unconstitutional because the university punished only those who disagreed with its goal of racial integration and gender neutrality while permitting and even encouraging speech that would further the university's goals. The university also argued that the Court should weigh fraternity conduct against the substantial interests in maintaining an educational environment free of racism and discrimination and in providing gender-neutral education. The Court agreed, but said the university had many other constitutional methods to do so, and the manner of its action could not consist of selective limitations on speech. The university must accomplish its goals in some fashion other than silencing speech on the basis of viewpoint.

Students have not been the only group punished by speech codes. The codes have also been used against faculty. A good example is *Levin v. Harleston*. Professor Levin, a Ph.D. in Philosophy, tenured for over 16 years at City College of the City University of New York, sued for violation of his First and Fourteenth Amendment rights. After a trial, the District Court found that Levin was punished in retaliation for and solely because of his ideas. One of Levin's opinions, published outside of his classroom, was that affirmative action programs have failed. He wrote that in spite of tremendous energies expended since 1954 to bring African Americans into the mainstream, there remained high rates of illiteracy among them, that they were absent from more prestigious disciplines, and failed in other forms of academic activity. He explained his belief by stating that

on average, blacks are significantly less intelligent than whites. The black mean IQ is slightly more than one standard deviation below the white mean. In more familiar terms, that amounts to a difference of more than 15 points of IQ as measured by standard tests... The significance of these findings for our profession (as for the rest of society) is that black representation in a field can be expected, absent any discrimination, to decrease as the intellectual demands of the field increase. Doctors and engineers are recruited from an IQ range of 114 or above; I do not know the corresponding figure for philosophy, but it is surely just as high, and for some specialities (e.g. logic) considerably higher. Only 3% of the black population (as opposed to 16% of the white population) has an IQ in this range. Making the most optimistic assumptions, given that blacks constitute 12% of the population, only 2% (not 12%) of the profession will be black. That is close enough to current figures for all philosophers to regard themselves free of any discriminatory guilt. (*Levin v. Harleston*, 1991)

Levin's opinion was publicly denounced by college officials. There had been no student complaints or allegations of academic misconduct or discrimination against Levin, but the college created additional sections of the classes Levin taught to provide alternative professors to insulate and protect students from his views. Letters were sent to potential students informing them of Levin's views and the alternative class sections.

For several years, organized student protests were directed at Levin. Students distributed pamphlets and demonstrated using bullhorns to express their opinions outside his classroom. Levin received anti-Semitic threats, and documents on his office door were burned. Students entered his classroom during class and called him a racist. Levin requested assistance from the university security chief, but no action was taken even after the chief observed the demonstrations. In response to a request for assistance from the Faculty Senate, the President said his hands were tied because the students also had academic freedom. Many of the student activities violated disciplinary rules but no action was taken by college officials. Levin was asked to withdraw from the remainder of his course by his Dean because of possible disruptions and potential student discomfort with his views.

The college President created an ad hoc committee of faculty to investigate Levin's writings. The committee was charged with the responsibility of reviewing the question of when speech becomes conduct unbecoming a member of the faculty, which, if found, could be the basis for revocation of tenure. The committee worked for ten months, during which time Levin turned down twenty speaking engagements and was not allowed to defend himself at the committee meetings. The committee issued a report that stated:

First, the Committee affirms its commitment to the principles of academic freedom and free speech...the College has an obligation to uphold students' rights to a supportive learning environment. It finds that there are utterances by faculty, even outside of class, that can have a detrimental impact on the educational process. In particular, statements denigrating the intellectual capability of groups by virtue of race, ethnicity or gender have the clear potential to undermine the learning environment and to place students in academic jeopardy.... [A] teacher's low expectations frequently have a negative effect on student performance.... [We] feel that there should be no disciplinary action taken...[but Levin's view has] the potential to harm the process of education in his classes.... [It] is appropriate for the College to continue to carefully implement ways to protect students from such harm.

The Court concluded that Levin's First Amendment rights were impermissibly chilled, impeded, and abridged by the college's actions. His Fourteenth Amendment property interest in tenure was violated by the stigma of the committee report and continuing scrutiny. Since Levin's views were protected expression and not punishable conduct, the court permanently enjoined the college from initiating any disciplinary action against Levin based on his views and from creating the additional sections of his classes. The court also ordered the college to take steps to protect Levin's classes from disruption. Tenure, the court stated,

is more than the right to receive a paycheck. Academic tenure, if it is to have any meaning at all, must encompass the right to pursue scholarship wherever it may lead, the freedom to enquire, to study and to evaluate without the deadening limits of orthodoxy or the corrosive atmosphere of suspicion and distrust.... (*Lenin v. Harleston*, 1991)

Conclusion

It is not necessary to read court cases to realize that speech is a powerful tool. But it is also a precious freedom, a fundamental right. Requiring some words, symbols, or viewpoints and banning others is harmful to the freedom of speech, whether it is called McCarthyism or political correctness. Enacting speech codes appeared to be the simple answer: a guide for equal treatment and opportunity for all, a way to rid minds of hate. But allowing repression of ideas lets those in power determine the "proper" way to think and believe at whim. Bigotry and hatred must be fought, not by suppression, but by example and role modeling, by communicating throughout society. "If there be time to expose through discussion the falsehoods and fallacies, to avert the evil through the processes of education, the remedy to be applied is more speech, not enforced silence" (*Whitney v. California*, 1927).

A lawyer's best advice for college and university professionals is this: stop legislating and start teaching. Realize that method is as important as content in the college classroom and learn different methods of communication, including listening skills so these can be taught to students. Find, learn, and use teaching and learning methods that encourage free and unrestricted exchange of ideas. As Hallie Lemon says elsewhere in this issue, think of the classroom as a contact zone where dissensus is tolerated and valued and respected; learn how to manage conflict and teach this skill to students. Bigotry may not disappear, but at least it will be exposed as the ignorance that it is.

REFERENCES

Brandenburg v. Ohio, 395 U. S. 444, 89 S. Ct. 1827, 23 L. Ed. 2d 430 (1969).

Chaplinsky v. New Hampshire, 315 U.S. 568, 62 S. Ct. 766, 86 L. Ed. 1031 (1942).

Doe v. University of Michigan, 721 F. Supp. 852 (E.D. Mich. 1989).

Iota Xi Chapter of Sigma Chi Fraternity v. George Mason University, 993 F. 2d 386 (4th Cir. 1993).

Kaplin, W. A. (1992). A proposed process for managing the first amendment aspects of campus hate speech. *Journal of Higher Education, 63,* 517-539.

Lenin v. Harleston, 770 F. Supp. 895 (S.D.N.Y. 1991).

Meritor Savings Bank v. Vinson, 447 U.S. 57, 106 S. Ct. 2399, 91 L. Ed. 2d 49 (1986).

Miller v. California, 413 U.S. 15, 93 S. Ct. 2607, 37 L. Ed. 2d 419 (1973).

New York v. Ferber, 458 U.S. 747, 102 S. Ct. 3348, 73 L. Ed. 2d 1113 (1982).

Papachristou v. City of Jacksonville, 405 U. S. 156, 92 S. Ct. 839, 31 L. Ed. 2d 110 (1972).

R.A.V. v. City of Saint Paul, 505 U.S. ___, 112 S.Ct. ___, 120 L. Ed. 2d 305 (1992).

UMW Post v. Board of Regents of U. of Wis., 774 F. Supp. 1163 (E.D. Wis. 1991).

West Virginia Board of Education v. Barnette, 319 U.S. 624, 63 S. Ct. 1178, 87 L. Ed. 1628 (1943).

Whitney v. California, 274 U. S. 357, 47 S.Ct. 641, 71 L. Ed. 1095 (1927).

REFERENCES

HATE-SPEECH CODES THAT WILL PASS CONSTITUTIONAL MUSTER

by
Lawrence White

It has been a trying few years for the drafters of hate-speech codes on college and university campuses. The University of Pennsylvania jettisoned its controversial speech code last fall after President Sheldon Hackney, during his confirmation hearing to be Chairman of the National Endowment for the Humanities, questioned whether such codes were the right approach to achieving civility on campus. This year, Central Michigan University became the latest institution to lose a court fight over its speech code. Continuing an unbroken line of victories by the American Civil Liberties Union, a federal judge held in January that Central Michigan had violated its basketball coach's right to free speech when he was disciplined under its "discriminatory harassment" code after he used a racial epithet during a closed-door team meeting. At Wesleyan University, the University of Michigan, and numerous other institutions, administrators have given up and repealed their codes.

Due largely to the court decisions, we now understand the arguments against campus speech codes: they use inherently vague terminology; they are overbroad, sweeping within their regulatory ambit not only pernicious language, but also language that enjoys constitutional protection. "It is technically impossible to write an anti-speech code that cannot be twisted against speech nobody means to bar," concluded Eleanor Holmes Norton, a former Georgetown University law professor who is now the District of Columbia's Delegate to Congress.

Despite the problems raised by speech codes, however, we must not forget that there are salutary purposes underlying the effort to draft codes banning derogatory and hurtful epithets. Such codes were intended to serve, and still serve, an important educational purpose: they are expressions of an institution's commitment to the victims of a pernicious and destructive form of behavior. Whenever anybody commits an act or utters a remark that is motivated by hatefulness, it causes harm to a real, flesh-and-blood victim. Hate-speech codes designed to protect victims are a noble endeavor. If institutions abandon the effort to draft policies against hateful speech, they are abandoning the victims the policies were meant to protect.

Campus administrators can learn important lessons from the court cases against the first generation of speech codes. In every instance, the codes that provoked court challenges were ambitiously, almost sweepingly worded. Several of them, including those at the University of Michigan and the University of Wisconsin, were modeled on the Equal Employment Opportunity Commission's guidelines on sexual harassment. They used concepts and terminology—"intimidating environment for education," "express or implied threat to an individual's academic efforts"-awkwardly borrowed from employment law. They treated the university campus as a single, undifferentiated "workplace."

The language they used seemed almost deliberately provocative to civil libertarians—phrases such as "expressive behavior" (University of Wisconsin) and other wording that equated physical behavior with verbal behavior (Central Michigan University)—as though there were no distinction under the First Amendment.

What we have come to refer to as "hate speech" takes many forms on the nation's college campuses. The most prevalent involves remarks by students. For every high-profile case involving a campus speech by Khalid Abdul Muhammad of the Nation of Islam, there are literally dozens, maybe hundreds, of incidents that occur behind the closed doors of dormitory rooms, in dining halls, or in the corridors outside student pubs. We know, regrettably, that a strong correlation exists between hate speech and alcohol abuse.

Colleges and universities must now craft a second generation of codes that will serve the important institutional objective of protecting the victims of hateful acts and utterances without violating constitutional principles. These codes would:

- Differentiate between dormitories and classrooms. In an article that appeared in the *Duke Law Journal* in 1990, Nadine Strossen, president of the ACLU, observed that the right to free speech applies with different force in different parts of a college campus. That right, she wrote, "may not be applicable to...students' dormitory rooms. These rooms constitute the students' homes. Accordingly, under established free-speech tenets, students should have the right to avoid being exposed to others' expression by seeking refuge in their rooms." A policy that disciplined students for hateful acts or utterances against other students in residence halls would probably bring three-quarters of all hate-speech episodes within the regulatory purview of college administrators without offending traditional free-speech precepts.

- Be tailored to the Supreme Court's decision in *R.A.V. v. St. Paul, Minn.* This 1992 decision suggests that anti-discrimination codes are on shaky ground constitutionally if they proscribe some hateful acts or utterances but not others. Any policy that prohibits categories of speech "because of" or "on the basis of" a specific factor—such as race, gender, or sexual orientation—runs the risk of violating the Court's stricture in R.A.V. that laws must not single out particular categories of hateful speech for penalties. As ironic as it sounds, the safest hate-speech code may be one that makes no mention of the very groups it is designed to protect.

- Use words emphasizing action and its effects, instead of speech. First Amendment jurisprudence recognizes an important distinction between speech and action and allows a greater degree of latitude when action is being regulated. The first generation of campus speech codes used vocabulary emphasizing speech, which virtually doomed them in advance—for example, they barred certain "comments" or "expressive behavior." By fostering the impression that these policies regulated pure speech, they made an easy target. The receptiveness of courts to arguments that the codes were overbroad—prohibiting speech that should be constitutionally protected along with utterances that deserve no protection (such as yelling "Fire!" in a crowded theater)—requires campuses to be more careful than they were in the past to draft constitutionally acceptable speech codes.

  The second generation of codes should favor "action" vocabulary—prohibiting hostile conduct or behavior that might "incite immediate violence" (the latter being the exact phrasing used in the Supreme Court's half-century-old "fighting words" case, *Chaplinsky v. New Hampshire*). Instead of calling them "hate-speech codes," colleges and universities should refer to the new policies as "anti-hate" or "anti-discrimination" codes.

- Enhance the penalties for alcohol-related hate mongering. Most campus conduct codes allow the imposition of disciplinary sanctions for disorderly conduct or violations of drug and alcohol policies. It would be constitutionally defensible to treat hateful acts or utterances as an additional factor to be taken into account when meting out punishment for code violations. For example, a student found guilty of public drunkenness could be sentenced to attend a program designed to treat alcohol abuse, but the same inebriated student could be suspended or expelled for hurling racial epithets or threats at fellow students.

Drafting a new generation of campus codes to curb hate mongering, codes that zero in on areas of highest risk (dormitories, drunkenness) while avoiding the vagueness and over-breadth that doomed the first generation of codes, is an exercise worth undertaking. Colleges and universities began attempting to regulate hate speech a decade ago for an important reason—to communicate a message of support to the victims of hate. That reason is still compelling today. If institutions abandon the effort to implement constitutionally acceptable codes, they will be sending a message chillingly and accurately expressed by the Stanford University law professor Charles Lawrence in an article that accompanied Ms. Strossen's in the 1990 *Duke Law Journal*:

"I fear that by framing the debate as we have—as one in which the liberty of free speech is in conflict with the elimination of racism—we have advanced the cause of racial oppression and have placed the bigot on the moral high ground, fanning the rising flames of racism."

We all understand civil libertarians' concerns when universities approach the delicate task of regulating certain forms of expressive conduct. But civil libertarians in turn should appreciate the message that is communicated when the rights of insensitive, viciously motivated members of college and university communities are placed above victims' rights to an education untainted by bigoted animosity. By trimming their drafting sails to incorporate the lessons of the first round of court cases, college administrators can satisfy constitutional concerns and at the same time curb the most egregious forms of hate mongering on campus. Then they can send an appropriate message to perpetrator and victim alike: Hateful utterances and behavior are repugnant forms of conduct that colleges and universities will not tolerate.

MEDIA DEPICTIONS OF ARABS

by
Jack G. Shaheen

In 1990, Operation Desert Shield transported more than 200,000 U. S. military men and women to Saudi Arabia. Thousands of armed forces from Egypt, Morocco, Syria, and other Arab countries were stationed alongside U. S. troops in the Saudi desert. How much did we, particularly members of our armed forces, know about the Arab peoples?

Prior to the Persian Gulf crisis, many people in the United States had probably never met an Egyptian, a Saudi, or a Syrian; most had never visited an Arab country. Our knowledge of Arabs came largely from the mass media, which has provided virtually all the images average U. S. citizens have of the peoples of the world.

Yet the media's Arab lacks a humane face. Images on television and movie screens present the Arab as a bogeyman, the quintessential Other. Little is shown of the Arab world's tradition of hospitality or its rich culture and history. We are shown almost nothing of value about its principal religion, Islam, the fastest growing of the universal religions, a faith embraced by 1.2 billion people, including 200 million Arabs in 21 nations. The American Muslim Council reports that between five and eight million Muslims live in the United States. "There are more than 200,000 Muslim businesses, 1,200 mosques, 165 Islamic schools, 425 Muslim associations and 85 Islamic publications, writes Steven Barboza in his text, *American Jihad* (p. 9).

Plato recognized the power of fiction when he said, "Those who tell the stories also rule society." In more recent times, Professor George Gerbner of the Annenberg School of Communications has said, "If you can control the storytelling of a nation, you don't have to worry about who makes the laws" (Cortés, p. 170).

For nearly two decades, I have studied how the Arab peoples are depicted in our culture, giving special emphasis to the entertainment images of television programs and motion pictures. My research has produced convincing evidence that lurid and insidious portraits and themes are the media's staple fare. An abhorrence of the Arab has embedded itself firmly in the psyche of many viewers. In more than 450 feature films and hundreds of television programs I have studied, producers have bombarded audiences with rigid and repulsive depictions that demonize and delegitimized the Arab. In the process, they have created a mythical "Ay-rabland," an endless desert with occasional oil wells, tents, 12th-century palaces, goats, and camels. Emotions are primitive, with greed and lust dominant; compassion and sensitivity are virtually non-existent. These images do not just entertain; they narrow our vision and blur reality.

Most Arabs are poor, not rich; they are farmers, not desert nomads; they have never mounted a camel, lived in a tent, or seen an oil well. After the 1973 oil embargo, media systems began promoting the "all Arabs are rich" myth. In 1979, Libya and the wealthier oil-producing countries of the Arabian Gulf—Saudi Arabia, Qatar, Kuwait, and the United Arab Emirates—had an average per capita income of slightly more than $12,000 (U. S. per capita income in 1979 was $10,600). According to a 1981 World Bank Development Report, the other Arab cultures had a per capita income of less than $850 per year (Law, 1980; Benson, 1980; Chung & Fouch, 1983).

Repetition of Arab caricatures, in both news and entertainment media, reinforce the limiting and demeaning stereotypes and serve as ritualized glue, teaching us whom to fear, whom to hate. On television and in motion pictures, for example, the media's sheik is projected as

169

uncultured and ruthless, attempting to buy media conglomerates (*Network*, 1977); destroy the world's economy (*Rollover*, 1981); kidnap Western women (*Jewel of the Nile*, 1985); use nuclear weapons against the United States and Israel (*Frantic*, 1988); and influence foreign policies (*American Ninja 4; The Annihilation*, 1991). The sheik image parallels the image of the Jew in Nazi-inspired German films. Just as the Jew was made the scapegoat for Germany's problems in such movies as *Jüd Sass* (1940), today the sheik appears as a swarthy menace lurking behind imbalances in our own economic life.

As for the Palestinian-as-terrorist image, the stereotype has evolved over a period of four decades. There are numerous similarities between the depiction of American Indians as savages in early Westerns and the dehumanized Palestinian portrayed in current movie dramas. In the 1980s ten of the eleven feature films that focused on the Palestinian portrayed him as Enemy Number One. Feature films such as *Wanted Dead or Alive* (1987), *Ministry of Vengeance* (1989), *Navy Seals* (1990), *Delta Force III: The Killing Game* (1991), and *Hot Shots! Part Deux* (1993) show Palestinians as sadistic caricatures. Made-for-television movies such as *Hostage Flight* (1985), *Terrorist on Trial* (1988), and *Voyage of Terror* (1990) augment the film image. Producers selectively frame the Palestinian as demonic, with neither compunction nor compassion toward men, women, or children.

What is forgotten in all this is that the great majority of Palestinians, like all other human beings, seek peace and abhor violence. On silver screens, however, Palestinians, adorned in fatigues and kuffiyehs, almost never appear as victims of violence or even as normal human beings. When, if ever, has the viewer seen a Palestinian embracing his wife or children, writing poetry, or attending the sick? Several years ago, when I asked 293 secondary school teachers to name any humane or heroic screen Arab they had seen, five cited past portraits of Ali Baba and Sinbad; one mentioned Omar Sharif and "those Arabs in *Lion of the Desert* and *The Wind and the Lion*." The remaining 287 teachers could identify none. As journalist Edward R. Murrow said, what we do not see is often as important, if not more important, as what we do see.

Print journalists help perpetuate the stereotypes. Meg Greenfield, the editorial-page editor of the *Washington Post*, has written that currently we "hear and see a tendency to invest all Arabs with the attributes of the vicious terrorist. If we succumb to this [stereotype] we will be doing in the very people we should be trying to protect." But in a *Newsweek* column, Greenfield wrote that Muslim women are slavish, submissive, and forced to stay at home. She noted "the contempt with which the Saudis treat women." One wonders where she obtained her information and how extensive her contacts with Saudis actually have been. A letter to the editor recently printed in the *Chicago Tribune* supplemented Greenfield's thesis: "In Saudi Arabia," the writer asked, "why should our female soldiers have to endure the baleful, lustful stares of the Arabs?" This question is on a par with past hate-mongering stereotypes of Jews and African Americans.

Although there are nearly 500 million Muslim women—the Muslim world ranges from Guinea on the west coast of Africa to Borneo in the South China Sea—the most distorted and misunderstood aspect of Islam concerns the status of women. For centuries Muslim women had property and legal rights greater than those afforded to women in Europe and North America. The media, however, usually portray Arab women as mute, uneducated, unattractive enslaved beings who exist solely to serve men. It is true that in Western eyes there are problematic aspects to the status of Arab women, just as there are problematic aspects to the status of Western women from an Arab perspective. In the United States and in the 14 Arab nations I have visited, I have come to know women, Muslim and Christian, who are protected, loved, honored, and respected for being physicians, teachers, journalists, architects, and/or homemakers. We almost never see Arab women portrayed in these roles in the entertainment media, much less anyone emulating the intellect of Palestinian spokeswoman Dr. Hanan Ashrawi, a prominent contributor to the Palestinian-Israeli peace process. Nor do we see women modeled after Jihan Sadat, Anwar Sadat's widow, whose life is clearly the antithesis of the prevailing stereotype.

Who benefits when people are denigrated? All groups contain some destructive, violent people, but they are in the minority. History teaches us that a major obstacle to world peace is the tendency of image makers to dehumanize others and to enhance myths. Prior to the Gulf War, a *New York Times* editorial addressed the negative portraits, stating: "Bigotry thrives on slanderous stereotypes, and the crazed Arab is today's version of the Teutonic hordes and the yellow peril.... To hold a diverse Arab world collectively responsible for a single leader's misdeeds traduces an entire people."

Members of the academic community often play an important role in producing and critically analyzing portraits of various groups. But most have ignored the harm done by the Arab stereotypes. College administrators and heads of departments actively and rightly seek out Jewish, Hispanic, Asian, African American, and female scholars to teach courses related to their particular racial, ethnic, and gender backgrounds. The presence of those faculty members reflects a university's sensitivity and commitment to increasing understanding of minorities and ethnic groups; yet, to my knowledge, no university offers courses on the Arab image in popular culture; no university actively seeks to recruit faculty members who could address that need. Only a few academics, notably film historians and those who study cultural diversity, are beginning to recognize the importance of including Arab portraits in their analyses of pervasive cultural images.

Soon after he launched Operation Desert Shield, President Bush said that the actions of Suddam Hussein went "against the tradition of Arab hospitality, against the tradition of Islam." The President's words help dilute prejudice by debunking prepackaged Arab stereotypes. We need more such high-level declarations to encourage us to examine carefully the realities of the region, both negative and positive. We need more scholars and teachers who can promote more accurate portraits of Arabs, who can challenge students and the general public to look beyond the obvious by focusing on the telling effects of myths. As President John F. Kennedy said: "The great enemy of truth is very often not the lie, deliberate, contrived and dishonest, but the myth, persistent, persuasive, and realistic" (1962).

Popular culture's messages teach us whom to love and whom to hate. There is a dangerous and cumulative effect when such messages remain unchallenged. I am confident that educators will eventually define, document, and discuss the racism prevalent in the media's images of Arabs. The ultimate result should be an image of the Arab as neither saint nor devil, but as a fellow human being, with all the potential and frailty that condition implies.

An earlier version of this essay appeared in *The Chronicle of Higher Education* (31 October 1990), B1, B3.

REFERENCES

Barboza, S. (1993). *American Jihad.* New York: Doubleday.

Benson, B. (1980, Winter). The selling of America. *Perspective.*

Chung, W. K., & Fouch, G. G. (1993, August). Foreign direct investment in the United States in 1982. *Survey of Current Business,* pp. 31-41.

Cortés, C. E. (1994). Knowledge construction and popular culture: The media as multicultural educator. In J. A. Banks & C. A. McGee Banks (Eds.), *Handbook of research on multicultural education* (c. 10). New York: MacMillan.

Greenfield, M. (1977, December). Our ugly Arab complex. *Newsweek,* p. 110.

Kennedy, J. F. (1962). Yale commencement address.

Law, J. (1980). *Arab investors: Who they are, what they buy and where.* (Vol. 1). New York: Chase World Information Corporation.

ANNOTATED BIBLIOGRAPHY

Abu Odeh, A. (1983). The American image in Arab mass media. In E. Ghareeb (Ed.), *Split vision: The portrayal of Arabs in the American media* (pp. 355-368). Washington, D.C.: The American-Arab Affairs Council.
  Abu Odeh suggests a Western misunderstanding of the effect of the Soviet press in the region, which he says is relatively weaker than assumed. He criticizes the use of Israeli propaganda through the Israel Broadcasting Authority, a powerful Arab language broadcast beamed from Israel to much of the Arab world.

Damon, G. H., Jr., & Michalek, L. D. (1983). A survey of political cartoons dealing with the Middle East. In E. Ghareeb (Ed.), *Split vision: The portrayal of Arabs in the American media* (pp. 143-156). Washington, D.C.: The American-Arab Affairs Council.
  Damon and Michalek analyze 226 political cartoons in four major U. S. newspapers during heightened tensions in the Middle East. Their findings indicate editorial cartoonists graphically depict propagandistic (read pro-Israeli) messages in a manner remarkably free of a writer's constraints, and, overall, their depictions are consistent with the overall tone of an opinion page.

Fife, M. D. (1981). The missing minority in mass communication research. In *In search of diversity: Symposium on minority audiences and programming research, approaches and applications* (pp. 19-32). Lenox, MA: Corporation for Public Broadcasting.
  Fife argues that the commentary and criticism in most content analyses about minorities have served to document a wide range of abuses and can be built upon. A weakness in this approach, says Fife, is that it "shows the residual of mass society and the passive audience because most of its face value exists only if one believes that the audience brings nothing to the mass communication process and takes away only what the media present."

Ghareeb, E. (Ed.). (1983). *Split vision: The portrayal of Arabs in the American media.* Washington, D.C.: The American-Arab Affairs Council.
  Recommended reading for anyone beginning to examine Arab stereotypes in the media, especially for news coverage. However, a tone of advocacy rings through the book, calling for a consideration of other opinions, especially Israeli views on U. S. media.

Hamilton, M. (1991, April). Images of Arabs in the sources of American culture. *Choice,* pp. 1279-1281.
  Comprehensive in scope and a true find for the itinerant researcher.

172

Jabara, A. (Ed.). (1989, April). *Cineaste: Supplement, The Arab Image in American Film and Television, 17*(1), 1989.

Credit should go to the editors of this journal, for it is the first of its kind in the film press. In addition to Michalek and Shaheen's articles, there are useful film and video reviews. A bibliography and a filmography for educational institutions looking to present a more balanced view of the Arab world.

Jarrar, S. A. (1983). The treatment of Arabs in U. S. social studies textbooks. In E. Ghareeb (Ed.), *Split vision: The portrayal of Arabs in the American media* (pp. 381-390). Washington, D.C.: The American-Arab Affairs Council.

Jarrar's particular content analysis in 1975 focused on 43 of the United States' "most used textbooks in four areas of the social sciences: world history, geography and world affairs, problems of American democracy and social studies." Using Evaluation Coefficient Analysis to identify evaluative terms or words "which express favorable or unfavorable value judgements" about Arabs, backed by a checklist including measures of validity, balance, and comprehension, Jarrar found "the treatment of Arabs was most unfavorable in the geography textbooks," followed in order by world history, problems in American democracy, and social studies texts. His criteria and methodology can be useful in evaluating more recent texts.

Lindenmann, G. N. (1983). Arab stereotyping in contemporary American political cartoons. In E. Ghareeb (Ed.), *Split vision: The portrayal of Arabs in the American media* (pp. 345-354). Washington, D.C.: The American-Arab Affairs Council.

Lindenmann is appalled at the gross exaggeration by various editorial cartoonists, particularly the *Washington Post's* Herblock, who, says Lindenmann, inflames anti-Arab hatred by jokingly ignoring human suffering.

Maalouf, A. (1985). *The crusades through Arab eyes.* New York: Schocken.

While not dealing extensively with the Arab image, reading through the many shocking accounts by Arab writers and historians at the time of the Crusades is an illuminating way to understand the viscousness on the part of some Europeans during the Crusades and may help explain the roots of Moslem rage against the West.

Michalek, L. (1988). *Cruel and unusual: Negative images of Arabs in American popular culture.* Washington D.C.: ADC Issues, The American-Arab Anti-Discrimination Committee.

Michalek surveys the negative Arab images created through popular songs, jokes, television programs, political cartoons, comics, and movies. To help explain our proclivity to stereotype Arabs, Michalak explores how our European folk heritage provided well developed stereotypes that were incorporated into contemporary U. S. popular culture.

Michalek, L. (1989, April). The Arab in American cinema: A century of otherness. In A. Jabara (Ed.), *Cineaste Supplement: The Arab Image in American Film and Television, 17*(1), 3-9.

A recurrent question in much of the study of the Arab image is: Are American Jews, and their prominence in the U. S. film industry, responsible for the negative Arab image? Michalek says no. He suggests blaming Jews is unsatisfactory because people in the U. S. in general tend to be pro-Israeli and because American Arabs have allowed this negative image to perpetuate itself.

Moughrabi, F. (1988). *American public opinion and the question of Palestine: An analysis of changes in American views based on polls taken from 1978-1988.* Washington D.C.: ADC Issues. The American-Arab Anti-Discrimination Committee.

Moughrabi cites polling data from two principal studies conducted in April 1988 by the *Los Angeles Times* and *Chicago Tribune,* that, for the first time, showed people in the U. S. in favor of Palestinian independence. He seems particularly interested in revealing a more balanced image of the political differences within the American Jewish community over the question of Palestine.

Mousa, I. S. (1987). The Arab image: *The New York Times,* 1916-1948. *Gazette, 40.*

Mousa chose the *New York Times* because of its elite position in the U. S. press, its wide circulation, and its influence on other papers, their editors, and their writers. His content analysis of 1256 themes covers eleven time periods.

Oxtoby, W. G. (1980). Western perception of Islam and the Arabs. In M. C. Hudson & R. G. Wolfe (Eds.), *The American media and the Arabs* (pp. 3-12). Washington, D.C.: Center for Contemporary Arab Studies, Georgetown University.

Oxtoby's essay provides a link between the 10th century and the 20th in terms of who shaped the Arab image and what vestiges remain today. It's a fascinating area.

Piety, H. R. (1983). Bias on American editorial pages. In E. Ghareeb (Ed.), *Split Vision: The portrayal of Arabs in the American media* (pp. 125-142). Washington, D.C.: The American-Arab Affairs Council.

Piety cites many factors as contributing to the trend toward bias, chief among them are large Jewish readerships in cities like New York and Chicago, a powerful pro-Israeli public relations lobby who regularly excoriate writers who express what they consider anti-Israeli sentiment, and an international foreign policy supporting Israel against its Arab neighbors.

Sabbagh, S. J. (Ed.). (1990). *Sex, lies and stereotypes: The image of Arabs in American popular fiction.* Washington, D.C.: ADC Issues, The American-Arab Anti-Discrimination Committee.

Sabbagh explores general plot foundations, historical distortions, and character development through a critical look at five popular contemporary novels about Arabs.

Said, E. W. (1978). *Orientalism.* New York: Pantheon.

Said defines Orientalism as "a system of knowledge about the Orient, an accepted grid for filtering through the Orient into Western consciousness." His exploration of the impact of Orientalism is thorough and insightful.

Said, E. W. (1990). Orientalism. In S. J. Sabbagh (Ed.). *Sex, lies & stereotypes: The image of Arabs in American popular fiction.* Washington, D.C.: ADC Issues, The American-Arab Anti-Discrimination Commmittee.

Shaheen, J. G. (1980). *The influence of the Arab stereotype on American children* (pamphlet). Washington, D.C.: American-Arab Anti-Discrimination Committee.

The publication of this monograph led Shaheen to write *The TV Arab.* General in nature, it shows a consistency in his approach to the study of the Arab image, for he constantly searches for facts to debunk the myths and introduce positive options.

Shaheen, J. G. (1991, November-December). Jack Shaheen versus the comic book Arab, *The Link, 24*(5).

In his survey of "218 Arab types appearing in 215 comic books," Shaheen found "149 characters portrayed as 'evil,' 30 characters portrayed as 'good,' and 39 characters portrayed as 'common people,'" a three-to-one ratio of bad to good. However, even the good characters are only good in as much as they are fighting the villains for the "right" side.

Shaheen, J. G. (1990, October 31). The Persian Gulf crisis gives scholars a chance to encourage more accurate depictions of Arabs. *Chronical of Higher Education, 37*(9), B1, B3.

Shaheen takes aim at academics for ignoring the study of the Arab image and critics who assert his work is biased because he is of Arab descent.

Shaheen, J. G. (1984). *The TV Arab.* Bowling Green, OH: Bowling Green State University Popular Press.

Shaheen mixes the results of eight years of content analysis, anecdotes, and myth-shattering facts to debunk the slew of negative stereotypes of Arabs on television. He documented over "100 different popular entertainment programs, cartoons and major documentaries telecast on network, independent and public channels, totalling nearly 200 episodes, that relate to Arabs."

Shaheen, J. G. (1989). TV: Arab as terrorist. In A. Jabara (Ed.), *Cineaste Supplement: The Arab Image in American Film and T.V., 17*(1), 10-12.

Shaheen's look at the made-for-television movies of the 1980s reveals fanatical plots by Arab extremists (read Palestinians) lurking "in the shadows with AD-47, bomb, or dagger in hand to seduce, beat, rape and murder innocents."

Signorielli, N. (1981). Content analysis: More than just counting minorities. In *In search of diversity: Symposium on minority audiences and programming research, approaches and applications.* Lenox, MA: Corporation for Public Broadcasting.

Signorielli calls for effects research to encompass the "overall picture" of media exposure and look for the stability of effects patterns, not just specific changes.

Simon, R. S. (1989). *The Middle East in crime fiction: Mysteries, spy novels, and thrillers from 1916 to the 1980s.* New York: Lilian Barber.

Reeva Simon pieces together crime fiction accounts from the Middle East over a sixty-year period, noting a veritable explosion of thrillers about the Middle East by 1985.

Suleiman, M. W. (1980). American public support of Middle Eastern countries: 1939-1979. In M. C. Hudson and R. G. Wolfe (Eds.), *The American media and the Arabs.* Washington, D.C.: Center for Contemporary Arab Studies, Georgetown University.

Survey data that details sudden shifts in public opinion due to specific events, pro-Israeli bias in wording questions by pollsters, and limited mention of Palestinians.

Terry, J. (1983). Images of the Middle East in contemporary fiction. In E. Ghareeb (Ed.). *Split vision: The portrayal of Arabs in the American media,* Washington, D.C.: The American-Arab Affairs Council.

For her study, Terry places Middle Eastern novels into "three categories: simple adventure stories; espionage or mystery thrillers; and those in which the plots revolve around international finance and the Arab petroleum reserves."

Woll, A. L., & Miller, R. M. (1987). *Ethnic and racial images in American film and television: Historical essays and bibliography.* New York: Garland.

The authors examine 11 ethnic groups represented on film and television as recorded by researchers; they include bibliographic information. About the Arab image, they suggest there are similarities to the German and Asian images of the World War II years though the Arab image is "more sharply etched in black and less subject to immediate modification and sophistication."

Zaremba, A. J. (1988). *Mass communication and international politics: A case study of press reactions to the 1973 Arab-Israeli War.* Salem, WI: Sheffield.

Zaremba's content analysis tabulated key categories like aggression, land legitimacy, peace seeking, and superpower/international culpability to show how difficult it is for the real picture to emerge for decision makers.

THE MICROCULTURE OF DISABILITY

by

Jacqueline C. Rickman

Freak shows are not about isolated individuals, either on platforms or in an audience. They are about organizations and patterned relationships between them and us. "Freak" is not a quality that belongs to the person on display. It is something that we created: a perspective, a set of practices—a social construction.

(Bogdan, 1988, p. x)

Higher education has a unique opportunity to assume a leadership position in the preparation of a generation of citizens with disabilities who have positive images of themselves and who are socially engaged, rather than socially estranged. To accomplish this task, postsecondary institutions must recognize the characteristics of students with disabilities as well as the level of disability stereotypes and misconceptions operating on campus. They must assume responsibility for meeting the needs of students with disabilities and for countering the stereotypes and misconceptions. Increasingly, postsecondary educators and administrators are assuming that responsibility; they are learning to respond resourcefully to a growing demand that the needs of students with disabilities be met and that they be helped in their efforts to develop positive self images and become socially engaged citizens.

Characteristics of Postsecondary Students with Disabilities

At present, approximately ten percent of students enrolled in U. S. institutions of higher education report that they have a disability. The microculture of disability is comprised of subcultures consisting of specific disabilities such as hearing impairment. Within each subculture are further subsets such as the totally deaf and the partially deaf. Individuals within these subsets reflect a great variety of medical diagnoses and are representative of the population at large in their heterogeneity.

Four major disability subcultures and five onset categories exist in postsecondary institutions. The most common disability subcultures and their subsets include: 1) learning disabilities (perceptual, perceptual-motor, and general coordination problems, disorders of attention and hyperactivity, disorders of memory and thinking, language disorders), 2) physical disabilities and other health impairments (neurological impairments, musculoskeletal conditions, chronic medical conditions), 3) visual disabilities (totally blind, partially sighted), and 4) hearing impairments (totally deaf, partially deaf). Onset categories include: a) special education early onset, b) special education adventitious onset, c) recently diagnosed d) self referral, and e) other referral. Each of these categories can be differentiated further depending on whether the conditions are permanent or uncertain and degenerative.

Although it would be illogical to assume that all students with disabilities have the same levels of independence and productivity or that they have identical needs for adaptations and services, all share the experience of interacting on a regular basis with social stigmas based on inaccurate assumptions and ambivalence. At present many drop out of college, and those who stay perceive themselves in a distinct marginal status with inequitable access to programs and services.

Reported stigmatic reactions from nondisabled faculty and peers have included: discom-

177

fort, admiration, patronizing or pitying attitudes, avoidance, fear, an assumption of low intelligence, an assumption of talent, treatment like that of a child, an assumption that all members of a disability subculture are alike, a public disclosure of special accommodations needed, and simply ignoring the situation. Most students practice self-advocacy and do not expect preferential treatment; most want faculty to ask about their disability and to collaborate with them for appropriate environmental and academic accommodations. Their expectations parallel those of their collegiate peers. They expect their post-secondary experience to provide them with the tools to achieve rewarding, productive, and integrated adult lives. They expect the institution to respect them and to be sensitive to their beliefs and experiences. I would like to examine the sources of disability stereotypes before discussing current stereotypes and misconceptions about postsecondary students with disabilities and then suggesting ways educators can help meet their needs.

A Chronology of Evolving Disability Stereotypes

In his book, *Freak Show: Presenting Human Oddities for Amusement and Profit,* Robert Bogdan (1988) suggests that "whenever we study deviance, we must look at who are in charge—whether self-appointed or officially—of telling us who the deviant people are and what they are like" (p. 279). Through the years, those who have been in charge of people with disabilities as well as the media have misunderstood, incorrectly categorized, and stigmatized individuals within the microculture of disability. Bogdan's pioneering text explores and evaluates the gradual evolution of those who were in charge of people we would identify today as having disabilities—from the managers, promoters, and audiences of "freak shows," through the administrators of professional organizations and charities, to medical practitioners, to present-day professionals and human service providers.

Freak Shows (circa 1840-1940)

Barbara Baskin sought to ban freak shows from the New York State Fair in 1939 contending that they were to disabled people as *Amos 'n Andy* was to African Americans and as the striptease show was to women (Bogdan, 1988). In the carnival culture, people with differences were seen as valuable presentations; indeed, their abnormalities and human variations translated into meal tickets and security. As exhibits, these individuals were part of the public domain. They were presented in two unique modes to their audiences: the exotic mode that exploited the public's curiosity about the unusual or sensational and the aggrandized mode that capitalized on the public's need for superior status and power.

The exotic mode was rooted in racism, imperialism, and handicapism. It presented people with disabilities as human curiosities—specimens to be feared and held in contempt. As exhibits, they were the devalued victims of institutionalized discrimination, hopelessly stigmatized and devoid of human dignity. Paradoxically, Bogdan's research revealed that these marginal citizens thought of themselves as having high status and as very elite carnival insiders who arrogantly viewed their audiences with disdain and contempt.

The aggrandized mode exploited the exhibits, that is the persons on display, as mere objects in a tainted amusement world. In doing so, it capitalized on the audience's need to maintain a sense of superior status and power. It contended that people with disabilities were not competent enough to be part of society. They were to be excluded and kept with their own kind. The most insidious features of this mode were the underlying contentions that exhibits were not capable of achieving, and that normal accomplishments by people with disabilities were to be flaunted as extraordinary. The aggrandized mode thereby served as the foundation for the perceptions of not only *Jerry Lewis's pitiful poster child,* the indigent *idiot,* and the blind *beggar,* but also the disabled *wonder-kid,* the *amazing crippled prodigy,* and the blind *genius.* All of these images were manufactured when audiences determined that people with disabilities were exhibits who were amusing, but tainted, incompetent, disgusting, and ultimately unworthy of inclusion in the larger world.

The Medical Establishment and Charities (circa 1940s-1960s)

A later conception of disability was basically *pathological* in that people with disabilities were seen as *patients.* Several premises were operant within this philosophy. They were: 1) people with disabilities could be treated and possibly cured; 2) people with disabilities were to be secluded from the public; and 3) people with disabilities were to be feared, and in many cases locked away to protect the *normal* citizenry from danger. The trend was followed by the emergence of organized charities, professional fund raisers, and poster children. It is likely that freak shows are perceived as repulsive today because members of society, including many with disabilities themselves, have embraced the pathological disabled imagery of pity as an artifact of the medical establishment's monopoly over the presentation of people with disabilities.

Freedom Movements: Rehabilitation Reform (circa 1960s-1970s)

Beatrice Wright (1960) was a pioneer in the provision of counseling and rehabilitation services for people with disabilities. Her mentor was Carl Rogers, who emphasized the importance of investigating the perspective of individuals with disabilities, of valuing what they were saying about their experiences. Her sensitization developed into an awareness of and objection to the presence of gross societal distortions and misconceptions about this population. Wright observed the medical establishment's presentation of people with disabilities as pathological cases and formulated the "fundamental negative bias" as a powerful source of prejudice that steers perception, thought, and feeling along negative lines to such a degree positives remain hidden. She reports that one's perception, thinking, and feeling regarding deviance will be negative if three conditions for the functioning of the fundamental negative bias are met. These conditions are saliency (what is observed stands out sufficiently), value (it is regarded as negative), and context (it is vague or sparse). Her view appears to be based on an integration of Heider's (1958) balance theory of sentiments and Sherif, Sherif, and Nebergall's (1965) social judgment theory. This theoretic combination suggests that when similarity with the self is perceived, the similarity will be exaggerated and liking and belonging will be induced; when differences are perceived, however, the dissimilarity will be exaggerated, resulting in a host of complex rejection reactions Wright, Dembo, and Leviton (Dembo, et al., 1975) identify as negative spread effects.

Perhaps an indication of these negative spread effects can be found in Zimbardo and Ebberson's (1970) observation that "the United States has spent millions of dollars on unsuccessful information campaigns to correct stereotypes about minority groups, to present the facts, and to help people get to know one another" (p. 101). Though U. S. universities were becoming beacons of protest against structural exclusion during the 1960s and 1970s, the fundamental negative bias against people who differed from the norm was too strong to overthrow, as evidenced in the spread effects of bigoted and prejudicial attitudes held by many postsecondary personnel and students. Many with disabilities were denied admission; and those who were admitted were perceived as dependent, unattractive, and not eligible for special services or adaptations.

179

Unawareness and Ambivalence as Sources of Negative Attitudes Toward Persons with Disabilities (circa 1980s)

During the 1980s, researchers began to report that the origins of conscious and unconscious negative attitudes toward disability range from full awareness to total unawareness. They emphasized that unawareness, or mindlessness, was the overwhelming determinant of negative societal attitude formation (Livneh, 1988; Langer & Chanowitz, 1988). At postsecondary institutions, an increase in mindfulness about the situations of students with disabilities was noted in females, younger personnel, faculty at institutions with disability service programs, faculty within education and the social sciences, and in faculty with previous extended contact with students with disabilities (Fonosch & Schwab, 1981; Yuker, 1988; Amsel & Fichten, 1990). Less supportive attitudes were held toward students with learning disabilities and socioemotional problems than for those with hearing, visual, or physical disabilities (Leyser, 1989).

In contrast, other findings during the 1980s discounted the notion of discriminatory practices based on a fundamental negative bias in favor of ambivalence. Ambivalence is best described as confusion about enduring cultural myths derived from freak show, medical, and rehabilitation images. Among those myths is the idea that disability and mainstream cultures exist without conflict within a harmonious world family, its Woodstock imagery reinforcing the false belief that interactions between members of mainstream and marginal cultural groups are easy. Ambivalence results when normal interpersonal discomfort and miscommunication occur, as they most certainly will, and mainstream individuals revive other myths that suggest persons with disabilities are eccentric (according to Bogdan's exotic mode) or inferior (as in Bogdan's aggrandized mode).

Sources of Stigma Identified by Consumers with Disabilities (1980s-present)

In the late 1980s and early 1990s, the seeds of Wright's client-centered emphasis began to blossom. Consumers with disabilities themselves began to speak on their own behalf. They presented intriguing arguments such as the idea that even a focus on disabled superstars, which implies more respect for disabled persons' accomplishments, can be a prejudicial reaction rather than a recognition of the person as an individual (Yuker, 1987). In contrast, protests against current counseling practices were illustrated in Kalter's (1991) caution against the treatment of disability exclusively as a drama of personal adjustment with no social context since the consequence would be the reduction of the issue to one of individual character and courage rather than of societal stigma and discrimination.

Legislation such as the 1990 Americans with Disabilities Act (ADA) has increased environmental and academic accessibility in both public and private postsecondary institutions and has enhanced employment opportunities for people with disabilities. However, negative attitudes towards students with disabilities on the part of faculty, administrators, and peers remains a challenging enigma. Unfortunately, current investigations have revealed that nondisabled students attributed fewer socially desirable and more undesirable traits to students with disabilities than to their nondisabled peers (Fichten & Bourdan, 1983). In fact, circumplex scales that tested for sameness and difference disclosed that the perception of traits of students with disabilities and their nondisabled peers were clearly opposite. Persons with disabilities were characterized as aloof-introverted, lazy-submissive, and unassuming-ingenuous, while nondisabled persons were seen to be more gregarious-extroverted, ambitious-dominant, and arrogant-calculating (Fichten & Amsel, 1986).

The microculture of persons with disabilities perceives social isolation and underparticipation in campus life as common and all-encompassing problems (Hanna & Rogovsky, 1991; Oakes, 1990; Jenkins, Amos, & Graham, 1988). A hypothesized cause for this exclusion can likely be found within the intersection of self-concept and a sociocultural system that encompasses the attitudinal barriers of apathy, paternalism, fear, curiosity, stereotyping, need for stability, and focus on disabled superstars (Pati & Adkins, 1981; Levi, 1975; Lenhart, 1976/1977). Low self-esteem resulting in social isolation as well as gross societal misconceptions and deep-seated discrimination must be addressed.

Assuming Responsibility for Meeting the Needs of Students with Disabilities

Higher education administrators, faculty, and staff must take responsibility to insure awareness and communication between nondisabled and disabled students and between university personnel and students with disabilities. Programming to counteract negative stereotypes and misconceptions can help. Fragmented and destructive interactions will continue, however, without vigorous and consistent upper administrative support. At the grass-roots level, formal in-services and workshops will be exercises in futility unless every participant believes he or she can be a change agent with the individual and collective power to make a difference. Fortunately, the higher education community has a history of solving problems, and student interest in social values is growing (Astin, 1991; Fichten & Bourdon, 1986; McLoughlin, 1982).

Higher Education Administrators, Faculty, and Staff

Disability awareness is now the responsibility of professionals in postsecondary settings who enjoy easy access to "a broad and rich literature on the lived experience of persons with disabilities, attitudes toward disability, stigma and discrimination, the disability rights movement, and laws and public policies affecting citizens with disabilities" (Hahn, 1991, p. 18). They are privy to action research from sociological, historical, philosophical, psychological, legal, educational, and scientific perspectives. But are universities willing to develop solutions to the marginal status of their students with disabilities? The facilitation of such opportunities means the surrender of the comforts of tradition and prejudice to close analysis, systematic evaluation, collaborative research efforts, and creative innovations (Vogel & Adelman, 1993; Feldman and Newcomb, 1969).

Campuswide assessment of needs and problems is the first priority. Recommended mechanisms are town meetings, surveys, interviews, and other interpersonal strategies designed to gather information from as many stakeholders as possible. Yuker's (1960) Attitudes Toward Disabled People Scale (ATDP) is one example of a survey that has been effectively used to reveal the level of disability stereotypes held in specific institutional contexts. Demographics should be investigated for retention rates and resiliency factors related to successful completion of studies on the part of students with disabilities. Former students should be surveyed for information on what worked for them. Myers' (1994) investigation, designed to reveal communication patterns and preferences of college students with visual disabilities, offers an excellent research base for a parallel inquiry.

The next priority is the generation of strategies to counteract the campus community's identified miscommunication patterns and misconceptions. Implicit in such counteraction is attention to the adjustment and refocusing of attitudes at every level: student workers, receptionists, custodial staff, faculty, and administrators, as the following case study illustrates.

Donna was a first-year student with learning disabilities (LDs) enrolled at an eastern university with a well known disability support service program. The legal documentation of her condition with an explanation of prescribed adaptations had been sent to her professors. She had forgotten to attend the orientation meeting for new students with disabilities, so she did not know the procedures for accessing accommodations. Her specific learning deficit, like that of the majority of adults with LDs, was in written language and necessitated a word processor with a spell check for written assignments and exams. She affirmed this need with each of her professors, including the one she had for U. S. history. He verbally agreed to allow her to take his essay exams using a word processor at the disability service center. On the day of the first exam, a graduate student was filling in for the professor. Nervously, Donna explained her circumstances to him and he reluctantly gave her a copy of the exam and excused her.

When she arrived at the disability service center, she asked the receptionist for directions to the word processors explaining she had to take an exam. The receptionist scolded her for not having faculty authorization to take the test under special circumstances. The student attempted to protest but the receptionist threw a faculty authorization form at her, frowned, and went back to his typing. The student meekly trekked back to get the required signature. The graduate student, however, was confused and unsure of what to do and ended up refusing to sign, stating he hadn't been given the authority. He suggested she return to the disability service center. When she arrived at that office, the clerk was on the phone and chose not to acknowledge her presence. She broke into tears, dropped the exam, and fled. When she returned to class the next week, the professor refused to give her a makeup exam. She dropped out shortly thereafter.

The smugness of one clerk, the lack of concern of a faculty member, the ignorance and confusion of a graduate student, forgetfulness, and inadequate procedural communication between a student and disability service personnel were combined factors culminating in one student's failure to make it through the maze of higher education. Could these causative variables have been avoided? Are proactive strategies possible for counteracting negative stereotypes and discriminatory interactions? I believe so.

Receptionists and Other Front-Desk Personnel

Anti-discriminatory procedural safeguards need to be built into job descriptions and monitored and evaluated on a regular basis. Because of their highly visible interactive positions, receptionists and other front-desk personnel merit extensive training in how to guide and direct students who may not do things the way they do. To practice creative resourcefulness and sensitive responsiveness, they would ideally possess flexibility, interest in problem solving and networking, and openness to new strategies for meeting students' needs. It is absolutely critical their success be acknowledged and rewarded by superiors to generate respect for themselves and those they were hired to serve. If the first priority of the receptionist Donna met was the student, an alternative scenario would have included his timely and undivided attention to her specific problem. While Donna did not fulfill her own responsibilities to learn and follow through on test-taking procedures, her unawareness did not warrant the treatment she encountered.

Faculty and Graduate Assistants

While large scale institutional reform is underway, specific changes can be made by faculty that will make a major impact on students. Attention needs to be given to the way language, environment, and course methodology perpetuate myths. Language in course descrip-

182

tions and lectures must not isolate people who are not in the mainstream. Consider, for example, the following course description for an introductory U. S. history course:

...investigate the great heterogeneity of the population in the U. S. in the 1960s, from powerful citizens like those in positions of medicine, politics, and business to the disabled and infirm who struggled in less fortunate situations.

Discussing those in successful positions and those who were struggling without considering the impact each had on the other is aggrandizing behavior. Those who struggled did not suffer oppression in isolation; those who succeeded did not acquire power through natural giftedness and physical inheritance. We need to talk about the balance sheet—to note that social disadvantage not only limited some individuals, it also enhanced the self-esteem and opportunities of others.

Like language, environment can help or hinder the interaction among students with disabilities and those without. According to Sherif, Sherif, and Nebergall (1965), students are likely to sit and socialize with those who most resemble them. By changing the seating arrangement purposively and often, faculty can build in opportunities for a variety of interactions that provide extended contact among nondisabled students and students with disabilities and opportunities for them to learn from each other. Carefully facilitated classroom interactions may have afforded Donna a more focused and proactive test-taking action path.

Recommended course adaptations to access individual abilities (versus deficits) fall into two categories: methods utilized to disseminate course content and methods used to measure subject mastery. The case of an educator at a large Midwestern university illustrates both.

The faculty member observed nonverbal reactions to the peer-tutoring method she routinely used in her political science course. Students who achieved mastery over specific content were paired up to drill those who were struggling. She saw an attitude of superiority developing in the tutors and a concurrent lack of confidence and helplessness in those being tutored, many of whom were students with learning disabilities. It became apparent the tutors perceived themselves as solutions to the "problem" of inept students.

Because grouping for the learning of rote facts and principles was the only type of peer tutoring within her course, the industry of the tutors, who were very capable of sequential organization of information, was operationalized at the expense of the academic identity of the tutorees whose ordering tendencies were less linear. She did not consider the tutorees incapable of the work, having observed their streaks of brilliance in class discussions and their creativity in problem solving and relating real-life case studies. She also noted untapped abilities in role playing, technological aptitude, critiquing films and readings, debate, research, interviewing, mediation, and oral presentations. Once aware of this, she began using a variety of creative pairings and team work to recognize and exercise the strengths.

Similarly, to level the playing field of evaluation, faculty who always use timed, computer-scored, multiple-choice tests may want to add alternate evaluative formats. The heterogeneity of students' learning styles are responsive to taped, project, portfolio, self-paced, developmental, collaborative, computer assisted, oral, short answer, and untimed assessments. These types of course adjustments do not necessitate additional cost or extreme revisions in planning or teaching style for most faculty, yet they benefit all students, not just those with disabilities.

Disability Support Service Personnel

The directive to disability support administrators is clear. While one might expect them to be directly responsible for programs counteracting identified miscommunication among students, faculty, administration, and staff, it must be stated it is no easy task to combat rampant negative bias, arrogance, mindlessness, ambivalence, and delivery system breakdowns. In order to implement effective interventions, collaboration with students with disabilities and representatives from all campus departments and services is imperative.

The content of disability awareness interventions should be innovative and include: a) the college's legal responsibilities, b) characteristics of disabilities, c) methods of providing reasonable architectural and academic adaptations, and d) ways to gain and maintain productive communication and collaboration. They should contain clearly defined short- and long-term anticipated outcomes to be used for formative evaluation. Additionally, a chorus of researchers recommends campus interventions that attend to the credibility of the presenter. Successful attitude modifying in-services have included talk show, panel discussion, and interview formats featuring qualified students with disabilities, expert speakers from off-campus sites, and university personnel who have effectively collaborated with students to achieve productive academic and physical accommodations (Gerber, 1990; Wright, 1988; Yuker & Block, 1986; Cortez, 1983; Pomerantz, 1983; Donaldson & Martinson, 1977; Dembo, 1970).

Summary

Assessing campuswide needs and problems, building in procedural safeguards, and recommending changes are the first steps toward the successful inclusion of students with disabilities within the campus community. Subsequently, campuswide programming must be designed as a direct response to identified institutional exclusion since every communication, environmental, and attitudinal barrier has a critical effect on students with disabilities. It is only when we gain a comprehension of the inherent challenges in our interactions with students with disabilities that we can engage in the construction of images of disability that dismantle the shameful and destructive freak show and pathological patterns. Bogdan has identified and contributed to the growth and success of all our students in his imperative to move beyond appearances, first impressions, stereotypes, and misconceptions to get to know our students, not as they have been presented but as they are.

REFERENCE

Amsel, R., & Fichten, C. S. (1990). Interaction between disabled and nondisabled college students and their professors: A comparison. *Journal of Postsecondary Education and Disability, 8,* 125-140.

Astin, A. (1991). The changing American college student: Implications for educational policy and practice. *Higher Education, 22* (2), 129-144.

Bogdan, R. (1988). *Freak show: Presenting human oddities for amusement and profit.* Chicago: University of Chicago Press.

Cortez, D. M. (1983). A study of the effects of an inservice program for postsecondary faculty on mainstreaming handicapped students (Doctoral dissertation, New Mexico State University, 1983). *Dissertation Abstracts International, 39,* 2865A.

Dembo, T. (1970). The utilization of psychological knowledge in rehabilitation. *Welfare Review, 8,* 1-7.

Dembo, T., Leviton, G. L., & Wright, B. (1975). Adjustment to misfortune: A problem of social and psychological rehabilitation. *Artificial Limbs, 3,* 4-62. (Original work published 1956)

Donaldson, J., & Martinson, M. C. (1977). Modifying attitudes toward physically disabled persons. *Exceptional Children, 43,* 337-341.

Feldman, K. A. (1972), & Newcomb, T. M. (1969). *The impact of college on students.* San Francisco: Jossey-Bass.

Fichten, C. S., & Amsel, R. (1986). Trait attributions about college students with a physical disability: Circumplex analyses and methodological issues. *Journal of Applied Social Psychology, 16*(5), 410-427.

Fichten, C. S., & Bourdon, C. V. (1986). Social skill deficit or response inhibition: Interaction between disabled and nondisabled college students. *Journal of College Student Personnel, 27,* 326-333.

Fonosch, G. G., & Schwab, L. O. (1981). Attitudes of selected university faculty members toward disabled students. *Journal of College Student Personnel, 22,* 229-235.

Gerber, D. A. (1990). Listening to disabled people: The problem of voice and authority in Robert Edgerton's *The cloak of competence. Disability, Handicap, and Society, 5*(1), 3-23.

Hahn, H. (1991). Alternative views of empowerment: Social services and civil rights. *Journal of Rehabilitation, 57*(4), 18-20.

Hanna, W. J., & Rogovsky, B. (1991). Women with disabilities: Two handicaps plus. *Disability, Handicap, and Society, 6*(1), 49-63.

Heider, R. (1958). *The psychology of interpersonal relations.* New York: Wiley.

Jenkins, C., Amos, O., & Graham, G. (1988). Do black and white college students with disabilities see their worlds differently? *Journal of Rehabilitation, 54*(4), 71-76.

Kalter, J. (1991). Good news: The disabled get more play on T. V. Bad news: There is still too much stereotyping. In E. Lessen (Ed.), *Exceptional persons in society* (pp. 55-6). Needham, MA: Ginn.

Langer, A. L., & Chanowitz, B. (1988). Mindfulness/mindlessness: A new perspective for the study of disability. In A. Yuker (Ed.), *Attitudes toward persons with disabilities* (pp. 69-81). New York: Springer.

Lenhart, L. C. (1977). The stigma of disability (Doctoral dissertation, The University of Oklahoma Health Services Center, 1976). *Dissertation Abstracts International, 37,* 5439B.

Levi, V. (1975). *Disabled persons; attiudes formation and the effect of the environment: An experimental research.* Unpublished manuscript, York University, Toronto.

Leyser, Y. (1989). A survey of faculty attitudes and accommodations for students with disabilities. *Journal of Postsecondary Education and Disability, 7,* 97-108.

Livneh, H. (1988). A dimensional perspective on the origin of negative attitudes toward persons with disabilities. In H. Yuker (Ed.), *Attitudes toward persons with disabilities* (pp. 35-47). New York: Springer.

McLoughlin, W. P. (1982). Helping the physically disabled in higher education. *Journal of College Student Personnel, 23,* 240-246.

Myers, K. (1994). *Preferences of communication styles and techniques of persons with visible visual disabilities: Implications for higher education.* (Doctoral dissertation submitted for publication, Illinois State University, 1994).

Oakes, J. (1990). *Lost talent: The underparticipation of women, minorities, and disabled persons in science.* Santa Monica, CA: Rand.

Pati, G., & Adkins, J. (1981). *Managing and employing the handicapped: An untapped potential.* Chicago: Brace & Jovanovich, Human Resource Press.

Pomerantz, R. M. (1983). *The effectiveness of training modules designed to improve the attitudes of college faculty toward students with disabilities: An evaluation study* (Doctoral dissertation, Temple University, 1983). *Dissertation Abstracts International, 44,* 1604B.

Sherif, C. W., Sherif, M., & Nebergall, R. E. (1965). *Attitude and attitude change: The social judgment-involvement approach.* Philadelphia: Saunders.

Wright, B. A. (1960). *Physical disability—A psychological approach.* New York: Harper & Row.

Wright, B. A. (1988). Attitudes and the fundamental negative bias. In H. Yuker (Ed.), *Attitudes toward persons with disabilities* (pp. 3-21). New York: Springer.

Yuker, H. (1987). Labels can hurt people with disabilities. *Et Cetera, 44*(1), 16-22.

Yuker, H., & Block, J. R. (1986). *Research with the attitudes towards disabled persons scales (1960-1965).* Hempstead, NY: Hofstra University, Center for the Study of Attitudes Toward Persons with Disabilities.

Yuker, H. E. (1988). *Attitudes toward persons with disabilities.* New York: Springer.

Zimbardo, P. G., & Ebberson, E. (1970). *Influencing attitudes and changing behavior.* Reading, MA: Addison-Wesley.

UNDERREPRESENTED STUDENTS ON PREDOMINANTLY EUROPEAN AMERICAN COLLEGE AND UNIVERSITY CAMPUSES: THE STRUGGLE FOR EQUALITY AND A VIABLE VOICE

by

Pearlie Strother-Adams

Colleges and universities represent a microcosm of the larger society (Tryman, 224). That racism and discrimination find their way into colleges and universities in much the same way that they find their way into other institutions such as housing, employment, and the criminal justice system is not surprising. Racism and other forms of discrimination, particularly sexism, have a long history in our schools (Nieto, 20). As the numbers of underrepresented students have increased on predominantly European American campuses, so have the incidences of violence emanating out of conflicts between these groups and the dominant group. This is particularly true on campuses where the enrollment of African American students has steadily increased. The Center for Democratic Renewal, an organization out of Atlanta that monitors hate-related violence and other race-related acts of hostility, chronicled 2,919 such incidents of harassment and violence from 1980 to 1986. The number has grown significantly since (Federal Bureau of Investigation, 1994).

Though it would be insensitive and limiting to overlook European American students falling victim to violence perpetrated by African American students, the largest number of such injustices has been directed toward African Americans. These acts of violence and/or hostility are important as we study the success and/or lack of success of underrepresented students at these institutions. In the case of African American students, their graduation rates lag far behind their European American counterparts. For too many, such institutions are revolving doors. "Nurturance, confidence building, and positive identity formation are sometimes stifled on these campuses. An environment filled with prejudices and stereotypes provokes tentativeness, suspicion, restriction, and harsh self-examination" (Love, 1993, 28). The effects of campus discomfort are cumulative on African American students. The results are often failure to graduate, a lowering of self-esteem, and a loss of confidence. Many who go back home without a degree are viewed as failures among their families and in their communities, for often there is a lot riding on their success. Often the first to attend college in their families and sometimes in their communities, their coming back without a degree reinforces a belief held by many African Americans that education beyond high school is still unobtainable.

It is essential to note that the increase in racial and other types of violence and hostility towards underrepresented groups, African Americans particularly, between 1980-1986, the Reagan era, is no coincidence: The substance and symbolism of this administration reflected anti-civil rights policies and may have created an environment in which a "White backlash" was inevitable at the college level (Tryman, 1992, 223). This "trickle-down effect" was significant since Reagan was a charismatic leader and one of the most popular presidents in the history of our nation. "Students…read the attacks on affirmative action and civil rights as license to act in a heretofore unacceptable fashion. They get their cues from the top" (Tryman, 1992, 223). This trend was carried over to the '90s since President Bush vetoed the Civil Rights Act. Two years earlier it had been ruled that educational fellowships for underrepresented students were unconstitutional; thus the fellowships from public institutions of higher learning were no longer available to these students. This struck multiple blows to many underrepresented students. The most obvious was a lessening of available funds for tuition, fees, and living costs (Tryman, 1992, 223). Perhaps, more devastating, however, was the spotlight shone on underrepresented groups, again African Americans in particular, who are often perceived as receiving far greater than their share of financial assistance.

Given this scenario, in 1995 a key concern is the charismatic presence of Speaker of the House, Newt Gingrich, as well as the often inflammatory and frequently divisive political satire of syndicated commentator, Rush Limbaugh, and others like him. In 1995 affirmative action, for example, surfaced as one of the most controversial political topics to occupy the media. This issue is, not surprisingly, a source of debate and discussion on many U. S. college and university campuses since a widely held assumption is that underrepresented students are not only taking jobs from European American males but are also taking seats away from them at predominantly European American colleges and universities. Dubbed "new racists" who want preferential treatment for jobs and college entry without competition, underrepresented students exist shrouded in arguments about affirmative action, among them the contention that preferential treatment harms individuals by stigmatizing them and creating a hostile atmosphere in society at large (Smith, 1995, 20). "It is no wonder that young whites...would have no sympathy for affirmative action programs and thus often perceive them as preferential treatment" (Tryman, 224).

Perhaps the most damaging effect of such thoughts, feelings, and accusations is the notion that many underrepresented students are only at these institutions because of affirmative action. This belief damages the self-esteem of the individuals within underrepresented groups and leaves them vulnerable and open to attack on many levels from both insensitive students and faculty. "Mobility by means of affirmative action breeds tenuous respect and questionable peer acceptance for...blacks" (West, 1994, 77). In essence, the very existence of faculty and students in what might be termed intellectually challenging and stimulating environments does not necessitate or insure a change in attitudes and values since we bring our racial and other psychological baggage with us to those environments (Tryman, 1992, 223-224). As an underrepresented U. S. citizen who attended at least three predominantly European American universities, I have firsthand experience with prejudice. As an African American, one of the loneliest and most frightening moments for me at college was walking into a classroom of European American students, staring into the face of a European American professor, and discovering I was the only one, the only African American there. At such moments, I became the center of attention, if not to the rest of the class, in my own mind. Always, I embodied a feeling of being alone, an alien who did not belong. Like a spirit, I walked among cold, white stares, often invisible but often visibly disdained.

I hold a peculiar fondness for one incident, perhaps because it occurred in a literature class and I love literature. I had been told by the professor that I had great interpretative skills, indeed a compliment, as all his comments to and about African Americans in my presence had been insulting and/or sarcastic. The one that stands out in my mind came when he blurted out sarcastically as he lectured: "People do different things in different places. Why, in Africa people wear bones in their noses." He laughed and added: "Mayor Daley, who is a great man that I admire and respect, hails gospel singer Mahalia Jackson the greatest singer in the world and says she is his favorite singer." This too ended with a grin. Finally, he observed that Dr. Martin Luther King Jr.'s mother was murdered by a young, black man as she sat at the piano in church. "This is terrible," he chuckled. I was left numb. This was, however, not the most damaging of my university experiences.

The experience that cuts like a knife was, in every sense, a personal attack on me and others of my group. It was Friday. The European American male professor walked in, looked around and asked indignantly, "Where are the other black students?" Though four of us were enrolled in the course, I was the only one present. "Well," he shouted angrily, looking directly at me as the rest of the class looked on, "today was the day we were to talk about the issues involved in dealing with diverse student populations in the classroom, but I find that hard to do with the black students absent. Let's just talk about this issue anyway." I could not help feeling his anger as it burned through me, anger that was obviously directed at me alone. It was as if I were responsible for the other students' absence. I was gripped by a horrible feeling that started as a knot in my stomach and spread through my whole body, eventually consuming me physically, mentally, and spiritually. I felt raped, stripped of all dignity and pride. I struggled against the weight and followed through as usual, taking my pen and notebook out to take notes. "Blacks are really the worst group of all," he continued, as the class looked on in horror. "They keep dirty houses and whenever they move into a neighborhood, it always goes down. Even the Indians are thought of more highly than blacks. I know I wouldn't want to live next door to a black person."

Such experiences leave indelible marks. My worst fears were realized: I was not welcome. From that day to my graduation, I felt no connection with the university. As I looked around, I saw no African American faculty. I saw no African Americans or women in key administrative positions. Essentially, I felt alone. I developed a sense of great urgency about finishing my course work and graduated a semester early. Who could I turn to? There were European American faculty members who were nice, but could I trust them? Would they simply choose sides based on color? I felt very small and unprotected. Unfortunately, many students of diverse backgrounds (racial, sexual, gender) find themselves in similar situations in the 1990s. Acts of discrimination are often less blatant, more subtle, but the blow delivered to the psyche and the self-esteem of the victim is no less harsh.

How then do we begin to make the needed changes? We are indeed a multicultural society. The demographic trend indicates there is no turning back, though the number of African American students enrolled in colleges and universities remains disproportionate to their percentage of the total population. Today, most African Americans enrolled in institutions of higher education are enrolled at predominantly European American schools (Allen, 1992). African American, Latino American, and female student enrollment on undergraduate and graduate/professional levels at Illinois universities and colleges, for example, increased slightly in the fall of 1992 and the fall of 1993; interestingly, female student enrollment exceeds male enrollment (See State of Illinois Board of Higher Education, 1995, Section IV of this volume).

The existence of discriminatory practices in predominantly European American institutions is taken as a matter of course (Allen, 1992, 28). Many situations communicate to us that we have not come very far since the 1960s towards what might be termed true integration; it is as if we have agreed to disagree to a great extent, to live apart, to socialize and play separately although we play in the same playground. We need to intensify our dialogue. Awareness is central to understanding. I remember Rev. Jesse Jackson telling the nation during the Carter administration in the late '70s that we needed to do away with the no-talk policy held towards Palestinians in the Middle East if we were to solve the problems between the Palestinians and Israelis in that region. Jackson received a tremendous amount of backlash as a result of his cry for justice. His life was threatened, as were the lives of his wife and children. However, as a result of his efforts, lines of communication were opened, resulting in greater opportunities for peace. If we are to be multiculturalists, defenders of and advocates for diversity, we too must talk to each other. We must share experiences, experiences that teach us while giving us a turn in the moccasins or shoes of others, experiences that will not replicate another's but can, if we walk with patience, understanding, and compassion, teach tolerance. Listen, for instance, to students' shared feelings and concerns about university life.

I am the first in my family to go to college. It means a lot to me. I am the summation of all of my ancestors. This in itself is affirming. College has been enlightening. There is, however, a downside. As an African American I feel a sense of struggle,...an omnipresent feeling of being subpar, of not being expected to succeed.... Then, there is the pressure of being able to afford an education. I had to borrow money. This is hard in light of so much talk about financial aid cuts and affirmative action. It hurts to hear European Americans as well as African American conservatives discuss these issues. It is as if they are telling me that I am not worthy and that I should not be here.

Studies show "Black families earn less than Whites, at the same time Black students receive less financial aid. Major factors include federal financial aid policies, such as shifts from grants to loans" (Love, 1993, 30).

Another student argued there needs to be greater accountability on the part of the media on college and university campuses since in some instances campus media have fueled the fires of prejudice by printing information from irate students that is obviously not true. He pointed to one such statement that asserted African Americans go to school free while others work to get the opportunity.

It is up to the newspaper to check this information. When it is seen in print this is validation for those who hold such racist stereotypes about African Americans. If you look around the campus, you see African American students holding jobs in large numbers.

He cited campus law enforcement as another issue of concern.

Police pose a problem to African American male students. In situations where there are altercations between European and African Americans, the African Americans' word is not worth much. In most cases I have witnessed European American students walk away and African American students are arrested.

In essence, African American students are often subjected to the same tactics of harassment by campus police that they suffer in the larger society. This police state follows them almost everywhere they turn in the U. S. College status does not afford the black male the luxury afforded white males of quietly, yet somewhat carelessly, stepping into adulthood. The African American male's life at college is not a charmed existence.

Another African American male student contended African American students are not part of the campus as a whole and still tend to eat together, study together, and socialize together. Many, he reported, still refuse to work with other groups.

We isolate ourselves by choice in many instances. There is a general feeling that other groups do not see our reality. African Americans have a sense of urgency about being together because for so long we were oppressed and could not turn to European Americans for friendship; there was no trust. We sometimes seek such relationships based on color only. By doing this we shut ourselves off from the larger picture.

However, he conceded, existence on a predominantly European American campus can be a double-edged sword. He recounts good and bad experiences with both African American and European American students.

I found myself a victim of racial stereotypes perpetrated throughout society. A major part of Resident Assistant training has to do with respecting your co-workers enough to come to them if there are ever any internal problems. After smelling marijuana my white co-workers automatically assumed it was me. None of them came to me and asked.

He rememberd one European American male who always slammed his door as he approached. On the other hand, he found many of the African American students calling him a "token Negro." Such comments as "You work for the man" were quite common.

It was as if many of the African American students felt I should be more lenient toward them because I was African American. It was as if they were saying, "It's our chance to be treated special since one of our own is in."

Students need, as they pointed out themselves, something that all students can rally around, a center or central body that works for everyone. To move toward true equity, student organizations, especially student government associations (SGAs), must take a more active, political and perhaps philosophical role. Such bodies must become genuinely representative of all students. A case in point, at historically African American institutions students naturally feel a greater sense of belonging. At Howard, Spellman, and Morehouse, for instance, "a comfort level is achieved that puts students at ease" (Love, 28). While this is to be expected, from a cultural perspective, its most telling strength has to do with inclusiveness: African American students have a viable voice on these campuses. One way that the underrepresented can obtain such status on predominantly European American campuses is to become more involved in student organizations such as SGA.

Many underrepresented groups see SGAs as the place to be. A recurring complaint among underrepresented students, however, is they receive little or no real representation. Gay and lesbian students, for example, complained that such absence of representation is indicative of anti-gay and lesbian or homophobic sentiments. Rejection at the top may heighten stereotypes and reinforce fears. "People fear the unknown," said one gay student. It is important, he reiterated, that SGAs support increased programs in residential halls, Black History month activities, International Student programs, and Gay-Lesbian Awareness Day activities. In short, taking every opportunity to educate people can accelerate the process and bring about change and a better campus environment. "Homosexuals, once hesitant about declaring their sexual orientation and fighting discrimination, are now demandng equal treatment (*CQ*, 1993, 193). This quest for equality among gays is necessary at the college level.

Student involvement and representation in key organizations can provide a sense of belonging as well as serve as an opportunity for students to gain experiences that will be helpful professionally. Many African American students expressed discomfort in attending SGA meetings, a definite disadvantage when the SGA is considered to be the real student power base on campus. More cynical students view the SGA as a closed club that provides a way of padding the resumes of a few. However, steering articulate underrepresented students to SGA is a major concern. That they must be strong is evident in how easily they can be identified as being one dimensional in their interests when they speak up for their group. Both faculty and students observed that SGAs often appeal to a need to be broad and mainstream when diversity issues are raised so a student representing an ethnic group, for example, is perceived as too self-interested even though they more frequently participate in discussions that are broader than a group interest. Given the typical structure, which involves designated senators or representatives bringing issues to the table, this is no surprise. Because it poses a problem for underrepresented groups that feel left out or too narrowly defined, SGAs sometimes find themselves in an adversarial role with such groups.

Indeed, SGAs can play a major role in helping to create harmony among the various cultural groups in a university or college's diverse setting if, as was suggested by one student leader, everyone works together as a functioning team. Color and cultural diversity do not have to matter if each group in such diverse populations can find a common cause to rally around. In some cases restructuring SGA may be necessary to create a more comfortable climate for all students. One university proposal calls for organizing its SGA under academic departments to allow for more equal and culturally diverse representation. This structure could also add an academic focus. Departmentally students would have an opportunity to reach their individual senators and make their concerns known. Previously underrepresented groups would then be responsible for making their senators work for them across the board.

This would help to build bridges across traditional interest groups since each senator would then be responsible to the more diverse population within his/her academic department.

Culturally identified groups such as Black Student Unions (BSUs), Latin American student organizations, and Asian groups, as well as women's and gay-lesbian organizations, still play an important role on college and university campuses. Though student participants are sometimes viewed as practicing a form of self-segregation, these associations "often foster a positive sense of group identity, awareness, cultural pride, increased self-esteem and decreased social isolation" (Tryman, 1992, 228). On many campuses, for example, BSUs still attract a fairly large segment of African American students that feel a need to keep the organizations operative as home bases and places of advocacy. For students who find themselves "in a world not at all their own," they become an integral part of campus life. As one student said, "They provide a comfortable outlet where students can deal with others like themselves." However, multicultural organizations that can function on a larger scale are also a must; they are clearly a missing piece of the puzzle on too many campuses. To integrate monocultural centers and organizations into the total fabric of campus life so they are not "used as a tool for resegregation" of students (Tryman, 1992, 228) is important.

Finally, students from all groups will tend to be most successful and comfortable in environments where they feel welcome. However, many from underrepresented groups still choose to enroll in predominantly European American institutions. Not surprisingly, diversity in faculty and staff of these institutions could contribute to both recruitment and retention of underrepresented students as well as to making the campus environment appear more friendly. Attempts have been made at several Illinois institutions of higher learning to increase the number of underrepresented faculty and staff within those campus communities (See State of Illinois Board of Higher Education, 1995, Section IV of this volume). Many current Illinois college and university administrations express support for such growth even though most statistics fail to show this because we have such a long way to go before the faculty and administrations of colleges and universities mirror the general population in ethnic and gender representation. The administration at Western Illinois University, Macomb, Illinois, for example, increased underrepresented faculty and staff during fiscal year 1994-1995, including the hiring of staff at the highest administrative levels. Such support for diversity across the board is certain to have long-term positive effects on the campus environment as a whole, but the effort must continue.

Race matters and so does cultural diversity. Hearts are touched each day because it all matters. If I could deliver a short message to this country in the form of a collage of words that would best describe the sting of prejudice and discrimination, this is how it would look:

I am both African American and Native American of Choctaw and Seminole descent. I cannot tell you about all Native Americans.... Some professors made me feel like a show-and-tell project.

I had to take a high-level course. The teacher was openly pessimistic about my ability to do well. What really made me mad was that a white student was trying to get into the same class and the teacher said he should catch on quickly. She made an assumption that the color of my skin would cause me not to do as well as a white person.

In a sexuality class where I was one of a few blacks, I was said to be playing up to the professor because I participated. It is not uncommon for anger and indifference to create problems within or among the same group.

Dr. Doolittle had a speech he wanted to share with us about a slave and his feelings. He chose Tom to read it. When Tom stumbled he quickly handed it to Randy. Randy could not read well either, so the professor huffed up to the podium saying, "Thought these were honor students, guess I'll have to read it myself." I was really hurt that he decided not to let anyone else try. He never took me seriously. I was a woman. Race is not the only factor that can cause professors, students, and administrators to label or brand university students. "In American culture, gender is the most salient feature of one's identity" (Cyrus, 59-60).

People tend to mistake me for being black which I don't understand, but it doesn't bother me. One thing bothers me. I try to socialize with my Chinese people, but they tend to alienate me as if I am a leper. They don't converse with me or even look at me. Maybe they think I am too different (Chinese-American). Our need to become culturally aware and sensitive extends far beyond the classroom and teacher/student interaction.

I am the daughter of an African father and an African American mother. African American students treat me no differently than they do other African Americans, but this friendliness is not extended to my foreign brothers and sisters, African students. I also have a Chinese American boyfriend. I hate people who judge you without knowing you. When someone calls me a sell out, I get very upset.

Not only is there a fear of black students but a fear of what others will do to black students. When I am walking on campus some people look at me and quickly turn the other way as if I want to bother them. When I see fear on a white person's face because of my presence, it makes me sad. When I look into someone's face and see terror, I feel that my life story has been written by someone who does not know me.

Just about everyday when I walk to class, people put their heads down or look in the other direction to avoid eye contact. Many times I feel uncomfortable talking to people of another race, knowing they show signs of being afraid of me. I was one of three blacks in a class and was stereotyped or referred to as 'one of those guys'. I spoke to a white guy sitting next to me in a class, and he showed fear. I only wanted to ask him about a paper that was due.

Two people in the residence hall where I live are constantly yelling insults from their window. Faculty can also be insensitive. A male professor announced to the class one day, "Two men attracted to each other are disgusting." The same professor also criticized the logic in having a gay/lesbian rights awareness day. Gays and lesbians, like African Americans and other ethnic groups, are subject to both verbal and physical abuse that results from ignorance, insensitivity, and political trends. AIDS has devastated the gay community in more ways than one. As a result of the AIDS epidemic, gays are regarded by many as the "scourge of the earth," a metaphor akin to the "wretched of the earth" used to describe African Americans. Such feelings are apparent on college campuses. A gay European American male admitted that he is often the victim of verbal attacks and that he is fearful of physical attack from heterosexual males.

Crimes committed against individuals because of their race, gender, religion, ethnic origin, or sexual orientation appear to be on the increase. Whether the offenses are homophobic slurs, or racially motivated assaults, experts agree that bias-motivated crimes have an especially devastating effect on society in general and on individual victims in particular (*CQ*, 1993, 1).

In 1995 we stand in the middle of a battle over affirmative action. Students at the University of California looked on as the university's mostly Republican, white male

University of California Board of Regents" (Smith, 1995, 20) abolished affirmative action initiatives throughout the system. This turn-around coming from one of the first public university systems to embrace affirmative action in the 1960s could, ironically, be the beginning of similar protests on campuses throughout the country, for as one protester warned: "Change anything and you'll have a new civil-rights movement on your hands" (Smith, 1995, 20). If ever there were a need for dialogue among all students as well as faculty and administrators, now is that time. This must be a dialogue of common concerns that can lead to progressive, inclusive campus coalitions. The real challenge will be holding on while easing tensions between the majority group and underrepresented groups.

If affirmative action is abolished, it will be crucial that the European American male majority understand the need to strike a compromise as underrepresented students struggle to hold on in environments where their presence is no longer a legal requirement. We can best fight campus violence and hostility if we expand student and faculty understanding of prejudice and instill within them the need to fight against it (Ransby, 1989,410). As an educator, one of the most rewarding experiences I have ever had was to have a European American student who had never encountered an African American as an instructor express great joy with having me as an instructor. He even bought me a copy of a U-2 recording that celebrated Dr. Martin Luther King, Jr. Perhaps a small accomplishment, you say, but a major accomplishment in a society where so often we choose not to cross cultural lines. Educational institutions can and should make the difference. Colleges and universities must turn the tide, exposing students to true multiculturalism; the trickle-down effect must become a trickle-out effect as society becomes a microcosm of our higher educational institutions, reflecting the positive behaviors and tolerance shown to all groups regardless of race, gender, or sexual orientation.

ACKNOWLEDGEMENTS

Special thanks to the following people who helped make this article possible: Adjoa Appiah, Nichole Barnes, Rogers Battle III, Marcus Beckman, Marvell Beckman, Gilbert Belles, Anthony Bradford, Eldon Brown, Belinda Carr, Karisa Fairchild, John Langan, Jim Miner, Robert Smith, Carmen VanBuskirk, Brent Watters, and Edward J. Yee.

REFERENCES

Allen, W. R. (1992, Spring). Color of success: African-American college student outcomes at predominantly white and historically black public colleges and universities. *Harvard Educational Review, 62*(1), 26-44.

Cyrus, V. (1993). Experiencing race, class, and gender in the United States. Mountain View, CA: Mayfield.

Federal Bureau of Investigation: Criminal Justice Information Services Division (1994). *Hate-crime statistics 1993: Uniform crime reports.* Washington, D.C.: Department of Justice.

Gay rights. (1993, March). *CQ Researcher, 3*(9), 193-216.

Hate crimes. (1993, January). *CQ Researcher, 3*(1), 1-24.

Love, B. J. (1993, April). Issues and problems in the retention of black students in predominantly white institutions of higher education. *Equity and Excellence in Education, 26*(1), 27-

39.

Nieto, S. (1992). *Affirming diversity: The sociocultural context of multicultural education.* New York: Longman.

Phillips, S. (1994, January). Racial tensions in schools. *CQ Researcher, 4*(1), 124.

Ransby, B. (1988, March). Black students fight back. *The Nation, 246*(1), 410-412.

Smith, R. M. (Ed.). (1995, June 26). California forecast: Storms on campus. *Newsweek,* p. 20.

State of Illinois Board of Higher Education. (1995, January). *Report to the Governor and General Assembly on underrepresented groups in public institutions of higher education in Illinois.* Springfield, IL: Author.

Tryman, M. C. (1992). Racism and violence on college campuses. *The Western Journal of Black Studies, 16*(4), 221-228.

West, C. (1994). *Race Matters.* New York: Vintage Books.

Section IV: Multicultural Education Initiatives in Illinois

COMMUNITY COLLEGE PROGRAMS AND SERVICES FOR SPECIAL POPULATIONS AND UNDERREPRESENTED GROUPS FISCAL YEAR 1994

(Abridged)

Illinois Community College Board

REPORT: The Illinois Community College Board has provided special populations grants to community colleges for nearly two decades. These grants are designed to assist with the funding of programs and services that community colleges need to provide to serve better the students that have special needs. The purpose of the grants has been expanded in recent years to provide special programs and services for minorities and underrepresented groups. The General Assembly passed Public Act 85-283, which required public colleges and universities to develop plans and strategies to increase the participation and advancement of underrepresented groups and to report annually on their progress. This report summarizes the community colleges' reports of these efforts, the programs and services they provide with special populations grants, and the programs and services funded by other grants for underrepresented groups.

State Support

Community colleges budget considerable resources to support the development of special services and programs designed to recruit, retain, and graduate students from underrepresented groups. The Illinois Community College Board (ICCB) supports efforts to address the needs of students from underrepresented groups. A major resource for community colleges is the ICCB **special populations grant program** (SPG). Funded at slightly over $9 million annually, this grant supplements many special support services offered by community colleges.

In fiscal year 1994, community colleges reported expenditures from special populations grants totaling $9.1 million. Each district annually receives a fixed sum of $20,000 per college plus an additional allocation based on student credit hours generated in remedial, adult basic education, and adult secondary education courses. Individual grants ranged in size from $35,900 to $5.5 million. Typically the highest expenditures under this grant are for direct services to students—instruction, counseling, and tutoring. Administrative costs are below 30 percent of the colleges' grant expenditures.

The SPG program helps colleges provide a variety of tutoring services designed to improve reading comprehension and computational skills. Such services are offered on an individual or group basis, by faculty or peer tutors, through computer-based instructional systems that cover discipline- and/or vocational-specific content (e.g., accounting or engineering) or basic skills (e.g., English or math). Of the nearly 370,000 students who received support services in fiscal year 1994, 101,500 students participated in tutoring services offered at the colleges. Additional support services for special populations students include counseling, assessment and testing, referrals to external agencies and organizations, and recruitment and outreach. Table 1 below shows a summary of the SPG services provided to students.

Table 1. Summary of Special Populations Grant Services in Fiscal Year 1994

Types of Service	# of Colleges	Total Contact Hours	Students Served
Tutoring	35	1,564,086	101,493
Counseling	30	102,762	100,769
Assessment & Testing	30	261,260	104,739
Referrals to External Agencies	23	6,124	6,259
Direct Support Services for Students with Disabilities	29	48,191	4,186
Outreach Services	17	27,309	36,505
Other Direct Support Services	20	51,428	16,041
Total		2,061,160	369,992

The total number of service contact hours provided to students was over two million. Colleges' primary support services efforts were in tutoring and assessment and evaluation. These two services comprised 88.6 percent of the total contact hours of service provided to students. In fiscal year 1994, SPG supported remedial, ABE, ASE and ESL instruction for approximately 71,000 students. Credit hours generated from these courses totaled 234,000.

Special populations grant monies included $400,000 to fund special state initiatives. These funds were used to support seven **Centers of Excellence in Adult Education.** Each center serves as an exemplary demonstration program for the delivery of adult basic and adult secondary education in the Illinois community college system. The centers accomplish their mission by (1) effectively using instructional technology; (2) providing seamless educational opportunities, from beginning literacy levels to baccalaureate transfer; and (3) participating in research and information-sharing activities in teaching and learning and assessment. **Richland Community College, Malcolm X College, Waubonsee Community College, College of DuPage, Illinois Central College, College of Lake County, and South Suburban College** are the participating colleges in this program.

In 1992, the Illinois Community College Board initiated an education and employment program that serves students in underrepresented groups. The **Opportunities** program is an

Richland Community College renovated and opened an off-campus center in a depressed Decatur neighborhood. By opening the Center, Richland provided greater accessibility for Opportunities students. Services such as child care are available to students at the main campus or the neighborhood site. The Center's opening has stimulated a community outpouring of contributions and economic development for the area. In addition to classes, the center is open to the public for neighborhood meetings and community workshops.

important segment of Illinois' JOBS (Job Opportunities and Basic Skills) program serving recipients of Aid to Families with Dependent Children (AFDC). Opportunities provides comprehensive education and support services as the means to move individuals from welfare to work. The program, in its third year, represents a unique state/local partnership, involving two state agencies and ten community colleges. In its first three years of operation, Opportunities has brought in over $9 million in federal funds and served over 4,600 students annually. The colleges that participate are **Black Hawk College, City Colleges of Chicago, Danville Area Community College, Illinois Central College, Lewis & Clark Community College, Lincoln Land Community College, Prairie State College, Richland Community College, Rock Valley College, and South Suburban College.**

Minority Student Transfer Centers operate in twenty-five community colleges. Funded by the Illinois Board of Higher Education, community colleges report that transfer centers make a difference in minority students' awareness of opportunities and rewards in pursuing a baccalaureate degree. Each center is centrally located in a highly visible area on campus for easy access. Directors of the centers provide information about course schedules; make referrals for student support services, including financial aid, academic advising, and counseling; schedule meetings between students and representatives from four-year institutions; and arrange for students to visit university campuses. Many centers offer services such as mentor-

> Joliet Junior College increased its minority transfers from 157 in fiscal year 1992 to 254 in fiscal year 1994. The College of DuPage reported that minority transfers increased by 194 over last year to 474. Moraine Valley Community College had a 38 percent increase in numbers of minorities served, from 350 to 560, and City Colleges of Chicago, with six Transfer Centers, had a 75 percent increase to 8,371 students served.

ing and peer advising. For the 1993-94 academic year, transfer center officials reported serving nearly 25,000 students.

Some improvements in minority student transfers are becoming evident. From fall 1988 to fall 1993, selected data on African American and Latino students showed increased transfers of 30.7 percent and 102.8 percent, respectively. In fall 1993, the total number of community college transfers was 16,679, a 19.9 percent increase from fall 1988. Of that number, African Americans and Latinos represented 11.3 percent (1,872) and 4.7 percent (783), respectively. More than half of the minority community college student transfers are to public institutions.

Community College Services and Programs for Underrepresented Student Groups

Community colleges have developed a variety of services and programs to facilitate success of underrepresented students. In fiscal year 1994, programs for underrepresented students served over 89,000 ethnic minorities; nearly 8,500 females; and 4,500 physically challenged students. In fiscal year 1994, personnel assigned to these programs was equivalent to 827.45 staff years an increase of 8 percent over the previous year. The total budget allocation was $25.3 million. The ICCB special populations grant program supplemented these programs with $1.6 million. The next section offers examples of the variety of programs and activities developed and implemented for underrepresented groups.

Institutional Commitment to Enhance Academic Climate for Minority Students

Several colleges have created committees as the overseeing entities to address matters related to college climate. Many of these committees include college administrators, faculty, nonacademics, and professional support staff, including key campus leaders in different academic departments and divisions. **Danville Area Community College's** Human Relations Council comprises minority leaders from the community and minority and other staff at the college. **Parkland College's** Committee on Access, Equity and Cultural Diversity includes key campus leaders in international, intercultural, and multicultural education, as well as personnel from administration, faculty, nonacademics, and professional support.

Committees of these types must address a variety of tasks, including developing strategies to improve the college climate for minorities, females, and students with disabilities; recruiting and retaining students, faculty, and staff from underrepresented groups; and promoting major activities and events to heighten awareness and sensitivity to cultural differences within the colleges. **Prairie State College's** Diversity and Human Relations Committee is charged with examining the diversity of campus life and interaction, identifying areas that discourage greater respect for cultural diversity and pluralism, and recommending steps that create a campus environment conducive to positive human interactions and relations.

Through these committees, activities and programs designed to recognize and celebrate diversity in the United States are encouraged or carried out. **Truman College** celebrates diversity throughout the year with events such as Hispanic Week, Black History Month, American Indian/Alaskans Week, African Week, and International Week. **William Rainey Harper College** had its first annual **AHANA** (Asian-Americans, Hispanic, African-American, and Native Americans/Alaskans) Pre-Orientation Program. The main purpose of the AHANA Pre-Orientation is to provide an opportunity for new ethnic/minority students to meet each other, as well as Harper faculty and staff who have a special interest in the minority education experience. The program includes presentations on special support services and financial aid, a panel of continuing minority students, and small group discussions.

Morton College's "We Care" Multicultural Initiative includes offering *Tertulias* sessions featuring Latino students and hosting visits of international educators to discuss aspects of the cultures of Latin American countries.

Curriculum Transformation

Several colleges are addressing climate issues in instructional areas as well. The impetus for this is the passage of Public Act 87-581, which requires public colleges and universities to include coursework on race, ethnicity, gender, and other topics designed to improve human relations in their general education requirements. Some colleges have identified existing required courses in social sciences and humanities that include topics specified by the legislation. **Parkland College, Sauk Valley Community College, Rend Lake College,** and the **College of Lake County** have incorporated human relations topics in their first-year composition and/or speech courses. **Highland Community College** has developed a required two-credit-hour course on human relations covering topics on sexual harassment, racial sensitivity, and ethnic differences. **Elgin Community College** created a special orientation component to emphasize diversity at the college, and now offers a diversity unit within all sections of four of its general education courses—Psychology, Sociology, Anthropology, and Speech.

Faculty and Staff Development.

Colleges are coupling matters related to inclusiveness in the curriculum and other areas with faculty and staff development efforts. Workshops and faculty orientations over the state have included topics on diversity in students' learning styles and reorientation in pedagogy and content. **Parkland College** has provided statewide leadership in faculty and staff development with the first annual multicultural and gender-balanced conference, attended by over 500 faculty, teachers, staff, and students from Illinois community colleges and secondary schools. The college also has provided leadership through its intensive three-week institute on curriculum transformation. At the summer 1994 institute, participants learned how to integrate multicultural women's topics into existing course content. **Morton College's** "We Care" initiative involved modifying courses that covered topics on race and human relations and offering those courses to college personnel free of charge. College officials also arranged a visit to Cuauhnahuac Institute in Mexico, and many faculty and staff went at their own expense. **College of Lake County's** Learning As a Challenge Committee sponsored several diversity workshops, including one conducted by Claude Steele, a social psychologist from Stanford University who focused on "stigmatization" as a barrier to academic achievement.

Programs Designed to Help Minorities on Campus

Over 100 minority programs were available to students in community colleges in fiscal year 1994. **Highland Community College's** African-American Male Mentoring program targets minority males by matching students with African-American male professionals who advise and encourage students in pursuing their educational goals. Academic success in this program leads to scholarships or part-time employment as student workers. **Harold Washington College's** Individual Needs (IN) program targets those needing special assistance in completing English. The IN program student receives in-class tutoring by an aide, instruction on critical-thinking skills, and cultural supplement instruction. IN students complete their courses at a higher rate than students in regular English 100 courses and return to classes the next semester at higher rates than new students. **Olive-Harvey College's** Future Teachers of Chicago program is a partnership with Chicago public and nonpublic schools and organizations formed to recruit and encourage minority students to consider teaching and leadership positions in Chicago schools. Partially funded by the U. S. Department of Education, the program gives Olive-Harvey students internship and scholarship opportunities.

Community Outreach

Community colleges work closely with community-based organizations and local elementary and secondary schools to help in preparing the next generation of minorities for college. **Kennedy King College's** Benjamin E. Mays Academy helps students who need additional support in reading, writing, and computation. Selected students are allowed to enroll in college credit courses while earning their diploma, thus easing their transition from high school to college. **Malcolm X College's** Personalized Curriculum Institute serves high school students needing basic skills development in mathematics, communications, reading, critical thinking, and study skills. The Institute focuses on improving needed skills through highly interactive ten-minute instructional sessions. Students who follow the Institute's requirements find median grade level gains of two years for every 20 hours of instruction. **Kaskaskia College's** Pre-College Enrichment Program serves students in grades four through twelve. Activities of the program have included trips to public universities, attendance at computer workshops on campus, a two-day math enrichment class, a two-day science enrichment class, and a career seminar conducted by representatives from Eastern Illinois University. **Richland Community College's** College Futures program served over 800 minority youth through its programming and activities. Tutoring, campus visits, and exercises in reasoning and critical thinking were a few of the activities offered by the program.

Several community colleges have attempted to address literacy problems by encouraging families to view learning as a family affair, since the parent is in the best position to encourage and be actively involved with his/her child's education. **Joliet Junior College's** Families About Success engages parents with their children in activities designed to reinforce the value and benefit of education. **Kankakee Community College's** Parents as Partners in Reading is the umbrella program for several networked, grant-funded programs that also promote literacy by involving the entire family. Through prepared curricula, lesson plans, videos, and parent/child activities, parents are encouraged to make reading a participatory and exciting family event.

Minority Faculty and Staff Efforts

Community colleges use a variety of resources to recruit and retain faculty, including advertising in community-based newspapers and drawing upon minority staff members, as well as ministers and community leaders who have contact in minority communities. In fall 1994, **Danville Area Community College** held a part-time job fair to attract minorities. College officials felt that they would be more successful in increasing the minority representation in the full-time faculty ranks by first bringing in minority candidates through part-time positions. **William Rainey Harper College** experienced significant progress in its efforts to increase the representation of minorities on its staff when an Affirmative Action Committee member began serving on the Search and Screen Committee as advisor and proponent for hiring to achieve diversity. Ten minority hires, including full-time faculty, were made by the college in the past two years.

Programs for Female Leadership and Nontraditional Programs

Community colleges have implemented several programs designed to encourage women to consider nontraditional program areas. The statewide Building Fairness Program is carried out in several community colleges across the state. The program encourages female and male students to consider occupations that are traditionally identified with persons of the opposite gender. **Belleville Area College's** Gender Equity Program is an innovative vocational education approach that integrates academic achievement and occupational competencies. The activities incorporated in the program include a series of women's issues workshops, celebration of Women's History Month in March, and a women-in-technology project. **Kishwaukee College's** strategies to encourage females to enroll in nontraditional programs included establishing scholarships to attract women in manufacturing technology and CAD mechanical drafting programs and creating a nontraditional career counselor position that resulted in 52 females enrolling in highly technical occupational programs. The **College of DuPage** designed activities to recruit female students into technological programs, including the Expanding Horizons program, a career development activity for young girls, and the Partnership for Excellence program offered in cooperation with Fermilab and Argon Labs.

Services to Female Students

Most colleges have begun services to help simplify women's attendance, including day care services for their young children. **Parkland College** has created an Office of Women's Programs and Services that focuses on women's needs. **Prairie State College** has expanded its programming in support of returning women by establishing an ombudsperson specifically for females. **Spoon River College** has facilitated the development of a support group for female victims of domestic violence.

Services and Programs for Students with Disabilities

Many colleges have developed and implemented major plans to improve physical facilities and accessibility for students with disabilities. Handicapped accessible elevators, electrically operated doors, new parking areas, improved walkways and toilet facilities, and relocation of offices are included in the changes being made on campuses. Special services to students with disabilities included purchases of access equipment, including reading machines that allow students with visual impairments immediate and independent access to printed materials via audio output/large print. Computer software packages designed to enlarge the print of most computer programs and amplified stethoscopes, which assist hearing impaired students in their medical programs, are among the many pieces of equipment being purchased to help students with disabilities in the teaching and learning process at community colleges.

Spoon River College has enabled many of its students with disabilities to move into college-level courses via the Maximum Benefits Team approach which involves all service support agencies, secondary schools, and college personnel in working with students with special needs. **William Rainey Harper's** English as a Second Language Program for the Deaf and Hearing Impaired meets students' needs through an innovative approach that includes second language instruction, and a bilingual/bicultural team-teaching situation in a self-contained classroom. **McHenry County College** provides an orientation to disabilities through an Institute Day on Disability Awareness for all faculty, staff, and students. As part of the program, a wheelchair obstacle course is set up for able persons to negotiate.

Summary

Community colleges have a mission to serve those who need special assistance in reaching their educational goals. This report indicates that colleges are attempting to address the diverse needs of underrepresented groups by offering a variety of programs and services within their institutions. Minority enrollments are improving, but colleges still need to focus their efforts on retaining and graduating students, particularly in the transfer programs (ICCB *Report on Enrollments and Completions-Fiscal Year 1994,* January 1995). Female students are well represented in the community colleges. Efforts to encourage females in nontraditional fields of study are applauded. As demographic changes occur in Illinois, it is anticipated that enrollments of students with disabilities will increase. Pressures to address the needs of students in this underrepresented group also will increase. Colleges are encouraged to develop and implement more effective strategies that meet the needs of these student groups and to share this information and expertise through consortia meetings and conferences.

REPORT TO THE GOVERNOR AND GENERAL ASSEMBLY ON UNDERREPRESENTED GROUPS IN PUBLIC INSTITUTIONS OF HIGHER EDUCATION IN ILLINOIS

(Abridged)

State of Illinois Board of Higher Education

TRENDS IN ENROLLMENT

Minority Students

The sections below present information about Black and Hispanic enrollment. This information has been highlighted because of the degree of Black and Hispanic underrepresentation in higher education and the size of these minority populations in Illinois....

Black Students

In fall 1993, total Black undergraduate and graduate/professional enrollment at Illinois colleges and universities increased slightly by 0.6 percent, the fifth consecutive year in which total Black enrollment rose. As in recent years, Black enrollment grew at the graduate/professional level. Undergraduate enrollment decreased this past year because of declines at both community colleges and private institutions. In part, the decrease in Black undergraduate enrollment reflects the 9.6 percent decline in the number of Black students that have graduated from Illinois public schools from 1986 to 1993. Since 1986, total Black undergraduate and graduate/professional enrollment has increased by 9.9 percent.

Major developments this past year include...
- *Total Black undergraduate and graduate/professional enrollment* increased by 0.6 percent from 72,112 in fall 1992 to 72,557 in fall 1993 and remained at slightly less than 12 percent of total enrollment.
- *Black undergraduate enrollment* decreased by 0.3 percent from 64,418 in fall 1992 to 64,236 in fall 1993.
- *Black graduate /professional enrollment* increased by 8.1 percent from 7,694 in fall 1992 to 8,321 in fall 1993.
- *Black enrollment at public universities* increased by 3.8 percent from 23,444 in fall 1992 to 24,338 in fall 1993. Eight of 12 public universities had increases in Black enrollment. The largest enrollment growth occurred at Chicago State University. The largest percentage increase in enrollment occurred at Governors State University.
- *Black enrollment at private institutions* increased by 1.6 percent from 18,474 in fall 1992 to 18,774 in fall 1993.
- *Black undergraduate enrollment at community colleges* decreased by 2.5 percent from 30,194 in fall 1992 to 29,445 in fall 1993. *Black student transfers* from community colleges to four-year institutions increased by 4.8 percent.
- *Black undergraduate and graduate/professional male enrollment* decreased slightly in the past year from 26,386 in fall 1992 to 26,361 in fall 1993. Black representation in higher education remains heavily female as males account for less than 40 percent of total Black enrollment at community colleges, public universities, and private institutions.

Hispanic Students

This past year, total Hispanic undergraduate and graduate/professional enrollment again showed significant growth increasing by 4.5 percent. In contrast to recent years, enrollment growth was greatest at the graduate/professional level increasing by 9.1 percent. Undergraduate Hispanic enrollment increased by 4.1 percent. Since 1986, Hispanic enrollment at Illinois colleges and universities has increased by 71.5 percent.

Major developments this past year include...

* *Total Hispanic undergraduate and graduate/professional enrollment* increased by 4.5 percent from 30,022 in fall 1992 to 31,385 in fall 1993 and increased to 5 percent of total enrollment.
* *Hispanic undergraduate enrollment* increased by 4.1 percent from 27,418 in fall 1992 to 28,545 in fall 1993.
* *Hispanic graduate/professional enrollment* increased by 9.1 percent from 2,604 in fall 1992 to 2,840 in fall 1993.
* *Hispanic enrollment at public universities* increased by 7.6 percent from 8,424 in fall 1992 to 9,065 in fall 1993. Hispanic enrollment grew at 11 of 12 public universities. The largest enrollment increase occurred at the University of Illinois at Chicago. The largest percentage increase in enrollment occurred at Eastern Illinois University.
* *Hispanic enrollment at private institutions* increased by 7.2 percent from 10,522 in fall 1992 to 11,278 in fall 1993.
* *Hispanic undergraduate enrollment at community colleges* decreased by 0.3 percent from 11,076 in fall 1992 to 11,042 in fall 1993. *Hispanic student transfers* from community colleges to four-year institutions increased by 7.0 percent.

Female Students

In Illinois higher education, female enrollment exceeds male enrollment. In fall 1993, 409,655 females represented 55.3 percent of total higher education enrollment compared with 330,550 males who represented 44.7 percent. Despite high levels of female enrollment, historically, a decline in female representation occurs in professional and doctoral programs, as well as in science, mathematics, and engineering programs. In recent years, these traditionally low rates of female participation have raised equity and occupational supply issues. In particular, it is advocated that the quality and number of persons entering science, mathematics, and engineering disciplines will need to increase if the nation and state are to improve economic growth and productivity. White males, who traditionally have accounted for a high proportion of new entries into science, mathematics, and engineering occupations, will be unable to meet this need because they represent a declining proportion of the population—a consequence of a decrease in White birth rates after the baby boom years.

This past year, the percent of female students increased at most educational levels. Over the past decade, female representation at Illinois colleges and universities has increased annually. These decade-long increases have occurred at all degree levels at public universities, community colleges, and private institutions.

There have been steady increases, in particular, in professional and doctoral female enrollment.

Minority and Female Employees

Data on minority and female employees at institutions of higher education are collected

208

biennially by the Board of Higher Education as part of the federal Integrated Post Secondary Education Data System (IPEDS).

The data indicates that for Blacks but not Hispanics, staff representation at institutions of higher education is comparable to representation in the general population. In addition, females comprise more than half of all employees in all three higher education sectors. However, as discussed below, Black and female representation is not evenly distributed and is lower in faculty and executive positions.

IPEDS data indicate that female representation among all public university staff increased during this period, as did female representation in executive, professional, and faculty positions. For example, females represented 24.0 percent of all faculty in 1981 and 31.3 percent of all faculty in 1993. Females comprised 25.3 percent of all executive, positions in fall 1981 and 40.0 percent of these public university positions in fall 1993.

Only limited progress has occurred in minority staff representation at public universities. Black representation showed improvement in executive and professional positions, and a decline in clerical and all other occupations. Some improvement has occurred in the number of Black faculty who increased from 3.2 percent of all public university faculty in 1989 to 4.3 percent of all public university faculty in 1993. Nevertheless, Black faculty representation remains very low. Hispanics represent less than 3 percent of public university employees, and few occupational categories exhibited meaningful improvement in Hispanic representation from 1981 to 1993. Information on institutional efforts to improve faculty representation is presented later in this report.

Students with Disabilities

Public higher education institutions in Illinois enroll significant numbers of students with disabilities. These students include those who are visually impaired hearing impaired, mobility impaired, speech impaired, learning disabled, or affected by chronic health and other problems so as to require special institutional assistance. Public institutions offer these students an extensive array of services to enable them to participate more fully in educational and non-educational programs. Services include academic support, such as interpreting for the deaf and book taping for the blind; student support, such as advising, counseling, and vocational assessment; and assistance in facilitating access to campus buildings.

Enrollment figures of students with disabilities from the annual institutional reports on underrepresented groups submitted to the Board of Higher Education are either institutional estimates of the total disabled population or counts of the number of students who receive services from campus programs. Totals differ significantly from campus to campus in part because of institutional program variations. For example, some institutions have specialized programs serving students with specific kinds of disabilities, such as mobility impairments or learning disabilities. Further information on programs and services for these students appears later in this report.

Trends in Persistence and Degree Completion

Increasing the enrollment of minority students at Illinois colleges and universities is a goal of utmost importance for Illinois higher education. However, once minority students enroll at these institutions, it is equally important that they succeed and graduate.

Recently, Illinois public universities and community colleges established procedures among themselves for sharing enrollment and graduation information in order to better understand student patterns of persistence, retention, transfer, and degree completion. These merged data currently cover the period fall 1982 through spring 1993. They contain information by racial/ethnic group and show that minority students, overall, were less likely than other students to remain in school. Eighty-two percent of Black first-time Freshmen continued beyond the first year. After three years, 55 percent of Black students were still enrolled in college. Among Hispanic first-time freshmen, 83 percent persisted beyond the first year and 63 percent were still enrolled after three years. Among all other students, 91 percent enrolled past the first year and 76 percent enrolled beyond the third year.

A lower proportion of minority students than all other students achieve a baccalaureate degree and fewer Black and Hispanic students than majority students achieve their degrees in the traditional four years. After six years, 31 percent of Black first-time freshmen who entered in 1987 earned degrees compared with 58 percent of all other students. The gap is less severe for Hispanic students; 37 percent earned degrees within six years. Although the proportion of Blacks and Hispanics who earned degrees within six years increased since 1983, the proportion who earned degrees in four years has changed little. Time-to-degree is affected by a variety of factors such as full versus part-time attendance, the choice of program majors, switching majors, and transfers among institutions. Given the variability of factors affecting time-to-degree, there is no one standard to which all students can or should conform. Institutions should promote and facilitate minority student academic progress while being sensitive and responsive to student differences. Institutions should consider what kinds of appropriate actions might be taken to assist minority degree completion and reduce their time-to-degree.

Black Student Degree Completion

The total number of higher education degrees (i.e., certificates through doctoral degrees) awarded to Black students by Illinois colleges and universities increased by 7.2 percent in the past year. The number of Black degree recipients increased at all levels except the baccalaureate. Since 1986, higher education degrees awarded to Black students have increased by 23.5 percent. During this period, the greatest growth in Black degree recipients occurred at the master's and advanced certificate (71.5 percent), doctoral (35.1 percent), and bachelor's (25.1 percent) levels.

Major developments in degree completion this past year include:
- *Total Degrees*—Total degrees awarded to Black students increased by 7.2 percent in the past year from 10,732 in fiscal year 1992 to 11,501 in fiscal year 1993.
- *Certificates*—Black students receiving certificates increased by 5.0 percent from 2,790 in 1992 to 2,929 in 1993.
- *Associate Degrees*—Black students receiving associate degrees increased by 19.2 percent from 2,433 in 1992 to 2,901 in 1993.
- *Bachelor's Degrees*—Black students receiving degrees decreased by 1.1 percent from 3,890 in 1992 to 3,847 in 1993.
- *Master's Degrees and Advanced Certificates*—Black students receiving master's degrees and advanced certificates increased by 11.2 percent from 1,383 in 1992 to 1,538 in 1993.
- *Doctoral Degrees*—Black students receiving doctoral degrees increased by 8.5 percent from 71 in 1992 to 77 in 1993.
- *First-Professional Degrees*—Black students receiving first-professional degrees increased by 26.7 percent from 165 in 1992 to 209 in 1993.

<u>Hispanic Student Degree Completion</u>

The total number of higher education degrees awarded to Hispanic students by Illinois colleges and universities increased by 2.2 percent in the past year. Strong growth in the number of Hispanic students earning associate degrees and first-professional degrees was tempered by a decline in master's degrees and little change in the number of bachelor's degrees. Since 1986, higher education degrees awarded to Hispanic students have increased by 72.4 percent. Over this six-year period, doctoral degree recipients increased by 20.0 percent and all other degree recipients increased more than 60.0 percent.

Major developments this past year include:

- *Total Degrees*—Total degrees awarded to Hispanic students increased by 2.2 percent in the past year from 4,794 in fiscal year 1992 to 4,900 in fiscal year 1993.
- *Certificates*—Hispanic students receiving certificates decreased by 5.0 percent from 1,327 in 1992 to 1,260 in 1993.
- *Associate Degrees*—Hispanic students receiving associate degrees increased by 11.1 percent from 1,243 in 1992 to 1,381 in 1993.
- *Bachelor's Degrees*—Hispanic students receiving bachelor's degrees increased by a small amount from 1,618 in 1992 to 1,622 in 1993.
- *Master's Degrees and Advanced Certificates*—Hispanic students receiving master's degrees and advanced certificates decreased by 2.6 percent from 431 in 1992 to 420 in 1993.
- *Doctoral Degrees*—Hispanic students receiving doctoral degrees increased by 7.7 percent from 39 in 1992 to 42 in 1993.
- *First-Professional Degrees*—Hispanic students receiving first-professional degrees increased by 28.7 percent from 136 in 1992 to 175 in 1993.

<u>Black and Hispanic Student Degree Completion in Select Disciplines</u>

In recent years, higher education has given increased attention to the issue of improving minority participation and degree completion in science, mathematics, and engineering disciplines. These are fields with low minority participation that require occupational growth to sustain future economic development. At the baccalaureate level, Blacks and Hispanics earned fewer degrees in computer science and mathematics, while they earned more degrees in engineering and life sciences. Blacks also earned more degrees in physical sciences this year, while Hispanics showed little change. At the graduate level, degrees earned by Blacks and Hispanics decreased or remained the same in all areas except life sciences for Blacks.

At the doctoral level, there have been few Black and Hispanic degree recipients in mathematics, engineering, and science disciplines. Fourteen Black and Hispanic students received doctoral degrees in these disciplines in fiscal year 1993.

For a number of years, colleges and universities have sought to increase the number of minority students who enter the fields of elementary and secondary education. There is widespread agreement that increasing the pool of minority school teachers can further the academic progress of minority students since minority teachers act as role models and help encourage and support minority student academic achievement. Unfortunately, there was a decline of interest during the 1980s in education as a field of study. In recent years, however, this trend has reversed, in part, due to the aging and retirement of the teacher workforce. Degree data collected by the Board of Higher Education showed significant increases in the number of Black and Hispanic students receiving bachelor's and master's degrees in education in 1990 and 1991. In 1993, this trend tapered off. The number of Black students receiving bachelor's

211

degrees in education has decreased from 339 in 1992 to 281 in 1993 and the number of Hispanic bachelor's degree recipients decreased from 164 in 1992 to 112 in 1993. Master's degree recipients also decreased among Hispanics, but increased for Blacks—from 566 in 1992 to 666 in 1993.

Female Student Degree Completion

The percentage of female degree recipients in the three education sectors changed little between 1992 and 1993. Females accounted for 60.0 percent of degree recipients in the community colleges, 50.1 percent in public universities, and 53.0 percent in private universities in 1993.

Although there was no appreciable change this past year, the number and percentage of women receiving degrees from Illinois public institutions of higher education have increased over the past decade. In particular, female degree recipients have increased over the past ten years at the doctoral and first-professional levels. On the other hand, little change has occurred in the proportion of females receiving bachelor's, master's, and doctoral degrees from 1986 to 1993 in mathematics and science disciplines.

EFFORTS TO IMPROVE REPRESENTATION

Statewide Activity in 1994

The state of Illinois has created various programs to help advance minority participation and achievement in higher education. These include minority projects funded by the Higher Education Cooperation Act (HECA) through the Illinois Board of Higher Education; Special Population Grants that are administered by the Illinois Community College Board; the Minority Teacher Incentive Grant Program administered by the Illinois Student Assistance Commission; and two financial aid programs for graduate students—the Illinois Minority Graduate Incentive Program (IMGIP) and the Illinois Consortium for Educational Opportunity Program (ICEOP). Grants are awarded annually by the Board of Higher Education under the Health Services Education Grants Act for the enrollment of minority students in health professions programs at private institutions.

A number of other statewide programs serve a general population but have special import for minority participation and achievement. For instance, the Medical Scholarship Program, administered by the Illinois Department of Public Health, awards significant numbers of scholarships to minority students who agree to practice in medically underserved areas of the state. Also, the federal Dwight D. Eisenhower Mathematics and Science Education Program sponsors projects for the improvement of science and mathematics instruction in elementary and secondary education, with many projects addressing the needs of underrepresented students. The state's Monetary Award Program (MAP), which provides need-based financial aid to undergraduates, also represents a significant state resource for under-represented students.

In its Priorities, Quality, and Productivity initiative, or P*Q*P, the Illinois Board of Higher Education has identified minority student achievement as one of the statewide priorities that deserve special attention by Illinois colleges and universities. The Board's budget recommendation for Illinois higher education for fiscal year 1995 contained additional funding of $2.0 million for minority student achievement at public universities and $1.1 million for Special Populations Grants at community colleges. The 1995 state budget passed by the General Assembly and signed by Governor Jim Edgar included these recommended funding increases. Also, the state budget appropriated an additional $180,000 for the Minority Teacher Incentive

Grant Program and $100,000 for ICEOP. Under HECA, funding for Minority Educational Achievement Projects was increased by $300,000 and Minority Articulation Projects by $50,000. Finally, in an important initiative, public universities have received allocations of $46 million from a fiscal year 1994 appropriation of $100 million for remodeling activities necessary to bring state facilities into compliance with the federal Americans with Disabilities Act (ADA). Nonappropriated funds have been used by both public universities and community colleges to undertake additional remodeling activities.

Funding for minority students under Health Services Education Grants also significantly increased during the past year. HSEGA has offered incentives to promote minority participation in medical and dental programs at Illinois nonpublic institutions. In 1993, a comprehensive study undertaken by the Board concluded that HSEGA grant rates have not been large enough to stimulate minority enrollment. A new Board policy, implemented in fiscal year 1995, increased minority grant rates and extended these rates to all health education fields. As a result of this change, minority incentive funds increased from $357,500 in fiscal year 1994 to an estimated $1.1 million in fiscal year 1995. It is projected that programs in medicine ($617,000), nursing ($271,300), and allied health ($136,200) will receive the largest minority incentive grants in fiscal year 1995.

Higher Education Cooperation Act

Through the Higher Education Cooperation Act the Illinois Board of Higher Education annually allocates funds for programs and projects that involve cooperation among higher education institutions. Two HECA programs are designed to increase minority representation at Illinois colleges and universities: the Minority Educational Achievement Program and the Minority Articulation Program.

For fiscal year 1995, the Board of Higher Education has allocated $4.5 million for Minority Educational Achievement projects from the precollegiate to graduate/ professional levels. Funding supports 33 projects including seven projects funded for the first time in fiscal year 1995. Twenty projects involve precollegiate students. The largest precollegiate project is sponsored by the University of Illinois at Chicago in cooperation with seven Chicago universities, the City Colleges of Chicago, and other Chicago civic and educational organizations. This project will provide academic and social support for secondary and postsecondary students through the establishment of "Future Teachers" programs at 89 public and nonpublic city high schools and cooperating colleges and universities. If successful, this project could substantially expand the number of minority teachers in Chicago schools

Another new pre-college project is Project Hope co-sponsored by Governors State University and Prairie State College to improve the general academic preparation of Hispanic high school students and to increase their awareness and interest in higher education. Also, a project led by the Native American Educational Services College supports academic skills development of Native American students enrolled in Chicago elementary and secondary schools. Other new projects involve architecture, art, urban planning; general career preparation for minority students in grades seven to twelve; and the development of critical thinking skills in the areas of mathematics, science, and communication.

For fiscal year 1995, the Board of Higher Education has awarded $2.3 million in the Minority Articulation Program to continue funding 25 transfer centers and 10 short-term projects. Each center provides services and activities to help encourage the successful transfer of minority students. The centers also work with faculty and staff at community colleges and regional colleges and universities to ease student transition. All transfer centers funded in fiscal year 1993 were continued for fiscal year 1994.

Five of the ten short-term Minority Articulation Program projects are new. The new projects range from a faculty/mentoring program at John A. Logan College to the Hispanic Program for Educational Advancement at McHenry County College. Also funded is a cooperative private/public project involving Millikin University and Richland Community College and a minority recruitment project sponsored by Southern Illinois University at Carbondale and six community colleges. The University of Illinois at Chicago also has received funding for a project involving minority graduate and professional student recruitment and placement.

Public Institutional Activity in 1994

Public institutions offer many special programs to improve student representation. These programs encompass diverse activities, serve extensive student populations, and involve considerable staff and funding. Almost 700 programs served students from underrepresented groups at Illinois public universities and community colleges in fiscal year 1994. Program expenditures totaled over $83 million. The following pages offer highlights from the institutional reports submitted each October to the Illinois Board of Higher Education. The reports are on file at each higher education system office.

<u>Minority Students</u>

A number of public institutions formulated new plans to enhance minority student representation and implemented associated administrative structures and procedures. For example, Eastern Illinois University announced a long-term goal to expand minority student enrollment to 12 percent and established a campus-wide committee to facilitate meeting this goal. Sangamon State University formulated an enrollment management plan which seeks significant annual progress in minority enrollment. The University of Illinois at Urbana-Champaign also announced plans to increase minority enrollment under its "Academic Plan for the Year 2000." William Rainey Harper College and the College of Lake County also established campus-wide committees to enhance minority retention.

Many institutions also undertook curricular initiatives in 1994. Western Illinois University and the University of Illinois at Chicago, for example, added a multicultural component to their general education requirements. The University of Illinois at Urbana-Champaign developed eight additional courses that address subjects related to nonwestern cultures and minority subcultures. The Urbana campus now offers 55 such courses. Southern Illinois University at Edwardsville formed the Diversity Advocates Program "to prepare students for cultural and racial issues on the SIUE campus and for the future." Many community colleges, such as Kankakee Community College, Elgin Community College, and Oakton College, pursued multicultural curricular development. Lakeland College also reviewed the race/ethnic composition of its programs as part of an effort to ensure that there was no bias in counseling and advising students.

Faculty development activities included Western Illinois University sponsoring a week-long institute to assist faculty in formulating strategies to advance teaching effectiveness with students from underrepresented groups, and Oakton Community College's semester-long faculty seminar entitled "Multiculturalism in the Classroom." Also, Parkland College was the site of a summer institute and a fall conference funded by the Ford Foundation on reforming curriculum for community colleges. The conference, entitled "Making Gender Balanced, Multicultural Education a Reality in Illinois Schools," was attended by 500 faculty, staff, and students. Northern Illinois University has created the Multicultural Curriculum Transformation Institute, which conducted a four-day workshop on how to develop a stronger multicultural curriculum.

During the past year, many institutions expanded or strengthened their minority student support programs and activities. Northern Illinois University, for example, dedicated a new facility for the Center for Black Studies. The Center and the Black Graduate Student Association hosted the "First African-American Leadership Conference" on the subject of cultural issues in the black community. Eastern Illinois University announced plans to build four houses in its Greek complex for four historically Black sororities and fraternities. The campus also sponsored its first multicultural job fair. Southern Illinois University at Carbondale implemented a tracking and monitoring system that is intended to support minority retention. The university also established a single administrative unit for a number of student affairs programs that previously had operated independently, and initiated a program to increase minority graduate student enrollment. Also, two community colleges, Kankakee Community College and the College of Lake County, undertook activities to enhance student articulation with historically Black colleges and universities.

Other new minority support programs included: a Latino student recruitment program and companion student scholarship program at Governors State University; *Los Amigos*, an organization for Latino students, at Sauk Valley Community College; and new graduate assistantships for Black and Hispanic students at Sangamon State University. The University of Illinois at Urbana-Champaign intensified minority graduate/professional student recruitment in the first year of a four-year program supported by additional funding of $864,000. Southern Illinois University at Edwardsville announced plans to form the Johnetta Haley Scholars Academy. The Academy will offer scholarships, mentoring, tutorial, and possibly cultural activities. Governor State University initiated "Teaming for Success," a program to support the personal and social development of its minority students. Danville Area Community College, Western Illinois University, and Southern Illinois University at Carbondale also expanded their mentoring programs, and other institutions reported considerable activity in this area.

In recent years, many new programs to improve representation have started at the college and department level. In 1994, the College of Business at Southern Illinois University at Carbondale established a minority executive-in-residence program which complements other support programs in the college such as a minority advisory board and an active minority student association. Other exemplary initiatives to enhance recruitment and retention occurred in the business and engineering schools at Northern Illinois University and the engineering school at Southern Illinois University at Edwardsville. The University of Illinois at Urbana-Champaign also began new minority support programs in the colleges of applied science and law. At Northeastern Illinois University, a Ford Foundation grant to promote diversity has begun to show increases in recruitment and retention in the department of special education and in the department of accounting, business law, and finance.

Finding new and more effective ways to improve communication between institution and minority community leaders remains an important issue. During the past year, Richland Community College established a Minority Community Partners Program and opened an off-campus center in an economically depressed neighborhood. Another interesting initiative occurred at the University of Illinois at Chicago where the Chancellor met with Black legislators and community leaders to review campus progress and to request assistance in recruiting and retaining Black students. Black government and community leaders also met with other campus administrators such as the deans for academic affairs and student affairs. The University reports that "this was the first such occasion for candid exchange of ideas regarding accomplishments, present concerns, and plans for the future... Information gleaned from this meeting will be valuable as UIC reexamines the goals that will prepare us for the next century."

Efforts to improve minority representation are of particular importance at institutions such as Chicago State University and the City Colleges of Chicago that have a large minority enrollment. During the past year, Chicago State University increased its Black enrollment by 744 students, or 10 percent. Black enrollment has grown by 3,050 students, or 60 percent, over the past five years. Retention among Black students has also improved during this period and further advancement is a major goal. One of Chicago State University's most recent initiatives is a department-based "retention in the major program." Another related emphasis is a writing-across-the-curriculum program. A recent initiative among the City Colleges of Chicago is a HECA and federally-supported program, Future Teachers of Chicago. This program is sponsored in partnership with Chicago public and nonpublic schools and has the purpose of recruiting minority students for careers in teaching. The City Colleges of Chicago also have emphasized increasing the number of minority students transferring to four-year institutions to complete a baccalaureate degree. The number of students served by its six transfer centers increased by 75 percent in the past year.

Female Students

Illinois public institutions of higher education offer various programs for female students and staff. In the past year, public colleges and universities strengthened existing programs and developed new programs to continue responsiveness to women's needs. One important initiative during 1994 was Sangamon State University's decision to create a Women's Center. The Women's Center is expected to "play an important role in supporting and guiding female students, faculty, and staff as they deal with issues affecting women on campus (e.g., safety, harassment, isolation)." The university has formed a coordinating council to develop a mission statement and goals for the Center. Funding and staffing levels have not yet been established.

Institutions implemented a variety of female support programs and activities during the past year. Lake Land College updated its sexual harassment policy and established four sexual harassment information centers. Kishwaukee College accepted a proposal from Greenlee Tool in Genoa to offer a scholarship to one student per semester. The scholarship goes to a financially needy student majoring in Manufacturing Engineering or CAD Mechanical Drafting, with preference given to women. Governors State University also now offers a scholarship to "encourage and reward bold, original, innovative or imaginative academic work by a woman student enrolled in a degree program." Two new community colleges joined the state-funded Opportunities Program. This program provides services to women who receive Aid to Families with Dependent Children, offering them special course work, job training, advising, and job placement. The program also provides childcare and transportation costs. Richland Community College established a mentoring program for women enrolled in its Options/Opportunities program. For precollegiate students, Danville Area Community College hosted a conference for eighth-grade girls in order to acquaint them with good jobs that require math and science skills. For staff, the Committee on the Status of Women at Parkland College conducted a survey of campus climate to determine employee perceptions of gender inequities.

Colleges and universities continue to monitor and to improve female student retention and to assist women in meeting needs to further their academic progress. Four community colleges reported this past year that they developed plans or updated policies to assure the achievement and retention of female students. Olive Harvey College established a strategic planning committee for female student retention. The committee addressed issues this year involving gender biases in instructional materials, the classroom, and support services.

Kishwaukee Community College also has noted that special efforts have been taken to help parents who sometimes miss classes due to sick children, including allowing them to make up missed assignments and tests.

All universities and colleges continue to respond to Public Act 87-581 which requires all degree-seeking students to meet general education requirements in courses that have content related to human relations issues. Beyond general education requirements, the University of Illinois at Urbana-Champaign received approval to offer a Women's Studies minor for master's and doctoral level students. Southern Illinois University at Carbondale reported increased enrollment in Women's Studies courses, and Parkland College sponsored a summer institute on "Multicultural Women's Studies Curriculum Integration in Illinois Community Colleges." Twenty faculty from several statewide colleges participated in the 2 1/2 week institute. They learned how to revise their courses in the humanities and social sciences in order to include contributions and perspectives from women. Faculty participants then shared their resources with their campus colleagues.

Students with Disabilities

Public colleges and universities continued this year to improve facilities and services for students and staff with disabilities in order to comply with the 1990 Americans with Disabilities Act (ADA). Sangamon State University, Moraine Valley Community College, Oakton Community College, Richland Community College, and Spoon River Community College reported physical renovations such as ramps to buildings, automatic doors, and water fountains accessible by those in wheelchairs. Other institutions—Eastern Illinois University, Western Illinois University, Southern Illinois at Edwardsville, the University of Illinois, and Lincoln Land Community College—reported the formation of committees and plans which will result in further compliance with ADA.

Several institutions reported purchasing new equipment for students with disabilities. Illinois State University acquired equipment that translates printed material into voice or braille. The University of Illinois at Chicago purchased screen enlargement technology for the visually impaired. College of Lake County added two specially-designed tables in the library for use by the wheelchair-bound and installed two large-screen monitors for the visually impaired. Moraine Valley Community College purchased a voice synthesizer and installed a TDD line. Morton Community College, Richland Community College, Rock Valley Community College, William Rainey Harper College, Belleville Area College, and Spoon River Community College also purchased equipment for use by the visually and hearing impaired.

Lake Land College sponsored a special needs open house for students with disabilities. The college reports that it also had a 64 percent increase in the enrollment of students with disabilities this past year, including a strong increase in the number of students with learning disabilities. Other colleges and universities also made progress toward aiding students with learning disabilities. Illinois State University, Northern Illinois University, Sauk Valley Community College, and Belleville Area College hired persons to coordinate services for students with learning disabilities. Moraine Valley Community College established a new Learning Development Support System.

Several institutions this year compiled information and distributed handbooks to students with disabilities to inform them of available services. Southern Illinois University at Carbondale, the University of Illinois at Urbana-Champaign, and Morton Community College each created such handbooks. William Rainey Harper College completed a career guide for students with disabilities. Some institutions, for example Belleville Area College, also distributed handbooks to faculty to help them advise students with disabilities.

Institutions also reported this year a variety of special support services for students with disabilities. For example, Harold Washington College offers a Vocational Transition Program to train adults with disabilities. The program includes placement tests, reading skills, and money management skills. Wilbur Wright College offers special training in office skills to students with disabilities.

Underrepresented Staff

Female and minority representation among faculty and staff is very low and a major concern of Illinois higher education. During the past year, a number of institutions designed comprehensive strategies to improve faculty and staff representation. For example, Southern Illinois University at Carbondale has requested each dean to formulate a three-year hiring plan for each unit and to become more actively involved in the search process. The Carbondale campus also has established an incentive fund that will assist in minority faculty recruitment. At Eastern Illinois University, each college has formed faculty committees to recommend new recruitment strategies. To enhance representation, the university has allotted a part-time faculty position to the affirmative action office, expanded its data base to monitor new hires and departmental hiring patterns, and offered workshops on the promotion and tenure process. Administrators meet with departing minority faculty and staff to elicit their opinions of campus climate and minority staff are asked to participate in focus groups on this topic. Also, President Stanley Ikenberry of the University of Illinois issued a "Statement on Inclusiveness" this past year which advocated, in particular, improving faculty and staff representation. In response, the University of Illinois at Urbana-Champaign has reviewed its affirmative action plans, adopted new affirmative action policies, strengthened its staff recruitment searches, and undertaken other actions to increase the number of female and minority administrators.

Another major initiative to improve faculty and staff representation occurred at Governors State University which hired five of ten top-level administrators this past year from underrepresented groups. Governors State University reports that it has a goal of filling 15 tenure-track positions with minority faculty. The university has obtained a consultant to assist in this process. Also, the University of Illinois at Chicago reports that it has exceeded its goal, established in 1989, for hiring new Black and Hispanic faculty members. The university is now emphasizing minority faculty retention as well as recruitment. During the past year, each college at the University of Illinois at Chicago examined hiring practices and established hiring goals for minority and female faculty as a part of a five-year recruitment and retention plan. The university reports that the "provost has incorporated commitment to diversity as an element of the performance evaluation for each dean." Other University of Illinois at Chicago initiatives this past year included: the creation of a faculty research support program, the allocation of seed money and release time for gender research, and the establishment of a new unit in the human resources office to improve representation among support staff.

Public institutions strengthened support programs and initiated new activities to improve faculty and staff representation. Danville Community College sponsored a part-time job fair to attract and employ minority instructors with the goal of promoting new hires to full-time positions as vacancies occur. Morton College, in cooperation with other institutions, helped form a minority resumé data base. A recent study at the University of Illinois at Urbana-Champaign showed a discrepancy "between national availability and UIUC (female) representation, indicating a need to focus on recruitment and retention efforts." In response to this finding, a faculty mentoring program for women and two new women's groups were founded.

The new Academic Women's Caucus, which now serves as an umbrella group for 37 organizations, currently is examining the needs of women on campus. Also, Southern Illinois University at Carbondale increased the number of administrative internships for female faculty members from two to five and allocated additional funds to support the research activities of female faculty and staff. In the coming year, the university will survey female faculty and staff to assess their perceptions of the campus climate. The university will incorporate survey results into program plans.

Studies and Program Evaluations

In the past year, the Board of Higher Education and public colleges and universities have undertaken a number of studies and program evaluations concerning underrepresented groups. Evaluation represents an important tool to better understand the obstacles confronted by underrepresented groups, as well as to understand how program efforts can help students overcome these barriers. Since public institutions allocate over $83 million for these programs, it is particularly important that colleges and universities assess program effectiveness, as well as how their investment of resources affects student success. The Board of Higher Education continues to emphasize the need for further progress in this area and the importance of coordinating study results with budget and program priorities.

The Board of Higher Education published a number of reports on underrepresented groups during 1994. Two of these concerned undergraduate education and included information and analysis about minority representation. *Undergraduate Education: Access and Preparation Reexamined* (March 1994) describes the preparation of students for college and their achievement in their first year in college. The report presents data on high school ACT scores for minority students. It also describes programs for minority students that offer outreach services, orientation for first-year students, preparation for students in the summer preceding their first year in college, and academic support.

Undergraduate Education: Transfer and Articulation Reexamined (May 1994) provides data on undergraduate student transfer and describes statewide articulation efforts and progress in majority and minority students transferring from community colleges to four-year colleges and universities. The report shows that Chicago State University and University of Illinois at Chicago enroll the largest number of Black transfer students, and the University of Illinois at Chicago, Northern Illinois University, and Northeastern Illinois University enroll the largest number of Hispanic transfers. Of the 21 community colleges that operated MAP-funded minority transfer centers prior to fall 1992, the report found that 14 colleges increased the number of Black students and 13 colleges increased the number of Hispanic students enrolled in their baccalaureate-transfer centers from fall 1990 to fall 1992.

Another May Board report, *Baccalaureate Student Graduation, Time-To-Degree, and Retention at Illinois Public Universities,* included retention and degree completion trend data from 1983-84 to 1987-88. In addition to major trends in degree retention and completion for Black and Hispanic students summarized above, this report also examines trends at individual Illinois public universities in degree completion and time-to-degree for Black, Hispanic, and all other students.

In July 1994, the Board of Higher Education issued, *Minority Students in Illinois Higher Education: A Review of Progress and Policy and Program Developments,* which examined the efforts that had been made to implement the Board's policy goals concerning minority student participation and achievement first formulated by the Joint Committee on Minority Student Achievement in 1988. The report described many recent initiatives including the development of new programs, such as the Minority Teacher Incentive Grant Program and the Minority Articulation Program under the Higher Education Cooperation Act; increased funding for minority student programs; and the creation of new statewide data collection and reporting systems that can monitor minority student progress.

As part of the July review, Board of Higher Education staff held two meetings with Illinois higher education and minority leaders in Chicago and Springfield to reexamine Board policy and statewide and institutional efforts to improve minority student representation. The participants at these meetings concurred that the joint committee's goals remain relevant. However, they also urged intensification of efforts to implement these goals and called for greater commitment and energy at the unit and program level.

The *Committee to Study Affordability Report to the Board of Higher Education,* whose recommendations were adopted by the Board of Higher Education at its November 1994 meeting, addressed a variety of issues concerning academic progress, student cost, and financial aid. The report emphasized that education is a continuum with the academic preparation at one level directly affecting the academic progress and success achieved at the next. It called for strengthening and expanding partnerships between schools and higher education institutions to support improved preparation. Among other recommendations, the report advocated that "college and university efforts to accelerate degree completion should address the needs of African-American and Hispanic, adult, and place-bound students, and any other student groups that historically have taken longer to complete their undergraduate degrees."

During the past year, the Board of Higher Education reviewed and evaluated minority projects funded under the Higher Education Cooperation Act and the federal Dwight D. Eisenhower Mathematics and Science Education program. Under the Board's procedures, applicants completing a project or seeking continued funding must submit a report that describes the results and progress of the project. The data required for this evaluation varies according to educational level and project type (e.g., precollegiate and collegiate level). Summaries of evaluations are included in Board of Higher Education reports that authorize HECA and Eisenhower Program projects—*Dwight D. Eisenhower Mathematics and Science Education Program: Federal Fiscal Year 1993 Grant Awards* (January 1994) and *Higher Education Cooperation Act-Fiscal Year 1995 Grant Allocations* (September 1994).

The Board's HECA evaluations demonstrate that these projects serve many precollegiate, college, and university students. Surveys of students and, in some cases their parents, reveal a high level of program satisfaction. Most important, many programs have enhanced student academic achievement as measured by tests in academic skills, such as reading, writing, and mathematics; high school grades and completion; college admission; and selection of college course of study. For example, Project Gain, a cooperative project in nursing education, reports that it has served 303 disadvantaged precollege, preclinical, clinical, and nursing students of whom 93 have graduated from Southern Illinois University at Edwardsville and 13 from State Community College. Of the 106 graduates, 94 percent passed the State Board Licensing Examination for registered nurses.

In the past year, Illinois public colleges and universities conducted various studies and surveys concerning underrepresented groups. As described in the 1993 Board of Higher Education report on Underrepresented Groups, institutional climate studies, as well as the equity assessments conducted by the Center for Higher Education at Illinois State University, particularly have helped institutions gain better understanding of minority student values and concerns. A number of campuses have used the findings of their climate studies to more effectively address minority student issues, while periodic studies have enabled institutions to identify and respond to particular problems.

In addition to campus-wide reviews, public universities and community colleges also conduct evaluations of programs serving underrepresented students and staff. The Board of

Higher Education has established a review cycle by program type, and institutions submit summaries of each review to the Board of Higher Education in their annual reports. Under this schedule, institutions were to review and report in fiscal year 1994 on support units that seek to improve the undergraduate retention of students from underrepresented groups.

Institutional reports indicate that colleges and universities are improving their data collecting and analytical abilities so that they can better track and explain the retention and degree completion of underrepresented groups. On the other hand, many institutions' reviews of units serving students from underrepresented groups appear perfunctory and do not thoroughly examine a unit's efficiency or effectiveness in facilitating student retention. One example of a thorough review was conducted by Southern Illinois University at Carbondale of its Center for Basic Skills (CBS). A committee of five individuals composed of three individuals from the university and two individuals from other universities spent three days on campus reviewing documents and interviewing students and staff, including President John Guyon. The Committee examined quality of instruction, predictor variables, characteristics of students, student evaluation of services, exploration of learning characteristics, and continuation rates. Among its recommendations, the review committee advised "career counseling should receive continued emphasis in CBS, since one of the major reasons these youngsters find little meaning in education is that they lack insight into its relevancy" and "identification with the institution is essential if the students are to be a part of the university community and profit significantly from this opportunity. Required attendance at some traditional cultural activities and discussion of its value could be beneficial."

Despite the shortcomings of some review processes, many institutions can demonstrate that their support units are effective in improving the retention of students from underrepresented groups. Illinois State University, for example, reported that 62 percent of all participants in its High Potential Student program are in good academic standing compared with 52 percent of all minority freshmen. The High Potential Student program provides opportunities to students who have the potential for success, but are at risk of not completing an undergraduate degree. Also, Kennedy King College of the City Colleges of Chicago reports that its extended orientation approach has raised retention of first semester freshmen from 47 percent in fall 1992 to 63 percent in fall 1993. A third example is Western Illinois University's Minority Achievement Program which encourages and supports academic excellence among minority students. In the past four years, the number of program participants has increased 44 percent with the program serving 266 undergraduate minority students in the past year; at the same time, student retention has improved and the mean cumulative grade point average for all students receiving services is 3.2 on a 4.0 scale.

1994 FOCUS TOPICS ON UNDERGRADUATE STUDENT RETENTION

Improving the retention of students from underrepresented groups is one of the major challenges facing Illinois higher education. As described earlier in this report, Black and Hispanic students have retention and degree completion rates significantly below the level of majority students. Also, female students enrolled in mathematics, science, and engineering programs, as described below, face special degree completion problems, and students with disabilities have needs that require institutional assistance. This section focuses on three areas of particular importance to the undergraduate retention of students from underrepresented groups: academic programs, noninstitutional services and activities, and support from faculty and staff. All public institutions have provided information on these topics in their October 1994 reports to the Board of Higher Education.

Academic Programs

In collecting information on this topic, the Board of Higher Education asked institutions to report on how ongoing academic programs and classroom activities, as well as special support programs, seek to improve the retention of students from underrepresented groups. The Board sought information on the full range of institutional activities, as well as a description of special efforts and activities that have proven effective. Responses demonstrate that institutions rely on basic undergraduate programs as the first resource for improving underrepresented student retention. For many underrepresented students, the strength of an undergraduate program is particularly important since a higher proportion of underrepresented students than majority students enter college with poor high school academic preparation and need to make significant educational advances in their first year of study in order to succeed at college level work.

A recent study by the University of Illinois at Chicago illustrates the relationship between undergraduate education and the academic advancement of students from underrepresented groups, as well as how institutions can restructure their educational program to improve retention. This study, conducted by a university task force, concentrated on the freshman year when more than half of the institution's students drop out. Its principal recommendation called for adoption of a "more systematic, comprehensive, and intrusive approach to providing the best academic support environment for all new students." The task force established goals for course availability and support, and academic advising and monitoring. In order to build a good foundation for academic success, it advocated guaranteeing seats in English composition and mathematics for all new students. The task force also recommended that students who are enrolled in difficult courses should receive greater guidance and support through supplemental instructional sessions, the establishment of prerequisites, and the creation of a peer tutoring center. Other recommendations included: improved use of math and chemistry placement tests, department-based training for teaching assistants, and creation of a comprehensive advising system for first-year students.

In the past year, the University of Illinois at Chicago has implemented some of the recommendations identified above, as well as related measures to promote undergraduate retention. Other institutions have initiated similar programs, and a smaller group have undertaken comprehensive studies to better understand the total impact of their academic programs upon student retention. Strategies and activities to improve retention vary according to tradition, institutional mission, and scope of operation. Simple efforts can prove very effective. For example, Lake Land College and Shawnee Community College report that personal contact with faculty, such as telephone calls to students who have been absent from class, can significantly affect student persistence.

Public colleges and universities also structure their undergraduate education programs to aid the retention of students from underrepresented groups. As discussed below, faculty, teaching assistants, and support staff have a strong impact upon the academic success of students from underrepresented groups, and institutions offer developmental programs to help staff ensure that the contributions of underrepresented students are recognized and their participation encouraged. Outside the classroom, many institutions hire academic support staff in admissions, counseling, and placement offices who are sensitive to the needs of students from underrepresented groups. Northern Illinois University, for example, reports that its Colleges of Liberal Arts and Sciences, Business, and Engineering and Engineering Technology have support staff working with underrepresented students in admissions, pre-professional advising, and other counseling programs.

In recent years, many institutions have expanded and modified their academic programs to make them more inclusive of race, ethnicity, and gender. Faculty and institutions have broadened their academic offerings in order to make the curriculum more meaningful to contemporary students who will live in a more demographically diverse world than their parents. As part of these efforts, Sangamon State University, University of Illinois at Urbana-Champaign, Northern Illinois University, and other institutions have sponsored curricular projects to develop or modify courses to incorporate gender and ethnicity topics. Parkland College, Sauk Valley Community College, Rend Lake College, and the College of Lake County have incorporated human relations topics in their first-year composition and/or speech courses. Other institutions such as Eastern Illinois University and Southern Illinois University at Edwardsville have adopted new general education curricula that address multicultural perspectives and issues. Many institutions also now offer academic majors or minors in Women's Studies and cultural studies programs such as African American Studies. Data is not available on how such curricula changes have affected the retention of students from underrepresented groups. However, campus climate studies have shown that a major concern of minority students is the amount of course work and class discussion that is relevant to their experience.

Colleges and universities offer academic support programs that are specifically designed to meet the needs of underrepresented student groups. For instance, all institutions offer special academic support services for students with disabilities, now a requirement under federal legislation. Academic services include pre-admission and pre-enrollment planning, tutorial referral, reader/notetaker referral, taped textbooks, and adaptive computer equipment designed to accommodate students with vision, hearing, mobility, and other types of disabilities. Many institutions, like Southern Illinois University at Carbondale, also offer extensive services to students with identified learning disabilities such as dyslexia.

The largest array of special academic support programs serve minority students. These students come to college with diverse academic experiences and needs which institutions seek to accommodate through various program structures and activities. Illinois State University, for example, reports four academic programs that are designed, at least in part, to improve the retention of minority students. These include: 1) the Minority Professional Opportunities program that serves high achieving minority students who are encouraged to enter careers in underrepresented disciplines and graduate/professional study; 2) the Collegiate Opportunities Admissions Program that provides intensive support during the freshmen year for special admissions students; 3) the Student Support Services Program that offers comprehensive academic support to low income and/or first generation college students; and 4) the High Potential Students Program that offers opportunities to students that have the potential for success and can benefit from its services.

Academic support programs for women are concentrated in the sciences, mathematics, and engineering. Research cited by the University of Illinois at Urbana-Champaign shows that if female and male students in these disciplines are both treated indifferently, in a so-called "null environment," they do not react the same way. "Men have sources of external support from society, friends, parents and others to sustain them in a null environment. Women in traditionally male majors have much less support from these sources and are less likely to persist in a nonsupportive environment." To assist female retention, academic support programs in math and science generally address potentially harmful climate factors such as sexual discrimination and isolation while also offering positive assistance through role models, mentors, and peers.

Many new programs that serve underrepresented students are college- or department-based. For instance, Southern Illinois University at Edwardsville reports that it has special academic support programs for underrepresented students in the School of Nursing, the

School of Engineering, and the Department of Chemistry. The Chemistry program offers tutorial services in biology, chemistry, physics, and mathematics with study groups in chemistry and mathematics. The university reports that students in this program have experienced improved academic performance and retention.

A few colleges and universities report that the voluntary nature of support programs can limit effectiveness since students may not seek assistance until they have experienced academic difficulty. Some support programs, however, do have mandatory provisions. Eastern Illinois University, for example, reports that participants in its Minority Admission Program "agree in writing to regular advisement, intensive work with small groups of students throughout their freshman year, course work based on placement tests, weekly study-tables, and tutoring. They are also prohibited from joining Greek organizations while enrolled in the program, and are required to live in university housing." Undoubtedly, all support programs should not incorporate mandatory requirements. However, Eastern Illinois University has suggested that its Minority Admission Program is successful because of "the responsibility it places upon students." Students who are admitted under this program do not meet regular admissions criteria. Yet, in the program's five-year history students have achieved a grade point average comparable to the university average and have high retention rates.

It is very important that institutions are able to evaluate the success of programs and activities designed to improve the retention of underrepresented students. All programs may not have the types of activities suited to sophisticated analysis. When possible, however, institutions should conduct program evaluations and incorporate results into program improvements and resource allocations. Ideally, an integrated retention strategy should incorporate support programs, as well as general academic programs, of proven effectiveness.

Non-instructional Programs and Activities

Students persist in higher education for academic and nonacademic reasons. Often the two factors are combined so that a student who is struggling academically and has an unsatisfactory social life is more likely to leave college than a student whose positive social experiences compensate for academic challenges and disappointments. As shown, an institution's basic undergraduate program often has the most direct effect on the academic success of underrepresented students, notwithstanding the importance of special academic support programs and activities. Correspondingly, basic noninstructional programs and activities on a college campus also strongly influence student retention.

The campus climate for underrepresented students, that is, how the normal array of social, cultural, and recreational programs and activities welcome and value diversity and the contributions of non-majority students, is a topic which many public colleges and universities are currently addressing. In this process, the attitudes and sensitivities of institutional staff are of importance. Southern Illinois University at Carbondale, for example, reports that "programs designed to serve all students are encouraged to recruit staff sensitive to the needs of all students, and to implement strategic approaches which apply effectively to all students. Staff composition guidelines suggest inclusion of members who serve as role models and mentors to a diverse population. The strategies and approaches employed also recognize, and when feasible, respond to the unique needs of underrepresented populations."

Creating a favorable campus climate is particularly important in the freshman year since many entering students have not been exposed to students from other racial/ethnic backgrounds. Many institutions sponsor orientation programs that discuss and encourage students to understand and value diversity and to promote inclusiveness. Some institutions also offer special orientation sessions for minority students and students with disabilities. For example,

Illinois State University's coordinator of minority affairs organizes a number of fall orientation programs including a picnic for minority students and the *Illinois State Showcase* where college staff present overviews of their programs and services.

Student life in the residence halls can constitute an important part of an institution's campus climate. Eastern Illinois University reports that "as a large portion of the student body at Eastern resides in university housing, the staff and activities of the Office of Student Housing are critical in contributing to the retention of minority students. Minority representation among the residence hall advisors (19 percent), the housing graduate assistants (22 percent), and the full-time staff (25 percent) is greater than the percentages of minority students among the student body. This level of representation among the housing staff further ensures that there are mentors and role models for minority students and contributes to advancing a tolerant, sensitive environment in housing." In addition to ensuring a broad race/ethnic representation among resident hall staff, some institutions also hold staff training sessions which deal with topics such as promoting inclusiveness and respecting diversity.

Finding the financial resources to attend college can present a formidable challenge for some underrepresented students. Studies have shown that minority students are less likely to borrow funds to finance their college education, and availability of grant funding can influence their enrollment and retention patterns. To meet these needs and to improve minority enrollment, some institutions offer special scholarships, especially in disciplines with low minority representation. In the past year, for example, Northern Illinois University offered 137 institutional waivers for new and continuing minority students. Governors State University reported that many of its underrepresented students face special financial problems because state financial aid criteria prevent students who attend less than half-time from receiving grant assistance. The university, which has 80 percent part-time enrollment, is now awarding supplementary loans to minority students who cannot register due to financial constraints. It also awards special child-care grants to needy students, and ten female and eight minority students received grants in 1994.

There are numerous ways in which colleges and universities can modify their noninstructional programs to meet specific institutional needs and improve the campus climate. For instance, Southern Illinois University at Edwardsville recently conducted a survey which indicated that the availability of recreational sports and facilities strongly influenced student retention. Responding to the implication of this finding, the university has expanded its recreational programs and activities for underrepresented students by installing specific weight-training apparatus for students with disabilities; increasing aerobic exercise programming for women; and instituting on-site child care.

Public colleges and universities offer many special noninstructional programs and activities for underrepresented students. Students with disabilities, for example, often have access to dormitory rooms with adaptive equipment and other special services such as transportation. Also, all institutions have enhanced the accessibility of their campuses for the physically disabled, although some plans to improve accessibility are not yet complete. Institutions have also published brochures and sponsored outreach activities at local high schools and community organizations to increase awareness of the services and facilities that are available for students with disabilities.

The most common support services offered for female students are to ensure greater campus safety and to provide child-care services. Colleges and universities also offer information and counseling on sexual harassment and discrimination. Many institutions sponsor mentoring programs and social activities organized around colleges and departments with low female representation such as mathematics, science, and engineering. Some programs also hold activities for precollegiate female students. For example, a student group, the Society of

Women Engineers, at the University of Illinois at Urbana-Champaign runs a "little sister" day every spring in which incoming first-year students stay with members of the society and attend a day of classes.

Minority services offer opportunities for involvement, leadership, and social and cultural support. Many campuses have programs or centers that organize social and cultural activities. One example is the Office of Student Services and Activities at Joliet Junior College which reports that it seeks "to provide extracurricular programs that celebrate the different cultures represented on campus. We do this for a variety of reasons; to promote pride in the students' various cultures, to educate members of the college community about cultures different from their own, and to help create an atmosphere where students may comfortably pursue their education." Some institutions also offer additional minority support programs within noninstructional units, such as the Black Student Union at the University of Illinois at Urbana-Champaign, or more targeted programs such as the African-American Male Mentoring program at Highland Community College.

Many support programs for underrepresented groups seek to enhance student involvement and identification with the institution, factors that research has linked to student retention. The University of Illinois at Chicago's Latin American Recruitment and Educational Services program has developed a survey to determine the degree to which the university's Latino students become integrated into the campus community. The university will use this survey, which examines student involvement with faculty, support staff, and other students, to identify additional factors affecting student persistence and its design and modification of university retention programs.

Faculty and Staff Support

As the university members who have the most contact with students, faculty and staff can have much influence on student success. For this reason, many colleges and universities seek to assist faculty and staff in creating an environment that respects diversity and responds to all students' needs. Institutions use a variety of approaches. Most commonly, they sponsor workshops, seminars, forums, and other training sessions designed to introduce faculty and staff to the needs of students with diverse backgrounds. Chicago State University organizes its activities under a special committee. This year the committee "participated in a research project on learning styles of minority students,...developed a resource guide of CSU materials concerning people of color,...and started a study group devoted to the continued education of faculty and staff on multicultural issues."

Workshops, seminars, and forums can be a particularly effective means for training many people at one time. The newly acquired skills can then be applied to campus life. For example, Eastern Illinois University sponsored a one-day workshop for faculty on methods for introducing issues of diversity and race into the classroom. After the workshop, Eastern administered a survey to find out how faculty felt about the training. Faculty continue to meet to share ideas about dealing with these issues in the classroom. The College of Pharmacy at the University of Illinois-Chicago offered a symposium entitled, "Cycle of Conditioning— Understanding Racism," for faculty, staff, and students. Southern Illinois University at Edwardsville conducts workshops during faculty orientation that explore how it feels to be a racial or ethnic minority person on a predominantly white campus.

Among the community colleges, the College of DuPage designed two staff development courses: "Who's a Stranger Here?" focusing on cultural diversity and "Sociology of the Disabled." Specific departments and divisions at Heartland Community College plan activities to help faculty deal with cultural diversity in the classroom. Joliet Junior College created

226

two new courses in General Student Development. These courses were designed to allow faculty to serve as mentors to students. John A. Logan College sponsors several "development days" for faculty and staff. Recent topics have included meeting the needs of students with disabilities, conflict resolution, and consensus-building. Spoon River College has sponsored a comprehensive set of programming, including awareness and training on issues of sex equity, sexual harassment, cultural diversity, and the needs of disabled students.

In addition to staff development programming, some institutions provide specific instructional training so that faculty have a repertoire of instructional strategies that will increase the likelihood of student success. Western Illinois University employs a Multicultural Curriculum Associate who helps faculty to incorporate diverse perspectives and pedagogy in the classroom. A Multicultural Advisory Committee does similar work at Richland Community College. The University of Illinois at Urbana-Champaign has a comprehensive training program for teaching assistants which includes topics on diversity. Sauk Valley Community College and Shawnee Community College sponsored workshops on the different learning styles of students. Additionally, Sauk Valley Community College participated in a national teleconference on learning styles which was sponsored by the League for Innovation.

While a diverse repertoire of instructional strategies can aid the development of students in the classroom, some institutions initiated programs to provide more one-on-one interaction with students. Nine institutions reported that they established faculty mentoring programs. Most of these programs serve minority students and use faculty mentors from a variety of racial/ethnic backgrounds. Other programs are designed for specific populations. For example, Northern Illinois University matches male African-American students with African-American faculty.

Although faculty have the most contact with students, some workshops are also held for campus administrative and civil service employees. For example, Northeastern Illinois University designed a program called *Connections,* which focuses on "improving the attitude of positive customer service for those staff who have a high frequency of public contact with students." Northeastern also provides special training to campus police on issues of cultural diversity. Several other institutions reported that they provided special training for student affairs staff to cover such topics as race relations and sexual harassment. Eastern Illinois University has plans to expand this training to employees in food services, building services, financial assistance, the University Union, the bookstore, admissions, registration, and career planning and placement.

Although many colleges and universities offer similar programs and activities, some institutions sponsor programs that address specific needs. For example, McHenry County College offered beginning and advanced Spanish to faculty to help them communicate with the number of Spanish-speaking students there. Morton College offered a sequence of three courses designed to increase faculty and staff knowledge and understanding of Hispanic students.

Summary

This is the Illinois Board of Higher Education's seventh annual report on underrepresented groups. The report presents data and information on minority, female, and disabled students and staff in Illinois higher education. It describes changes in representation during 1994, highlighting special efforts to address the needs of underrepresented students.

As shown in the first section of this report, strong gains in representation continued in some areas this past year, such as:

- *Hispanic undergraduate and graduate/professional enrollment* increased by 4.5 percent, and since 1986 has increased by 71.5 percent.

- *Black graduate/professional enrollment* increased by 8.1 percent, and since 1986 has increased by 49.0 percent.
- *Black student transfers* from community colleges to Illinois four-year institutions increased by 4.8 percent, and since 1988 have increased by 30.7 percent.
- *Hispanic student transfers* from community colleges to Illinois four-year institutions increased by 7.0 percent, and since 1988 have increased by 102.8 percent.
- *Public university Black enrollment* increased by 3.8 percent and *Hispanic public university enrollment* by 7.6 percent; since 1986, Black public university enrollment has increased by 21.6 percent and Hispanic public university enrollment by 65.4 percent.
- *Black recipients of all higher education degrees* from associate to doctoral degrees increased by 7.2 percent, and since 1986 have increased by 23.5 percent. The strongest increase this past year was at the master's and advanced certificate level which increased by 11.2 percent.
- *Black and Hispanic six-year undergraduate degree completion rates* showed improvement for the fourth consecutive year, although four-year degree completion rates have not improved and Black and Hispanic undergraduate degree completion rates remain significantly below rates for majority students.
- *Female enrollment in first professional programs* for the first time exceeded 40 percent in both public and private education sectors; this is up from 25.5 percent in 1980.

Despite these gains, in the past year representation remained low in a number of areas and some declines occurred:

- *Black undergraduate enrollment* decreased by 0.3 percent; this was the second consecutive year that showed a decline in Black undergraduate enrollment and may reflect the impact of a 9.6 percent decline in Black public high school graduates since 1986.
- *Black undergraduate enrollment at community colleges* decreased by 2.5 percent, the third consecutive year of Black undergraduate enrollment decline in this higher education sector.
- *Hispanic undergraduate enrollment at community colleges* decreased by 0.3 percent, the first decline in undergraduate enrollment at community colleges since 1987.
- *Hispanic master's degree and advanced certificate recipients* declined by 2.6 percent.
- *Black, Hispanic, and female degree recipients in mathematics, science, and engineering disciplines* showed no improvement and remained very low. Small gains in enrollment in some disciplines were offset by losses in other disciplines. At the graduate level, degrees earned by Blacks and Hispanics decreased in most of these disciplines.
- *Black and Hispanic faculty* representation remained very low, Hispanic faculty representing 1.8 percent of all faculty at public universities, and Black faculty representing 4.3 percent, an increase from 3.2 percent in 1989.

The second section in this report contains information on major statewide and institutional initiatives undertaken during the past year to improve student and staff representation. The section summarizes state higher education budget increases that affected underrepresented groups, including new incentive payments under the Health Services Education Grants Act to increase minority student enrollment in health professions programs, and the allocation of $46 million to public universities for remodeling activities to bring state facilities into compliance with the federal Americans with Disabilities Act. A brief description is given of new HECA projects approved under the Minority Educational Achievement and Minority Articulation programs. A major portion of this chapter describes new programs and program expansions that were undertaken this past year to better serve female, disabled, and minority students and staff. The final section of the chapter highlights major findings from Board of Higher Education reports, as well as statewide and institutional program evaluations that pertain to underrepresented groups.

Each year this report examines in some detail a few topics that have special relevance to improving student and staff representation. The third section in the report concerns undergraduate student retention and provides information on how public universities and community colleges have structured and improved academic and noninstructional programs and extended faculty and staff support to enhance the retention of underrepresented students. The section describes special programs that are in place to assist these students. However, it emphasizes that the basic instructional and noninstructional programs that serve all undergraduate students are the first resource for promoting retention. The strength of an institution's undergraduate program is particularly important for underrepresented students since a higher proportion of underrepresented students enter college with poor high school academic preparation and need to make significant advances in order to succeed in college. The section shows how various institutions have shaped and modified their academic and noninstructional programs in order to serve all students better and help improve the retention of students from underrepresented groups.

For a copy of the complete *Report to the Governor and General Assembly on Underrepresented Groups in Public Institutions of Higher Education in Illinois,* including graphs and appendices, contact the Illinois Board of Higher Education, 4 West Old Capitol Plaza, Room 500, Springfield, IL 62701-1287.

ISCDA MEMBERSHIP

The Illinois Staff and Curriculum Developers Association (ISCDA) was founded to encourage research and an exchange of ideas on the professional development of college and university faculty and staff, curriculum change, and teaching effectiveness. It seeks to provide a forum, through workshops and its Dealing with Difference Summer Institute, that furthers discussion and understanding of issues of immediate and critical concern to educators committed to preparing students for the 21st century.

Name _____ Title _____

Institution/Organization _____ Position _____

Address _____

City _____ State _____ Zip_____

Daytime Phone ( ) _____ E-Mail Address _____

Membership Dues: $20.00 **payable by check to ISCDA** ___New or ___Renewal

Check # _____ Amount enclosed: _____

Indicate the skills and interests you have that would contribute to the ISCDA.

_____

_____

Indicate the kinds of support, programs, and/or information you want from ISCDA.

_____

_____

Return this form to:
ISCDA Multicultural Resource Development
and Advising Center
HH 80
Western Illinois University
1 University Circle
Macomb, IL 61455

Phone: 309/298-3387

FAX: 309/298-3367